ASIAN INDIAN OLDER ADULTS IN SILICON VALLEY

Quality of Life of Parents
Who Immigrate to
Reunite with their Children

Dr. Anita Jhunjhunwala Mukherjee

Copyright © 2012
Dr. Anita Jhunjhunwala Mukherjee
All rights reserved

ISBN-13: 978-1481027359
ISBN-10: 1481027352

DEDICATION

I would like to dedicate this endeavor to my extended family: the families into which I was born, the Jhunjhunwalas and the Khetans, and the family into which I married, the Mukherjees. Of special importance is the person who is no more, my sister, Anju. Only a couple of years older, Anju was my indirect teacher since early years. While she battled through various issues, I merely learned from observation and avoided many of the pitfalls. I am very much aware that there were resources that would have been hers but for the younger sister. And when it was time for her to go, I truly experienced what, in hindsight, seems like telepathy of souls. Unconscious strings were pulled, forcing me to her bedside on the other side of the globe, and I am truly grateful for the 30 hours I spent with her before she left. The seeds of my journey through the field of psychology took roots in those months five years ago, as I struggled to make sense of everything that was happening around me. I also want to dedicate this book to my parents, Shakuntala and Banwari Jhunjhunwala, for whom I could never be the ideal daughter; perpetually breaking the gender-role boundaries, I could never do what they expected, so I am offering what I have been able to do. And now, I come to my brother Ashok and my husband Animesh, the two men who had a vision for me, that of an engineer with Master's in Computer Science, that of an entrepreneur. *Bhaiya* (elder brother) often played the role that parents usually do, and Animesh took over where *bhaiya* left off. But the higher power had different plans and the destiny eventually found me, making the words of a television serial *Dhoondh Legi Manjil Hamey* come true. Hence, this work is also dedicated to the power of destiny!

TABLE OF CONTENTS

TABLE OF TABLES	viii
TABLE OF FIGURES	ix
LIST OF ABBREVIATIONS	x
PROLOGUE	xii
FOREWORD	xiii
ACKNOWLEDGEMENTS	xv
CHAPTER ONE: INTRODUCTION	1
Research Background	4
The Silicon Valley	4
Asian Indians in the United States	4
First-generation Asian Indians: The age groups	6
Older adults	7
The Role of Immigration	8
Immigration as trauma	9
Current Research on the Elderly AI Immigrants	10
The Research Problem	12
Gaps within the Literature	13
The Purpose of the Study	14
The Research Questions	14
Hypotheses	14
Significance of the Study	15
American Geriatric Population: Need for Culturally Competent Care	16
The Focus on the Under-Researched AI Community	17
Adding to the knowledge base on AI seniors	17
Limited community support structures	19
The Advantage of Silicon Valley	19
Limitations of the Study	22
Delimitations	23
Feasibility of the Study	23

Definitions of Terms	24
Asian Indians or Indians	24
South Asian	25
First- and Second-Generation Immigrants	25
Early Immigrants and Family-Sponsored Recent (or Late) Immigrants	25
CHAPTER TWO: LITERATURE REVIEW	27
Quality of Life	28
Defining Quality of Life	28
The common themes	29
Different perspectives	30
The WHO initiative	31
Summary	32
The History and Evolution of QoL	32
The functional status scales	33
WHO definition of health and the social science indices	33
Subjective well-being	34
Cross-over of social science QoL indicators into medical science	35
Impact of Food and Drug Administration (FDA) policy	35
Components of QoL	36
Constituents of QoL contrasted with factors that influence it	37
Terms Closely Related to QoL	38
Stability of QoL	39
The Theoretical Models of QoL	39
QoL of older adults	40
QoL models for ethnic immigrants	41
QoL and Asian Indians	41
The Political and the Legal Context	42
Immigration Policies of the United States	43
Pre-1965 scenario	43
The immigration and naturalization act of 1965	44

Post-1965 regulations: Embracing the diversity	45
Social Security and Welfare	46
The Older Americans Act (OAA) of 1965	46
The Medicare act of 1965, SSI, Medicaid, and other benefits	47
The 1996 Welfare Reform Act and the 1996 Immigration Act	48
Impact of the American Politico-Legal Context	50
Indian Laws that Influence QoL of Expatriates	52
The Asian Indians in the United States	53
Waves of Asian Indian Immigrants	54
Asian Indians in Silicon Valley	56
From Brain-Drain to Reverse Brain-Drain	57
Diversity within the Asian Indian Older Adults	59
Family-sponsored seniors: Characteristics of population under study	60
Barriers and perceived needs	61
The Asian Indian Cultural Value System	61
Individualistic Versus Collectivistic Culture	62
Disruption in the family hierarchy and power structure	63
Acculturative dissonance amongst family members	64
Perspectives on Aging	65
Wisdom and privilege	66
Responsibility for the Elderly	67
The 2007 senior citizens bill in India	68
Role reversal, unrecognized contribution	69
Spirituality and Religion	70
Role of karma	71
Stigma of Mental Health	72
Major Studies Relevant to this Research	72
Age-Neutral Studies on Asian Indians	73
An early study on the QoL of Asians	73
A study on ethnic identity and acculturation in SF Bay Area	73

Studies with AI Older Adults in the United States	74
A landmark study in New York	74
Early studies in Washington, D.C. and Chicago areas	75
Studies in the tri-state area of New York, New Jersey, and Connecticut	76
Studies in Atlanta	78
Gaps in the Literature	80
Factors Affecting Quality of Life	80
Identity or Sense of Belonging	81
Acculturation	82
Racism and prejudice	82
Acculturation strategies	84
Reason for coming to the United States	85
Length of residence in the U.S. and age at the time of immigration	85
Language proficiency	86
Perceived cultural gap	88
Autonomy and Independence	88
Sense of self-efficacy in the new culture	89
Access to transportation	91
Financial dependence	92
Dependence for interaction and communication: Language barrier	93
Political and Legal Context: Citizenship Status	94
Utilization of public resources	95
Social Capital, Support Network, and Isolation	96
Refueling: Access to AI culture	98
Extramural refueling	99
Intramural refueling	100
Role of ethnic organizations	101
The current programs for AI seniors	102
Religiosity, role of religious organizations	104
Marital status and living arrangement	105
Having a Role or Meaning in Life	105
Health	106

Physical health	107
Yoga and pranayam	108
Mental health	110
Anxiety, loneliness, and personality characteristics	110
Discrepancy between expectation and reality	111
Demographic Variables	112
Age	112
Education level	113
Gender	113
Summary	114
CHAPTER THREE: METHODOLOGY	116
Purpose of the Study and the Research Questions	116
Selection of Participants	117
Instrumentation	117
The Deficiencies of the Standard Instruments	117
The Chosen Instruments	119
WHOQOL-BREF	119
Pearlin and Schooler mastery scale	121
The PHQ-9: Mood scale of the BPHQ	122
GAD-7 anxiety assessment instrument	123
Psychosocial Questionnaire	124
Language	124
Identity	125
Financial condition	125
Transportation	125
Access to Indian culture: Refueling	126
Importance of religion	126
Physical health	126
Overall QoL and expectation	127
Isolation versus social support	127
Open-ended questions	127
Procedures	129
The Study Setting	129

Data Analysis	131
Methodological Limitations	132
CHAPTER FOUR: RESULTS	133
Participant Characteristics	133
Research Question 1 (RQ1): QoL of AI Senior Immigrants	135
Research Question 2 (RQ2): Loss of Autonomy or Independence	140
Hypothesis 2a: Self-efficacy or mastery	141
Hypothesis 2b: Access to transportation	142
Hypothesis 2d: Financial condition	144
Hypothesis 2f: Dependency due to language barrier	145
Hypothesis 2c and 2e: Comparison with situation in India	147
Research Question 3 (RQ3): Political and Legal Context	154
Research Question 4 (RQ4): Depression and Anxiety	156
Qualitative Analysis	157
Open-ended Questions: Themes	158
Summary of Findings	159
CHAPTER FIVE: DISCUSSION, CONCLUSIONS, AND RECOMMENDATIONS	162
Discussion	163
Participant Diversity: Representation of Indian States	163
Demographic Factors	164
Multilingual Capability, Hindi as the Most Common Language	166
Theoretical Models	167
QoL: United States versus India	168
Transportation	168
Financial dependence	170
Isolation	170
Frequent visits to India	171
QoL of AI Seniors and the Population Norms for WHOQOL-BREF	172
Impact of the Political and the Legal Context	175
Prevalence of Depression and Anxiety	177

    Connection with Children and their Families   179
    Peer Relationships, Meeting Places   180
        An ingenious solution   181
    Stay Here or go Back?   181
Implications for Practice   183
Directions for Future Research   186
Conclusions   188
Epilogue   193

REFERENCES   194

TABLE OF TABLES

	Table	Page
1.	Growth in Asian Indian Population in United States, California, and SF Bay Area Counties	20
2.	Demographic Profile of Participants	134
3.	Age, Number of Years in USA, QoL, Mastery, Depression, and GAD Scores	135
4.	Language Profile, Entertainment Preferences	136
5.	Self-Identification, Connection with India	137
6.	Health Insurance, Exercise, Expected versus Actual QoL	139
7.	QoL: Expected versus Actual (N = 109)	140
8.	Transportation in USA: Access and Satisfaction	142
9.	Most Common Mode of Transportation	143
10.	Source of Finance	144
11.	Language Barrier and Proficiency	145
12	Access to Transportation: U.S. versus India	148
13.	Finance: U.S. versus India	149
14.	QoL: U.S. versus India	151
15.	Social Support and Isolation: U.S. versus India	153
16.	ANOVA Analysis of QoL Dimensions by Citizenship Status	155
17.	Depression and Anxiety Profiles	156

TABLE OF FIGURES

Figure		Page
1.	Rise in AI population from 1990-2010	21
2.	Trend in Asian Indian Population Growth	22
3.	Number of Indians Obtaining Permanent Resident Status in the U.S.	50
4.	Flowchart of Research Procedure: Identifying Participants	128
5.	Flowchart of Study Procedure for Identified Participants	130
6.	Self-reported Mastery Scores by Gender	141
7.	Response to: Lack of English prevents access to services	146
8.	Response to: "I Communicate very well in English"	147
9.	Access to Transportation: U.S. versus India	149
10.	Finance U.S. versus India	150
11.	QoL: U.S. versus India	151
12	Feeling Isolated, Lonely, or Left out of Things: U.S. versus India	152
13.	Social Support in the U.S. is Better than in India	153
14.	Proposed QoL Model for AI Senior Immigrants	167
15.	Major Challenges faced by AI Senior Immigrants	190

LIST OF ABBREVIATIONS

AAFNY	Asian American Federation of New York
ADA	Americans with Disabilities Act
AOA	Administration on Aging
AI	Asian Indian
ANOVA	Analysis of Variance
BPHQ	Brief Patient Health Questionnaire
CAD	Coronary Artery Disease
CAPS	The Community Ambassador Program for Seniors
ECCAC	Ethnic and Cultural Community Advisory Committee
FDA	Food and Drug Administration
FEMA	Foreign Exchange Management Act
FERA	Foreign Exchange Regulation Act
GAD	Generalized Anxiety Disorder
HRQoL	Health Related Quality of Life
ICC	India Community Center
INSAF	Indian Seniors Association of Fremont
IT	Information Technology
JVSVN	Joint Venture Silicon Valley Network
NAMI	National Alliance on Mental Illness
NIAASC	The National Indo-American Association for Senior Citizens
OAA	The Older Americans Act
PHQ	Patient Health Questionnaire
PRIME-MD	Primary Care Evaluation of Mental Disorders
PRWORA	Personal Responsibility and Work Opportunity Reconciliation Act
QoL	Quality of Life
RQ	Research Question

SAHC	The South Asian Heart Center
SAMHSA	Substance Abuse and Mental Health Services Administration
SCCMHD	Santa Clara County Mental Health Department
SF	San Francisco
SPA	Senior Peer Advocate
SSI	Supplementary Security Income
SVCF	Silicon Valley Community Foundation
UCSF	University of California San Francisco
WHO	World Health Organization
WHOQOL	World Health Organization Quality of Life instrument
WHOQOL-BREF	World Health Organization Quality of Life instrument Brief version

ढूंढ लेगी मंजिल हमें
▶▶▶▶▶▶▶▶▶▶

PROLOGUE

Silicon Valley is known for innovative thinking, and engineers of Asian Indian origin make a substantial contribution in heralding new technology and implementing path-breaking ideas in the valley. Perhaps some of that creative thinking can be targeted towards improving the quality of life of the parents these engineers invite to this new land. With my background in computer science and engineering, it was not so long ago that I belonged to the community of Silicon Valley engineers and entrepreneurs. And for years I was quite happy with that profession. Yet, life brought me to a stage where I started questioning the worth of my existence, my training at some of the best institutions in the world, and my career. This book is based on my dissertation research, which was motivated by my desire to do something for my Indian community, and to bring the focus from physical health to mental health, from mere living to the quality of life. It is my sincere hope that this research will motivate like-minded people to take steps towards improving the life quality of our elders, which, in turn, will improve our own lives. If you would like to help in taking steps towards finding solutions, please contact me at anitaj@gmail.com.

Dr. Anita Jhunjhunwala Mukherjee
November 2012

FOREWORD

It was indeed a happy and welcome augury for me to have an opportunity of perusing the book, "Asian Indian Older Adults in Silicon Valley" authored by Dr. Anita Jhunjhunwala Mukherjee. This is an exhaustive and comprehensive commentary on all aspects of life of these older Asian Indian (AI) immigrants in new environs. Silicon Valley provides a fertile ground for conducting such a piece of social research. In the introductory chapter 1, the focus is on the scanty information about AI community, especially the recent (or late) immigrants.

Chapter 2 on literature review, is a commendable effort in presenting all such attempts undertaken earlier based on the financial and psychosocial aspects of the immigrants in general. It is a good compendium of the constitutional changes in immigration policies by the government since early 20th century. The legal framework had a salutary influence on the number of people seeking immigration and the facilities of healthcare and financial assistance available to the needy. There is ample discussion of the parameters that have a bearing on the quality of life of AI seniors, and need to be taken into account while comparing their lives in the U.S. and in the originating country. Their financial security, access to transportation for their mobility in daily living, and the position of subservience in the host country, were matters of concern. The language barrier and the cultural differences played havoc in developing closeness to their grandchildren. These are the real life problems in vivid comparison to their earlier life style back in India.

Chapter 3 deals with the methodology used for the study with a clear mandate to get rid of any possible source of bias. The questionnaire was devised to contain psychological parameters in addition to published instruments. The factors on which the selection of participants was based and the instruments employed for the investigation are discussed in great detail.

Chapter 4 on results pertains to the overall quality of life of AI senior citizens as adjudged from their financial condition, access to transportation, self-efficacy, language barrier, and loss of authority. In a nut-shell, immigration results in depletion of their social capital and dependence on children or government, depriving them of their dignity to some extent.

The last, but not the least, chapter 5, constitutes the epitome of the entire book as it pertains to the author's analysis, conclusions as well as recommendations based on this exhaustive study. The issues which were considered relevant to impacting the quality of life of AI seniors are: (a) political and legal context, (b) independence as characterized by access to transportation, financial health and language barriers, (c) social support network, (d) sense of belonging, (e) meaningful role, and (f) health. The citizens have a higher quality of life vis-à-vis the residents, since the citizens have been in the country for a longer period from the viewpoint of psychological health, environment domain, financial independence and social isolation. The conclusions are well reasoned out and are in consonance with earlier studies carried out in Europe, and North America.

The style of presentation is superb and the survey of literature is thorough and up-to-date. I sincerely appreciate the effort on the part of the author to create a highly useful database for AI senior immigrants. Its availability in a book form will be a good resource for future AI senior immigrants to acquaint and anticipate the realities of life that they have to cope with in the U.S. after this momentous step.

> Dr. S. P. Puri
> Former Prof. of Physics, Panjab University
> Chandigarh-160014
> November, 2012

ACKNOWLEDGEMENTS

First and foremost, I am grateful to the higher power that created circumstances propelling me towards an unknown destination and was there with me through the darkest and the brightest periods of this journey. And while the higher power is abstract, my husband, Animesh Mukherjee, is the concrete presence that has made this journey feasible as well as enjoyable. Animesh has this unique ability to see positive in the most negative circumstances, and without his help in numerous ways, I could never have reached where I am today.

I want to express my deepest gratitude to my dissertation committee members, Dr. Susan Guzzo and Dr. Wei-Chien Lee. Even before she agreed to chair the committee, I felt a strong connection with Dr Guzzo; both of us had technology background as well as similar values and interests, such as a desire to work with the older adult population. She always heard my perspective, patiently listening to the confusion and doubts I had, and then with a smile encouraged me to go on, showing confidence in my ability even when I did not feel it. Dr. Guzzo did not always give me the answer, but she empowered me and cajoled me to find the answer, and for that, I am extremely grateful. Dr. Lee came into my life at a time when I was feeling very discouraged, unable to decide how to proceed. She offered me a ray of hope and remained a guiding light in the rest of my journey. Her strength in research and statistical analysis was a very valuable resource.

One of the most important things that my foray into psychology has taught me is to see that our lives are more like a stage play. Various individuals come here, play a part, and then walk off. Coming from a large joint family, my traditional Indian values taught me to build close bonds, and to hold on to relations forever. My journey through the field of psychology while living in the Silicon Valley taught me new American values, the most important of which was to understand that individuals walk into our lives for a reason. They play their role and exit—there is no point in holding onto them; the stage has been emptied so that new actors can walk in. If only we can patiently live through the pause in the play while the stage is being set for the new act, then the new actors will play their role in our lives, tilting us towards the new direction that destiny has already chosen. While Dr. Hepworth, Dr. Hans, and Dr. Keller helped me in conceptualizing this research, Mr. Surti, Dr. Satyapal Puri, Dr. Ramesh Puri, B.G. Nair, and Manjula Gupta were instrumental in converting the dissertation into a book.

I want to particularly thank the entire Sharma family: Dr. Gopal and Shanta Sharma, and Dr. Shashi Sharma, who not only provided me a home away from home but also connected me to many potential participants. Special thanks go to Naren Bakshi and Edward Subega, who have been my mentors for many years and have supported me in diverse ways. My sincere gratitude also goes to the Indian senior community in the Bay Area, which welcomed my research initiative and participated with enthusiasm. I deeply appreciate the support provided by colleagues from South Asian Healthy Aging Initiative and by different Indian senior centers including India Community Center.

Amongst family and friends, I want to particularly thank my brother Dr. Ashok Jhunjhunwala, and friends Patrick Pracht, Dr. Vipin Kumar, Dr. Sreeharsha, Lien Cao, and Gopi. And that the next generation is now professionally our equal and will soon take over became evident when my nephew, Dr. Siddharth Jhunjhunwala, not only beat me by completing his doctorate several months ago but also provided some very thoughtful comments. And finally my gratitude to all those who played crucial roles in this journey but are too numerous for me to be able to name them here.

पिंजरे के पंछी रे, तेरा दर्द ना जाने कोय
▶▶▶▶▶▶▶▶▶▶▶▶▶▶▶▶▶▶

CHAPTER ONE: INTRODUCTION

An old person in general does not wish to move: it is painful to leave things that give him security; his past is much greater than his future; he always loses more than he gains. If he moves or emigrates because of adverse circumstances or to follow his children so as not to remain alone, he is very unhappy: he feels regressively dependent, like a child, but without a child's expectations and growth potential to reach new achievements. If it is true that every time we say goodbye we die a little, one dies a great deal in this case. (Grinberg & Grinberg, 1989, p. 128)

With these words, Grinberg and Grinberg succinctly captured the sense of loss and helplessness felt by many of the older adults who immigrate to a distant land in old age, such as Asian Indian (AI) parents who have come to the United States to be with their adult children.

The San Francisco (SF) Bay Area is one of the hubs for the AI population, especially because many Indians have immigrated to work in technology companies here (e.g. Hans, 2002; Shankar, 2003). Reasonably affluent (Sandhu, 2009; U.S. Census Bureau, 2008a), these working professionals have brought their parents from India to live with them, increasing the senior population of

Silicon Valley. Following their children into unknown territory, however, often requires that these seniors give up their extended family and friends, independence, and a sense of self-efficacy and self-confidence. In their home country, they belonged; they participated in the society; but with no experience in a new land, they are often forced to learn new values, a new culture, and sometimes even a new language at a time when they would have been more content with *aging in place* (Treas, 2009).

With no concrete job role that can provide fulfillment and many of the social roles left behind in their home country, they often stand on the bank of the river of life, watching and letting life slip by, unable to jump in and enjoy. Some of their issues are no different from what is associated with normal aging, but the rest stem from having to age in an environment where they are cut off from life as they knew it.

As the number of AI older adults grew in the SF Bay Area in the late 1990s (U.S. Census Bureau: American Fact Finder, 1990, 2000), it caught the attention of the local media. The San Jose Mercury News reported the story of a 70-year-old AI father who was a psychiatrist heading the department in a reputed hospital of Mumbai. He shared, "In India, I was in charge …. Now, I don't do anything. I have had to ask my daughter for money to go to the barbershop. It's very awkward" (Fernandez, 2005, para 2).

Lack of a meaningful role in life and helplessness that stems from having to depend on others for every small thing is reflected in the frustrated voice of this elderly interviewee. Although individual circumstances play an important role, retired seniors are one of the most vulnerable communities hit the hardest by the process of late-life immigration to a foreign land (Akhtar, 1999; Carlin, 1990; Grinberg & Grinberg, 1989; Kalavar & Van Willigen, 2005; Nandan, 2005, 2007).

In the foreword to the 1980 publication of *The Quality of Life of Asian Americans* (Nandi, 1980), William Liu raised an important point: many recent Asian immigrants experience *downward social mobility* rather than the much hyped and assumed *upward mobility*. His observation seems particularly applicable in the case of AI seniors who have relocated to live with their adult children. Liu argued in favor of further researching this important phenomenon:

> Studying downward as well as upward mobility of immigrants would lead us to ask many "common sense" questions in reverse. Instead of asking why some people move, the question is why they move when they already have superior status in their home countries; who would wish to immigrate in spite of the anticipated frustrations and relative deprivations after the move? Did they know about such realities? Does the "push and pull" hypothesis, so long well established in sociology since the days of Samuel Stouffer, really work in designing studies of new waves of immigrants from Asia? The consequences of not studying downward as well as upward mobility are serious in terms of developing adequate theory and description. (Liu, 1980, p. xii)

Yet, 30 years later, a recent search in various research databases yielded very few articles on downward social mobility. Meanwhile, the perception amongst policy makers, social scientists, and the general American public remains that immigrants are consuming important resources and public funds (Torres-Gil & Treas, 2009, Portes & Rumbaut, 2006).

The contribution made to American society by ethnic minority individuals who were highly educated and skilled in their own countries before migration is often ignored. Further, how immigrant seniors enhance the lives of their children and grandchildren by preserving their ethnic cultures, and the richness they bring to the pluralistic fabric of American society, is neither understood nor appreciated.

Research Background

The Silicon Valley

First coined by the journalist Don Hoefler in the early 1970s, the term "Silicon Valley" referred to the growing silicon chip industry in the Santa Clara Valley (Markoff, 2009). Although there is no consensus on the geographic boundaries of Silicon Valley, it usually denotes the southern part of the SF Bay, including all of Santa Clara County and adjacent areas in San Mateo, Alameda, and Santa Cruz counties (Joint Venture: Silicon Valley Network [JVSVN], & Silicon Valley Community Foundation [SVCF], 2010). Known at one time for its orchards and agricultural produce (County of Santa Clara, n.d.), over the last few decades, the valley has been transformed into the birthplace of innovative ideas and high technology industry. Meanwhile, the demographics of the region have undergone a major shift: more than one third of the region's 2.9 million inhabitants are foreign-born, and 48% people speak a language other than English at home (JVSVN & SVCF, 2010). With 40% white, 29% Asian and 25% Latino population (JVSVN & SVCF, 2010), it is a majority-minority region that is a microcosm of the growing diversity of the United States (Santamaria & Palma, 2008).

Asian Indians in the United States

The change in the immigration policies in 1965 and the persistent demand for skilled workers that could not be adequately met by domestic talent have led to tremendous growth in the AI population in the United States (e.g. Portes & Rumbaut, 2006; Rangaswamy, 2007). Whereas only 6,000 Indians took permanent residence in the United States between 1947 and 1965 (Rangaswamy, 2000), the numbers rose dramatically to almost 400,000 for the period of 1960-1989 (Department of Homeland Security, 2010). In last 20 years alone, the AI population has more than tripled, as it has grown from

815,000 in 1990 to more than 3,000,000 in 2010 (U.S. Census Bureau: American Fact Finder, 1990; 2011).

In Silicon Valley, a major contributor to AI population growth was the "dot com boom" of the 1990s, when professionals from India migrated in large numbers to work in the technology companies in the Valley (e.g. Hans, 2002; Shankar, 2003; Rangaswamy, 2007). As a result, from 20,000 in 1990, the AI population of Santa Clara County surged to more than 120,000 in 2010 (U.S. Census Bureau: American Fact Finder, 1990, 2011). The Alameda County saw a similar growth, from 15,000 in 1990 to 78,000 in 2010.

Along with engineers and technologists, not only did their families arrive but also their elderly parents in many instances. Further, the parents of the earlier wave of immigrants also arrived in significant numbers in the last couple of decades, resulting in a relatively high AI senior population in the Silicon Valley. Yet, very few empirical studies have been conducted and not much is known about the quality of life (QoL) of AIs nor their mental health condition (Hans, 2002).

Research in the cross-cultural counseling field has traditionally treated Asian immigrants as a homogeneous community (e.g. Mui & Kang, 2006; Mui & Shibusawa, 2008), and focused on East Asians as the subject of their research (e.g. Nandan, 2005; Singh, Arteaga, & Zea, 2002; Varghese, 2005). Sue and Sue are key authors in the field of multicultural counseling, yet the chapter on Asian Americans in the 2008 edition of their book, *Counseling the Culturally Diverse: Theory and Practice*, concentrates mostly on East Asian culture and research.

Despite their similarities, the culture of people from India and its neighboring countries, also known as South Asians, differs significantly from that of East Asians (e.g. Gill, 2008). As a result, their mental health issues are likely to be different, too. Many studies have commented on this lack of research on AI immigrants (e.g. Gill, 2008; Hans, 2002; Mehta, 1998), and some have attributed it to a paucity of initial research that can foster further research (Durvasula & Mylvaganam, 1994). Lack of researchers and mental health professionals who focus on this population and can mentor new students is cited as another cause (Durvasula & Mylvaganam, 1994). This study will, therefore, concentrate on the QoL of Indians living in the Silicon Valley, who are first-generation immigrants to the United States.

First-generation Asian Indians: The age groups. Relocating to a new country is the common experience that all first-generation immigrants share. The cause and effect relationship between immigration and stress or even trauma has been well-documented in the literature (e.g. Beckerman & Corbett, 2008; Harris-Reid, 1998; Portes & Rumbaut, 2006; Yakhnich, 2008). However, within the first-generation immigrants, different age groups—children, adolescents, adults, and seniors—face widely different challenges. The issues that adult professionals have are not the same as those of young children or adolescents, who come to this country with their parents, or of seniors, who relocate after retirement to reunite with their adult children.

Although the published literature is sparse, a number of dissertation studies have addressed acculturation issues that adolescents or children of South Asian immigrants face and the intergenerational struggle that occurs in these families (e.g. Ghosh, 2007; Mehta, T., 2005; Rajiva, 2005; Shankar, 2003; Shariff, 2006; Zaeem, 2007). Researchers have also focused on South Asian women facing the challenge of balancing the home and professional career, and navigating the shift in cultural norms (e.g. Agarwal-Narale, 2005; Badruddoja, 2007; Roshanravan, 2007; Samuel, 2008). Domestic violence is another issue that has received ample focus in the literature (e.g. Brommer, 2004; Grewal, 2004; Kallivayalil, 2006, Pillay, 2004; Sharma, 1998; Sharma, 2006).

What it means to be a South Asian, including self-concept and identity formation, either as a whole or for a subgroup of South Asians, seems to be the most well documented subject (e.g. Das Gupta, 1999; Deepak, 2004; Gupta-Carlson, 2007; Han,

2007; Rudrappa, 2001; Sen, 2002; Verma, 2004). Comparatively, there is very limited research on the specific struggles of the older adult subgroup (Nandan, 2005, 2007; Jonnalagadda & Diwan, 2005).

Older adults. Within the elderly AI population, two groups with very different needs exist (e.g. Prasad, 2009; The National Indo-American Association for Senior Citizens [NIAASC], n.d.). Those who arrived in their young age in search of education or jobs form the first group and are known as the *early immigrants*. The second group is that of *family-sponsored recent immigrants*, who arrived in their middle or old age. These two groups exist not just amongst AI older adults but amongst other immigrant communities in the United States (Treas, 2009). With their age cohorts of early immigrants, family-sponsored seniors share issues related to aging. However, the challenges they face are not limited to old age; rather, late-life immigration and culture shock are major factors that influence the life quality of this at-risk group (Treas, 2009).

The acculturation level of seniors in these two groups is very different. Early immigrants are mostly bicultural. Quite familiar with the U.S. laws, customs, and way of living, they can navigate the health care system and other social service agencies with ease (e.g. Nandan, 2007; NIAASC, n.d., Leach, 2009).

In stark contrast, family-sponsored immigrants are less educated, less proficient in English, and are poorer (e.g. Diwan & Jonnalagadda, 2001). They are also unaware of the resources available to them and are mostly dependent on their families (e.g. Leach, 2009). If they had aged in place in their home country, they would have been more content (Treas, 2009), autonomous and independent. Their mental health is heavily interlinked with the issues related to late-life relocation and Indian cultural values that are often diametrically opposite to that of American values (Khanna, McDowell, Perumbilly, & Titus, 2009; Nandan, 2005).

The Role of Immigration

Pointing towards a deep nexus between immigration and the aging population of the United States, Torres-Gil and Treas (2009) assert that the fields of gerontology and geriatrics have so far ignored this important link. They emphasize that professional societies and advocacy groups on aging have been silent even when the immigration reforms proposed in 2007 called for limiting the number of aging parents that are admitted to the country. Similar concerns have been raised in Europe where the older adult population is becoming increasingly diverse. Arguing that QoL of older ethnic minority migrants cannot be studied without taking into account the key aspects of their migration experience, and that existing QoL models are, therefore, not applicable to this population, Brockmann (2002) proposed a new model for the QoL of older minority immigrants in Europe. Yet, in the U.S., despite the voluminous literature on immigration, the needs of the elderly immigrants have been ignored in favor of the issues faced by working adults and their children (e.g. Burr, Gerst, Kwan, & Mutchler, 2009; Leach, 2009; Torres-Gil & Treas, 2009).

The timing of immigration also plays an important role in the lives of newcomers, as it determines the warmth of reception that they receive in the host country (Portes & Rumbaut, 2006; Torres-Gil & Treas, 2009). In 1986, some of the illegal immigrants were able to legalize, but since 1990s, the perception amongst the general American public that the older immigrants are "gaming the system" (e.g. Torres-Gil & Treas, 2009) and taking advantage of public benefits has led to debates and partial xenophobia resulting in the 1996 Welfare Reform Act, which has placed major restrictions on the eligibility of immigrants for social benefits (e.g. Portes & Rumbaut, 2006; Santamaria & Palma, 2008; Torres-Gil & Treas, 2009).

Further, a section of American society is of the opinion that "too much ethnic or national diversity threatens social solidarity" (Sabl, 2009, p. 90). AI seniors are conspicuous because of the color of their skin and their traditional ethnic clothes; as a result they often become the target of discrimination. Such hard-line stands and behavior of the host community makes acculturation of migrants more difficult than it already is (Portes & Rumbaut, 2006).

By emphasizing the role of the host community in making the acculturation process easier for the immigrants rather than putting the entire burden of adaptation on the individual, Santamaria and Palma (2008) echo the new thinking on improving immigrant integration. In San Jose, more than 58,000 jobs were created and upwards of $17 billion in revenues were generated in late 1990s by immigrant owners of technology companies (Santamaria & Palma, 2008). In 1998 alone, more than $26.8 billion in sales were posted by Silicon Valley businesses where Indian and Chinese engineers were senior executives (Saxenian, 2002), which makes a strong case for viewing immigrants as assets rather than liabilities. Recognition of such realities by the host community would reduce the barriers that exist in integrating the newcomers (Portes & Rumbaut, 2006).

Immigration as trauma. "Even under the best circumstances, immigration is a traumatic experience; like other traumas, it mobilizes a mourning process," argues Akhtar (1999, p xi) in the very preface of his treatise on immigration and identity. Although this seems like an extreme view not shared by many researchers, the difference is a matter of degree. Most scholars agree that there is a cause-and-effect relationship between immigration and mental health and that immigration causes stress, even though for some individuals, the stress could take the form of excitement and new opportunities (Beckerman & Corbett, 2008; Harris-Reid, 1998; Portes & Rumbaut, 2006). The terms *uprooting* and *immigration trauma* have been used in connection with seniors to portray the exceptional difficulties that some immigrants endure (e.g. Kalavar, 1998). Being an older adult and belonging to an ethnic minority has also been likened to *double* or *triple jeopardy* or disadvantages across multiple dimensions (Grewal, Nazroo, Bajekal, Blane, & Lewis, 2004; Kalavar, 1998; Sue & Sue, 2008).

How immigration affects an individual depends on many psychosocial variables as well as the unique circumstances of the person. However, the socio-demographic variables, such as the reason for migration, age at the time of migrating, the magnitude of cultural differences between the host culture and the home-country culture, and a sense of self-efficacy in the new culture, are all fairly good indicators of the result of the immigration (Akhtar, 1999).

Current Research on the Elderly AI Immigrants

In recent years, there is a growing awareness that the aging population in United States is becoming more and more ethnically diverse (e.g. Hayes-Bautista, Hsu, Perez, & Gamboa, 2002; Kalavar, 1998; Nandan, 2005; Torres-Gil & Treas, 2009) and that culturally competent services must be provided to them (e.g. Abramson, Trejo, & Lai, 2002; Periyakoil, 2004). Similar concerns have been raised for a number of years in the U.K. and Canada (e.g. Lai & Surood, 2008), where a sizable South Asian population resides, and studies on the mental health of older adults have been reported (e.g. Grewal et al., 2004; Kobayashi, 2003; Lai, 2010; Moffatt & Mackintosh, 2009; Rait & Burns, 1997). Choudhry (2001), for example, interviewed 10 elderly women who had immigrated to Canada from India and identified isolation and loneliness, family conflict, economic dependence, and issues with settling in, learning to cope, and a sense of loss of traditional values as the major themes in their narratives.

In contrast, since AI became a census category in 1980 (e.g. Lal, 2006), studies in the United States have been on Indians rather than the broader South Asian population. In an early study conducted during 1989-90, the life satisfaction of seniors was examined, and through surveys and semi-structured interviews, the effects of various demographic and other psychosocial variables on life satisfaction were studied (Kalavar,

1998). The acculturation and adaptation experience and the worldviews of elderly Indians were explored through qualitative studies in the tri-state (New York, New Jersey, and Connecticut) area (Kalavar & Van Willigen, 2005; Nandan, 2005) and Chicago (Rangaswamy, 2000). Although the standard of living or the material QoL of participants had improved, many lacked social, emotional, and spiritual fulfillment, and the mental health for some had deteriorated (Nandan, 2005). Lack of appreciation for their contribution in their children's successes, lack of social circle, generational differences in value system, and forced financial dependence on children are some issues raised in the Rangaswamy study.

A group of researchers investigated the physical and mental health conditions of English- and non-English-speaking Indians in the Atlanta area (e.g. Diwan, Jonnalagadda, & Balaswamy, 2004; Jonnalagadda & Diwan, 2005). They reported a link between depression, poor health, and sociodemographic factors, including gender, body mass index, perceived lack of social support, small social network, and acculturation level. Miltiades (1999, 2002) examined the filial bonding across the geographical boundaries between Indian immigrants in the U.S. and their parents, who still resided in India. She explored how the aged parents cope on a daily basis, whether they contemplate immigrating to the United States, or whether they expect that their emigrant children would eventually return to India to be with them.

In a landmark study conducted in 2000 in New York, the multiple dimensions of QoL of various Asian American groups, including AIs, were studied in depth and compared with each other (e.g. Mui & Shibusawa, 2008; Ryan, Mui, & Cross, 2003). Among other factors, this study explored how the acculturation and immigration experience affected the mental health of Asians, their perceived needs, and their formal and informal support networks. The resources available to these seniors and the key indicators of their well-being were analyzed in depth also. Clearly, there is a need to go further in this research direction; this study extended the work done by earlier studies.

The Research Problem

Within the senior AI immigrant population, the retired parents, who relocated specifically to be with the families of their adult children, face unique challenges. They neither have jobs nor accumulated assets, which force them to financially depend on their adult children or the state (Burr et al., 2009). Many communicate only in their native languages, and most of them do not drive; hence, they are dependent on their families or public transportation to participate in the community. This is especially difficult for these seniors, as most of them lived independently, had good jobs, family and friends, and a reasonably high standard of living in India.

Immigration forced them to leave their social capital behind and in a way demoted their social status. Further, the respect that the older generation commands and expects in the collectivistic AI culture is in stark contrast to the values of the individualistic American society (Kalavar, 1998; Lamb, 2009a; Nandan, 2005; Nandi, 1980; Rangaswamy, 2000). The resulting shift in the family power structure and the value system increases the gap between the pre-immigration expectations and the realities of older immigrants. As a result, isolation, loneliness, and helplessness can become key themes of their lives (Brown, 2009), yet due to their cultural value system, they often hide their mental health issues from the society (e.g. Durvasula & Mylvaganam, 1994; Lai & Surood, 2008; Patel, 2005). Instead of professional practitioners, they often turn towards religion (e.g. Chattopadhyay, 2005; Patel, 2005; Varghese, 2005). Further, even when they seek help, the community structures that could provide culture-sensitive care to this population are virtually absent (Hans, 2002). There is, therefore, a tremendous need to study the mental health condition and the life quality of this high-risk population.

Gaps within the Literature

As mentioned earlier, the AI older adults have been underrepresented in academic research. The age of participants in Nandi's study (1980) ranged between 21 and 60, and only one Indian was in the age category above 50. Even when the studies were exclusively on Indian seniors (e.g. Kalavar, 1998; Nandan, 2005; Jonnalagadda & Diwan, 2005), they included early immigrants, who have studied or worked in this country and as a result are much more acculturated; as discussed earlier, their needs are very different from those who came under the family reunification scheme (Prasad, 2009; NIAASC, n.d.).

Rangaswamy (2000) focused on elderly parents, but her focus group had only eight seniors. Kalavar's (1998) study examined life satisfaction, which is an aspect of QoL, but only English-speaking participants were chosen, and the fieldwork was mostly carried out in 1989-90. The demographics of the United States and the AI immigrant population have changed dramatically since then. Though Miltiades (1999, 2002) looked at the mental health of aged parents, she focused on those who had chosen to stay back in India rather than those who chose to immigrate.

While academic research on AI older adults is scarce, newspapers and popular media have published several stories on the silent plight of seniors living in the Bay Area (e.g. Padmanabhan, 2010; Hua, 2004; Fernandez, 2005, Brown, 2009). "Invisible Immigrants, Old and Left With 'Nobody to Talk To,'" published recently in The New York Times (Brown, 2009), gained considerable public attention. The articles highlight the isolation, loneliness, boredom, and depression among the elderly, notwithstanding the financial success of their adult children. For AIs living in the SF Bay Area, Hans (2002) examined the effect of acculturative stress on their mental health, but once again the age of the participants ranged between 18 and 81. Thus, so far, AI seniors relocating for family reunification has remained a neglected population for academicians. This study focused on Indian parents who (a) came to the United States in their middle or old age to reunite with their families, and (b) live in the SF Bay Area. Despite an extensive search, no study that focused exclusively on this population could be located.

The Purpose of the Study

The purpose of the study was to explore the current QoL of AI older adults in Silicon Valley who have immigrated to the U.S. to be with their adult children and grandchildren. Factors that relate to the mental health condition of this population were studied. Gaining an insight into the lives of these seniors and understanding their concerns, lifestyles, social-service needs, and psychological health was the objective of this research. The study particularly focused on understanding the effect of late-life immigration sequelae on the QoL of these seniors.

The Research Questions

1. What is the QoL of elderly AI immigrants who came to the United States to be with their adult children? Which psychosocial factors influence the QoL of such seniors living in the Silicon Valley?
2. How has the immigration influenced the self-reported autonomy or independence for this group of people? Specifically, how has the immigration experience impacted their physical and social mobility, including access to transportation, finances, and social interaction?
3. How does the political and legal context of the United States influence the QoL of these seniors? Specifically, does citizenship status impact their life quality?
4. What is the prevalence of depression and generalized anxiety disorder in this population?

Hypotheses

The QoL of AI seniors is affected by their (a) old age, (b) Indian cultural heritage, and (c) late-life immigration. The objective of the study is to understand how late-life immigration has affected the lives of these seniors. The study hypothesizes:

1. Descriptive statistics will be reported for research question 1 as there is no hypothesis.
2. Indian seniors who immigrate in late life to be with their adult children will experience a loss of autonomy or independence. They will:
   a. Have low self-efficacy or mastery.
   b. Not be satisfied with their current access to transportation.
   c. Have less access to transportation compared to when they were in India.
   d. Be financially dependent on their children or the government.
   e. Be more financially dependent compared to when they were in India.
   f. Experience a language barrier that would result in dependence for interaction or communication.
3. Indian seniors who are U.S. citizens will have a higher QoL compared to those who are not.
4. The prevalence of depressive symptoms and generalized anxiety disorder will be higher in Indian older adults under study compared to the general population.

Significance of the Study

Most of the studies on the mental health of immigrant AIs have researched women, children, young adults, or working professionals (Nandan, 2005; NIAASC, n.d.), which is consistent with the trend amongst other immigrant populations (Markides, Salinas, & Sheffield, 2009). Although research evidence on immigrant communities suggests that elderly Asians have worse mental health and higher depression compared to the general older-adult population (Markides et al., 2009), very few studies address this issue.

American Geriatric Population: Need for Culturally Competent Care

Considerable academic and policy attention has been focused on (a) the graying of America, which entails an increasing older-adult population as a result of higher life expectancy, declining fertility, and aging of baby-boomers (e.g. Brown, Bean, & Bachmeier, 2009; Myers, 2009); and (b) the browning of America, indicating the increasing ethnic diversity of the country, a consequence of the growing number of immigrants (e.g. Torres-Gil & Treas, 2009).

A number of studies and advocacy groups have put the two phenomena together to bring attention to the growing diversity of the geriatric population (Abramson, Trejo, & Lai, 2002; Community Partnerships for Older Adults, n.d.; Gupta & Pillai, 2002; Kalavar, 1998; Mui & Shibusawa, 2008). Describing it as *browning of the graying of America*, Hayes-Bautista et al. (2002) examined the ethnic composition of the increase in the 65-plus population from 1990 to 2000 in California and discovered that 70% of the increase came from the Hispanic and the Asian communities.

Further, the life expectancy of Asian/Pacific Islander older adults was nine years more than that of Whites in the 65-70 years age category, whereas that of African American elders was 1.5 years less than that of the White Americans. This indicates that one size does not fit everyone and that considerable group differences within ethnic minorities exist. This heterogeneity of the minority groups, coupled with the increasing diversity of the older American population, calls for new tools, research, and policies (Abramson et al., 2002; Community Partnerships for Older Adults, n.d.; Hayes-Bautista et al., 2002). However, very little empirical research exists on many ethnic minorities, including AIs.

In recent years, a growing body of literature has emphasized the need to provide linguistically and culturally competent care to ethnically diverse populations (e.g. Khanna et al., 2009; Mui & Shibusawa, 2008). On one hand it would improve the quality of services, and on the other hand it would reduce the health disparity amongst minorities (Mui & Shibusawa, 2008).

Evidence-based practice demands that studies are conducted to obtain more information and a better understanding of various cultures, their effect on mental health, and the problems that individuals perceive (Abramson et al., 2002; Mui & Kang, 2006). The ethnogeriatrics committee of the American Geriatrics Society (2004) also asserts that the ethnicity of the client should be an important factor in the "doorway thoughts" of the clinicians intending to provide culturally competent care to this growing segment of the population. By exploring multiple dimensions of the lives of a growing ethnic minority group in the United States, this study makes a significant contribution to the multicultural counseling field.

The Focus on the Under-Researched AI Community

Although considered *a model minority*, judging by the prevalent norms of American society, the AI community faces challenges in terms of recognizing the need for better mental health care and providing it through appropriate community support structures (Kalavar, 1998; Nandi, 1980; Patel, 2005). Calling the model minority a myth, scholars have commented on the large within-group differences, which often are ignored by the community at large (Mehta, 1994; Rangaswamy, 2007; Verma, 2004) as well as by prosperous members of the Indian community (Diwan & Jonnalagadda, 2001). Although the perception of society is that Indians take care of their own and do not need assistance from the state, many struggling immigrants do not receive the public support they require (e.g., Mehta, R., 2005; Nandan, 2007).

Adding to the knowledge base on AI seniors. Commenting on the lack of studies on immigrant older adults, Treas (2009) reasoned, "Arriving too late in life for the Americanizing influences of school and workplace, they remain invisible to the broader society and dependent on kin for support, companionship, and help in navigating U.S. society" (p. 40). Other researchers have also echoed the view that very little is known about the lives of elderly immigrants (e.g. Torres-Gil & Treas, 2009; Kalavar & Van Willigen, 2005). This study intends to make a small opening in the closed walls that surround the AI older-adult community.

There is a taboo against acknowledging or seeking professional help for psychological issues in this community (Chattopadhyay, 2005; Derry, 1996; Patel, 2005). However, if and when seniors do seek professional help, a lack of research on this population forces the service provider to treat them in a context where there is scarce research evidence.

Exploring the lifestyle, environmental, and psychological issues faced by AI immigrant seniors is likely to give psychologists, therapists and family counselors, an insight into the mental health condition of this high-risk population. It might focus their attention towards the depleted social capital, resulting isolation, lack of transportation, and other problems that affect the life quality of immigrant seniors, which could help them in designing programs targeted specifically towards this demographic population. The study could also herald changes in the policy of the local government and social service agencies as they are better informed about the needs, barriers, and the resources available to the AI older adults.

This study is also likely to build awareness amongst the seniors—it would normalize their psychological issues, as they would learn that they are not alone and many others have similar problems. Mental health practitioners would gain an insight on the kinds of issues these seniors face, and the seniors, in turn, would learn that professional help is available to them. The study could also be a resource in understanding what would contribute to successful ageing of this ethnic minority population simultaneously struck by multiple jeopardies of aging and immigration in late life. Further, the results of this study are likely to be applicable to the broader South Asian community with whom the AI community shares history and culture.

Limited community support structures. Physical health impairment is socially acceptable in the Asian culture, as a result of which non-profit organizations that deal with physical health issues, such as The South Asian Heart Center (SAHC) at El Camino Hospital in the SF Bay Area, have been established (SAHC Mission, n.d.). However, community support structures that build awareness, provide psychosocial education to prevent mental health episodes, and offer culturally sensitive therapeutic services are quite limited in the AI community.

Amongst what is currently available are organizations that address the domestic violence issues faced by South Asian women. Senior Centers operating several times a week have also been established in a few locations. Innovative programs that involve families and community members are also emerging, the details of which will be examined in Chapter 2. While these isolated efforts deserve recognition, there is a need for sustained efforts to help improve the QoL of seniors. By documenting the locations that seniors visit frequently, this study improves the knowledge about existing facilities and might even draw the attention of policymakers, thereby helping in improving the available infrastructure.

The Advantage of Silicon Valley

In 1990, the combined AI population in the six counties of Santa Clara, Alameda, Contra Costa, San Mateo, and Santa Cruz was 50,000, approximately 31% of 160,000, the total Indian population of California (U.S. Census Bureau: American Fact Finder, 1990, 2000). By 2000, there was a dramatic three-fold increase in the Bay Area Indian population so that the six counties were now home to 151,000 Indians, 41% of the 360,000 Indians residing in California. Similar population growth continued for the period 2000-2010, as is evident from Table 1, which shows the numbers for each county as well as the total figures for the United States and California.

Table 1
Growth in Asian Indian Population in United States, California, and SF Bay Area Counties (Based on the U.S. Census Bureau: American Fact Finder Data)

	1990	2000 AI alone or in any combination	2008 AI alone or in any combination	2010 AI alone	2010 AI alone or in any combination
United States	815,447	1,899,599	2,703,731	2,843,391	3,183,063
California	159,973	360,392	498,704	528,176	590,445
Alameda County	15,282	47,194	65,031	72,278	78,208
Contra Costa County	6,351	13,376	Not Available	22,328	24,816
San Francisco County	3,063	6,616	Not Available	9,747	11,583
San Mateo County	4,842	12,599	Not Available	13,486	15,933
Santa Clara County	20,164	70,159	102,693	117,596	123,182
Santa Cruz County	417	1,123	Not Available	1,077	1,400

Based on 2010 census data, approximately 255, 000 Indians live in the six SF Bay Area counties, which is 43% of the AI population of California, and 8% of the AI population of the U.S. Further, nearly 10-12% of the total AI population falls under the category of seniors including both early and recent immigrants (Prasad, 2009; NIAASC, n.d.). As a result, the number of Indian seniors in the SF Bay Area is now large enough so that sufficient participants of diverse backgrounds could be identified.

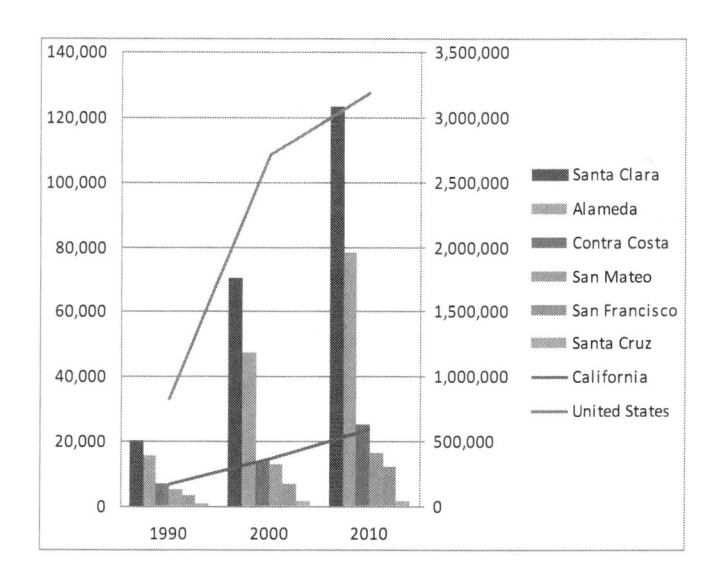

Figure 1. Rise in AI population from 1990-2010

Further, Figure 1 and 2 show the increase in AI population graphically in bay area counties as well as in California and U.S. The rise is above national average and is steepest in Santa Clara County followed by Alameda County.

The valley is now home to shops, restaurants, and movie theaters where Indian food, clothing, and entertainment are available. It has temples, *gurudwaras* (Sikh-temples), and community centers where seniors usually gather, and all major Indian festivals are celebrated throughout the Bay Area. Such events and locations helped in finding participants for the study.

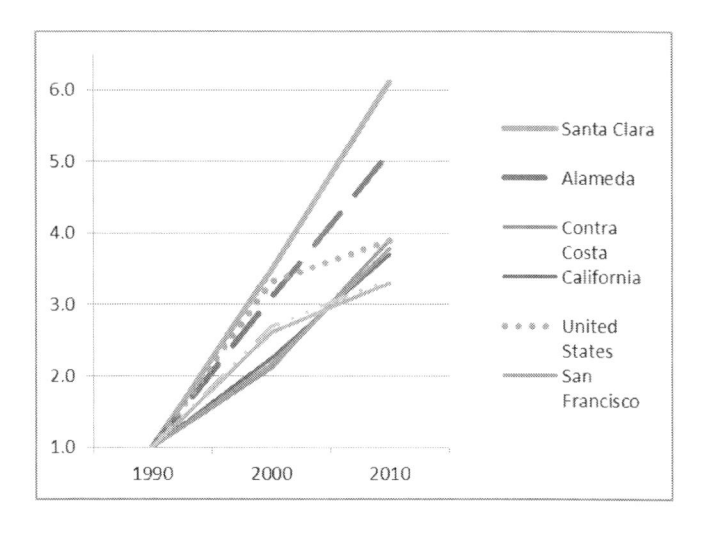

Figure 2. Trend in Asian Indian Population Growth

Limitations of the Study

The scope of this study is limited to the geographic region of the SF Bay Area, which has one of the highest concentrations of AI population in the United States. Ethnic enclaves act as a protective buffer for new immigrants by preserving the languages, culture, and customs of the home country (e.g. Torres-Gil & Treas, 2009; Nandan, 2005, 2007) as well as by providing social support that might mitigate the effect of economic hardship (Burr et al., 2009). The experiences of the seniors in this area are therefore likely to be different compared to those arriving in the Midwest or other regions with a low density of Indians. Further, within the SF Bay Area, the demographics of various cities are very different. Fremont, Milpitas, Sunnyvale, Santa Clara, and San Jose, for example, are cities with relatively large Indian populations, whereas cities such as Santa Cruz have a much lower density of AIs. The present study has not taken into account the impact of city of residence in the QoL of AI seniors.

Another limitation of this study is that the sample size of 109 is not large enough for generalization of the research results or for carrying out regression analysis because of the large number of variables involved. Further, only limited numbers of home-bound seniors participated in this research; hence, their issues need to be further studied. Moreover, because the study relies on structured interviews or survey responses, problems such as social desirability and agreeability to the interviewer (e.g. Campbell, Converse, & Rodgers, 1976) common to all survey designs exist in this study.

Delimitations

Although physical health is a major priority for this age group, especially if they are facing health issues, it is not a focus of this study. The factors that affect QoL seem to follow Maslow's pyramid—if health is poor, it becomes a priority for the individual, but the moment satisfactory health is achieved, other issues become important. Yet, there are apparent paradoxes as some people find happiness and peace even though their physical health is bad, as in the case of some cancer patients (Barron, 2000; Freedman, 1991; Greer, 1998). Further, stressful life events, especially bereavement due to the death of friends and family members play an important role in the well-being of the geriatric population, but this study did not focus on them.

Feasibility of the Study

Measuring the QoL of this ethnic, migrant, older-adult population presented unique challenges at conceptual, methodological, and measurement levels. The difficulties at the conceptual level were very well-articulated by Nandi (1980): "The concept of quality of life is so bound by time, class, ideology, and values that there is a general lack of consensus about what conditions are desirable and what are not, and to what extent" (p. 13). Chapter Two will explore these difficulties and examine the various definitions in the literature for QoL.

Recognizing that immigration in late life and the resulting acculturative stress plays a significant role in the QoL of these seniors and taking into account the argument put forward in the literature that acculturative stress should be looked at from a systemic framework (Beckerman & Corbett, 2008), this study attempted to do just that. By using an internationally standardized instrument from the World Health Organization (WHO) that not only measures Health Related Quality of Life (HRQoL) but also takes into account psychological, social, and environmental perspectives, the study gave an overall picture of the QoL of the research participants.

By using additional instruments for mastery, depression, and anxiety, it provided an insight into the mental health of the studied sample. The study zeroed in on the environmental aspects by examining psychosocial variables relevant to immigration, aging, and Indian culture. The impact that late-life immigration has had on the lives and in particular psychological health of these individuals remained an important purpose of this study.

Definitions of Terms

Some of the important terms that are used throughout this study are defined in this section.

Asian Indians or Indians

The term "Asian Indian" was used by the U.S. Census Bureau in 1980 to distinguish people of India from Native American Indians (Rangaswamy, 2000). Since then it has gained popularity in the academic literature. However, beyond academics, the term AI is hardly used. It includes individuals (a) who were born in India, or (b) whose ancestors came from India, even if they later resettled in other parts of the world; that is, the Indian diaspora. Since the context is quite clear, this study used both AIs and Indians interchangeably.

South Asian

The term South Asian refers to people from India and its neighboring countries (e.g. Lai & Surood, 2008). However, there is no consensus on exactly which countries are included in South Asia, and different agencies such as South Asian Association for Regional Cooperation and United Nations, define it differently. In this study, natives of India, Nepal, Bangladesh, Bhutan, Pakistan and Sri Lanka, and their diasporas were regarded as South Asians.

First- and Second-Generation Immigrants

Although there is some ambiguity regarding who should be considered the first- and the second-generation immigrant, for the purpose of this research, immigrants who were born outside the United States and immigrated as adults are considered to be first-generation, while their children are called the second-generation immigrants. That is, second-generation immigrants are those who are either born within the United States or immigrate as children with their first-generation parents.

Early Immigrants and Family-Sponsored Recent (or Late) Immigrants

Individuals who immigrated to the United States for higher education or employment are regarded as early immigrants (Prasad, 2009; NIAASC, n.d.). Most of them arrived in the U.S. as young adults; therefore, the term "early" is used to refer to them. In contrast, family-sponsored recent immigrants are those who arrived in middle to late age to reunite with their families. In literature, they are called recent immigrants as well as late immigrants. Some recent immigrants have been living in the U.S.

for 30-40 years. The major characteristic that distinguishes them from early immigrants is that recent immigrants are family-sponsored, while early immigrants arrive on student or employment visas. This study focuses exclusively on AI, family-sponsored, recent immigrants.

CHAPTER TWO: LITERATURE REVIEW

This chapter reviews the literature and is divided into several sections. It begins with an exploration of the amorphous concept of life quality, its history, how it evolved, what it means to different groups, and the factors that influence it. The theoretical models pertinent to ethnic immigrants and older adults are examined followed by their meaning in the special context of AI seniors who have relocated in late life. The second section deals with the impact of the political and legal context of the United States in the lives of AI older adults. The immigration policies, the evolution of social security, and welfare benefits as it relates to older adults is described along with a brief look at the Indian laws for expatriates.

The third section focuses on the history and diversity of Indian immigrants in the United States. The subgroups within AI seniors are then examined and the definitive characteristics of the study population are introduced. The nuances of Indian culture relevant in the study of senior immigrants, such as the family structure, perspectives on aging, and the responsibility for the elderly make up the fourth section of the chapter. This is followed up with a description of studies within the U.S. on AI seniors. A large number of factors and facets within each factor influence the life quality of an older adult, and the final section focuses on these.

Quality of Life

QoL has become an important construct not only in gerontology research (Chandler, 2009; Smith, Sim, Scharf, & Phillipson, 2004) but also in population studies and government policies (Brockmann, 2002; Campbell et al., 1976; Hawthorne, Herrman, & Murphy, 2006), and in health, psychology, and medical literature (Aggarwal, Agarwal, Gupta, & Jindal, 2010; Hawthorne et al., 2006; Hyde, Wiggins, Higgs, & Blane, 2008; Saxena, Chandramani, & Bhargava, 1998). The broad use of the term across multiple disciplines in diverse contexts has led to the publication of a large number of theoretical and empirical papers on the subject, and according to some estimates, the numbers are as high as more than 5,000 articles every year (Chandler, 2009). This section reviews the literature on QoL, including its myriad definitions, related terms, components of and influences on life quality, and the evolution of QoL and its instruments over the last few decades. The meaning of QoL in the context of older adults and AIs will also be examined.

Defining Quality of Life

Despite many articles that investigate the concept of QoL (e.g. Haas, 1999; Hensel, 2001; Prutkin & Feinstein, 2002), defining QoL turned out to be a much more difficult task than was originally envisaged due to several reasons. First, it is a multi-disciplinary term that is interpreted differently by different groups of people (Dissart & Deller, 2000, Nandi, 1980). On the surface, in colloquial terms, it simply refers to how good someone's life is (Brown, Friefeld, & Schiller, 1993), but defining "good" is not straightforward as what is considered good in one society is often not the same in other contexts and cultures; that is, QoL is a value-laden term (e.g. Hensel, 2001; Low, 2005; Nandi, 1980).

Second, QoL is associated not just with individuals but also with groups in terms of societal well-being (Campbell et al., 1976; Felce & Perry, 1995), and with locations to denote a good place to live (Dissart & Deller, 2000; Nandi, 1980). The planning literature is replete with QoL of a neighborhood or community, and how that can affect migration, employment opportunities and regional economic growth (Dissart & Deller, 2000). Governments and social scientists produce aggregate statistics by tracking QoL and well-being of populations through various social indicators (Prutkin & Feinstein, 2002).

Third, although several writers have attempted to define it, there is neither a consensus on what QoL really is, nor is there a single, agreed upon definition (Carr & Higginson, 2001; Smith et al., 2004). Some scholars have called it an elusive concept (Campbell, Converse, & Rodgers, 1976; Felce & Perry, 1995; Low, 2005) while others have found it a complex construct that defies definition, and have argued that a single definition is not even desirable (Nandi, 1980).

Commenting on the state of confusion, one author went as far as saying that as many definitions of QoL exist as there are people (Liu, 1976, as cited in Felce & Perry, 1995) while others argued that the number of definitions equal the number of researchers studying QoL (Baker & Intagliata, 1982, as cited in Wiggins, Netuveli, Hyde, Higgs, & Blane, 2008). This has led some theoreticians to say that as a construct, QoL is still in its infancy and that despite the progress in the last few decades, a lot of work remains pending (Brown, Friefeld, & Schiller, 1993).

The common themes. In spite of this lack of agreement on definition, several common themes emerge in the literature. Although some authors consider QoL in only subjective or only objective terms, there is a reasonably broad consensus amongst scholars that (a) QoL is multidimensional, and depends on factual and objective conditions as well as individual's subjective evaluation of these conditions; and (b) the perception of a person is paramount in the ultimate quality of his or her life (Bowling, 2005; Felce & Perry, 1995; Haas, 1999; Hepner, 2003; Nandi, 1980; Prutkin & Feinstein, 2002; Wiggins, Higgs, Hyde, & Blane, 2004). Further, the importance of expectations and aspirations in determining QoL, and comparing them against the actual experience of the individual is increasingly recognized (e.g. Bowling, 2005; Hepner, 2003).

Different perspectives. The debate over defining QoL is certainly not new. Thirty years ago, Nandi (1980) commented on QoL emerging as a major issue for both academicians and government agencies. The focus then was on understanding and measuring the well-being of both individuals and groups through social indicators. Nandi cited Ben-Chieh Liu:

> Quality of Life – QoL – is a new name for an old notion. It is a subjective name for the 'well being' of people and the environment in which they live . . . QoL expresses that set of 'wants' which after being supplied, when taken together, makes the individual happy or satisfied. (1980, p. 11)

Thus Liu's definition took into account only the subjective aspects of QoL, ignoring the objective ones. Nandi's (1980) conclusion based on the review of literature, however, included both components—the exogenous factual measures of living conditions, and the endogenous satisfaction of the individual. Felce and Perry (1995) came up with a rather comprehensive definition through a synthesis of various models presented in the literature:

> Quality of life is defined as an overall general well-being that comprises objective descriptors and subjective evaluations of physical, material, social, and emotional wellbeing together with the extent of personal development and purposeful activity, all weighted by a personal set of values. (p. 60-62)

They argued that the three elements—objective conditions, subjective satisfaction, and personal values—interact and influence each other so that change in any one of them affects the others. In addition, external factors influence the three elements independently. Hence, all three must be assessed to arrive at the QoL of a person, and knowing one set, others cannot be predicted since the relation amongst the three does not remain static.

"The degree to which a person enjoys the important possibilities of his or her life" (The Quality of Life Research Unit, n.d.), is how the Centre for Health Promotion at the University of Toronto defined QoL, and by doing so, it zeroed in on the unrealized potential in each human being. People have inherent abilities and talents, but the extent to which they can attain their potential depends on the opportunities that the environment provides. Thus, their life quality depends on the interplay between the personal and the situational factors. Focusing on the aspirations of the individual, Carr and Higginson (2001), define QoL as "The extent to which hopes and ambitions are matched by experience" (p. 1358) or as "Appraisal of one's current state against some ideal" (p. 1358).

The WHO initiative. Realizing the complex and broad nature of QoL and lack of a universal definition, the Quality of Life Group at WHO undertook a cross cultural study involving 15 field-centers across the world to define what QoL meant to individuals in these different nations, and to develop standardized instruments to measure it (WHO, 1998). The centers were specifically chosen to take into account diverse socioeconomic standards, levels of industrialization, availability of health resources, religion, family values, and cultural settings. The perspectives of sick and healthy individuals as well as health professionals and researchers were incorporated in this exercise. After extensive literature review and focus group discussions, the group defined QoL as "individuals' perceptions of their position in life in the context of the culture and value systems in which they live and in relation to their goals, expectations, standards and concerns" (1998, p. 3). This definition stressed on how people perceive and internally evaluate their lives, and deemphasized objective conditions of their lives.

Summary. Based on the review of the available literature, QoL seems to be an amorphous rather than concrete concept that individual researchers have tailored to suit the requirements of their study. It is a complex, multidimensional concept with psychological, social, emotional, spiritual, physical, functional, and environmental domains that may serve as simply influences on QoL or as content domains. QoL depends on the external conditions of people's lives; but the value that individuals attach to those conditions and how they interpret them affects it significantly more. Further, QoL does not remain static; as the life situation, aspirations, and objectives of the individual changes, so does the life quality.

The History and Evolution of QoL

This section reviews the history of significant events that affected the evolution of QoL as a concept and instruments that measure it. Although several articles reviewed provide a section on the history of QoL, none were as comprehensive and detailed as Prutkin and Feinstein (2002), which is the main source of information for this section.

QoL is not only a technical term used in literature but is also popular amongst the general public. Some researchers consider the 1889 article by James Set, "The Evolution of Morality," as the earliest known scientific paper utilizing QoL concept (Mazaheri, 2010), whereas others have stated that a clear origin of the term QoL cannot be established (Szalai, 1980, as cited in Dissart & Deller, 2000). Tracing the history of QoL in medical literature, Prutkin and Feinstein (2002) attributed the lack of clarity and consensus in defining and measuring QoL to the simultaneous development of QoL instruments in both the medical and the social science fields.

The functional status scales. A functional status scale that assessed how well a person can perform various activities, which are now classified as Activities of Daily Living (ADL), appeared as early as 1937 in the medical literature (Prutkin & Feinstein, 2002). A joint project of several agencies, the instrument was designed to assess the medical needs of seniors in New York City, who were receiving public assistance. It categorized people as "I, no obvious disability; II, up and able to get about; III homebound, and IV, bedridden" (Prutkin & Feinstein, 2002, p. 81). Similar instruments that examined the health status of patients suffering with different diseases, functional capacity and occupational skills of the elderly, and the physical disability, and emotional status of the soldiers in World War II were devised over the next few decades (Prutkin & Feinstein, 2002).

WHO definition of health and the social science indices. At the International Health Conference in New York on July 22, 1946, the representatives of 61 countries signed on a new definition of health, which in 1948 became a part of the WHO constitution. The definition, "Health is a state of complete physical, mental and social well-being and not merely the absence of disease or infirmity" (WHO, 1948, p.1), acted as a trigger for governments, which started looking beyond mortality and morbidity in quantifying public health in their national metrics. Surveys were designed to incorporate the social and personal impacts of diseases, and the steps taken for prevention of illness (Prutkin & Feinstein, 2002). Simultaneously, public satisfaction became a measure of the effectiveness of the social programs.

The social studies and urban planning literature, which had so far looked at the governmental policies, services, and how they improved the economic well-being of its citizens soon started including the psychological well-being and perceptions of citizens (Campbell et al., 1976). Led by psychologists and sociologists, the Social Indicators Movement advocated the inclusion of QoL statistics such as satisfaction that income brings while collecting statistics on earnings and distribution of income, and the incorporation of mental health and positive elements of health while reporting on death and diseases (Prutkin & Feinstein, 2002). This need to distance health from morbidity has been particularly justified in recent years in the light of studies that have shown that patients with chronic diseases often perceive health in a holistic sense realizing that there is a potential for health even within sickness (Haas, 1999), and report a much higher QoL than would be expected given their health condition (Carr & Higginson, 2001; Hepner, 2003).

Subjective well-being. Two publications in 1976, the seminal work of Campbell et al., *The Quality of American Life*, and of Andrews and Withey, *Social Indicators of Well-Being: Americans' Perceptions of Life Quality,* had a monumental impact on the growth of QoL (Prutkin & Feinstein, 2002). They showed how subjective aspects of QoL such as satisfaction with life can be measured. This sparked off an interest in examining the relationship between people's life satisfaction and their aspirations/expectations. The studies now started assessing satisfaction at a global level as well as in various individual domains such as employment and housing.

Drawing attention to erstwhile fixation of the nation with material possessions, Campbell et al. (1976) urged Americans to shift the focus from being well-off to psychological well-being. They echoed the growing sentiment that good life does not come from consumer goods as a result of which national goals were increasingly defined in terms of QoL rather than economic wealth.

Thus, QoL has evolved from a mere economic indicator to a complex construct that takes into account the individual's perception of his or her life (Hensel, 2001). Traditionally, psychological well-being was assumed to be directly related to economic growth but as discussed above, by 1950s the fallacy in this assumption was understood. By 1960s, social indicators such as health, leisure, and political activity were incorporated in the studies and 1970s saw the emergence of psychological indicators (Hensel, 2001; Prutkin & Feinstein, 2002).

Cross-over of social science QoL indicators into medical science. The social science indices designed to measure population characteristics were gradually employed in clinical research as the utilitarian approach of functional indices gave way to include patient's perception while comparing treatment interventions (Prutkin & Feinstein, 2002). The new definition of health by WHO in 1948 acted as a catalyst in this regard as emphasis was laid on measuring the effect of a disease on the QoL of patients (Haroon, Aggarwal, Lawrence, Agarwal, & Misra, 2007). For terminal illnesses such as cancer, the acceptability of the life quality after intervention became a measure in addition to longevity in 1960s and 70s. Factors such as inability to find or retain a job, or to care for children, or withdrawal of the spouse were considered in judging QoL. That is, both the quantity and the quality of survival gained prominence in the medical literature.

Impact of Food and Drug Administration (FDA) policy. The QoL research received another impetus when in 1980s the FDA decided that the new cancer drugs should include QoL data such as improvement in pain or other physiological or psychological symptoms (Prutkin & Feinstein, 2002). Further, when clinical studies comparing QoL of people taking different hypertensive drugs were published, and one medication performed better than others, the potential of selling drugs because of their impact on QoL was realized by the pharmaceutical industry (Prutkin & Feinstein, 2002). This spurred further research in QoL measures.

Thus, the commercial and regulatory incentives were an important factor in the evolution and growth of literature on QoL. Prutkin and Feinstein (2002) reported that the number of articles with QoL in the Medline subject heading showed a gradual increase from 1975 to 1988, which became a sharp increase in 1989, a trend that continues without abating.

Components of QoL

Although scholars do not agree on what constitutes QoL, there is a general consensus that it depends on exogenous or objective factors of a person's life as well as endogenous or subjective perceptions of the person about these objective conditions (Dissart & Deller, 2000; Felce & Perry, 1995; Haas, 1999).

Haas (1999) conducted an intensive literature review where she examined 27 book chapters and theory-based papers, and 88 empirical studies selected from more than 16,000 articles. She concluded that physical, psychological, social, and spiritual are the four dimensions of QoL, and that functional status and well-being are its objective and subjective components respectively.

By examining and synthesizing 15 key articles that have proposed models for QoL, Felce and Perry (1995) identified physical well-being, material well-being, social well-being, emotional well-being, and development and activity as the five main domains relevant to QoL. Several subdomains and sub-subdomains were identified within each domain, thereby completing a hierarchical picture.

The Quality of Life Research Unit at the University of Toronto uses a model that focuses on three life domains—being, belonging, and becoming (The Quality of Life Research Unit, n.d.). The *being* refers to "who one is" and is evaluated in terms of physical, psychological, and spiritual dimensions. The *belonging* is the individual's connection with the environment, and has the subdomains of physical belonging measured in terms of concrete connections such as home, neighborhood, and place of work; social belonging, which refers to family, friends, and co-workers; and community belonging, conceptualized in terms of access to education, employment, community events, and the like. Finally, *becoming* indicates achieving one's goals and aspirations through practical, leisure and growth potentials.

In contrast to above efforts to identify the common components is the view that emphasizes the individual nature of QoL and opposes the standardization effort. Carr and Higginson (2001), for example, posit that even if some content domains that definitely impact QoL are identified, the importance that the person attaches to these domains would vary depending on their culture and individual situation. Further, such influence would not be static as the person's priorities and expectations might change with time—a view that has been expressed by other scholars (e.g. Hepner, 2003).

The international initiative undertaken by WHO in early 1990s discussed earlier resulted in identification of broad domains, facets within each domain, and items within each facet that contribute to QoL. Physical, psychological, level of independence, social relationships, environment, and spirituality or religion or personal beliefs were the six domains identified by this unique, cross-cultural, developmental process (WHO, 1998). Each domain had several facets with a total of 25 facets, and with four items per facet, an instrument with 100 questions, WHOQOL-100 was developed. Later, two of the domains were subsumed within others and only physical, psychological, social and environmental domains were retained for a shorter version of the instrument, WHOQOL-BREF (Lin & Yao, 2009; WHO, 1997).

Constituents of QoL contrasted with factors that influence it. A number of publications (e.g. Andrews & Withey, 1976; Grewal et al., 2004; Low, 2005; Wiggins et al., 2004) have distinguished between what constitutes QoL compared to the factors that affect it. However, there is considerable overlap in the literature between the component domains and factors influencing QoL, and many authors do not discriminate between the two. The number of psychosocial variables and life conditions that impact QoL are "virtually limitless" (Dissart &

Deller, 2000), and some of the important ones will be examined in a separate section.

Investigators have also commented on whether various factors influence QoL making it the "effect," or whether QoL affects the factors, which makes it the "cause." For example, it is debated whether poor health reduces life quality or low QoL causes deterioration of heath.

Terms Closely Related to QoL

Not only is the definition of QoL debated, but a number of surrogate terms have also been used in the literature synonymously. Well-being, life satisfaction, happiness, HRQoL, and functional status are just a few of the most common ones (Dissart & Deller, 2000; Low, 2005). Arguments in favor of and against using these terms loosely and interchangeably have been presented by the scholars (e.g. Bowling, 2005; Haas, 1999). Although not synonymous, for older adults, the terms *active ageing* and *successful ageing* are closely linked to QoL (Bowling, 2009).

The fields of nursing research and medical science have zeroed in on people's ability to perform activities of daily living, diseases and their impact on the person, and treatments and their effect on the patients, all of which fall under the umbrella of HRQoL and functional status. While pointing out that functional status is not simply limited to physical domain, and that "spiritual functional status" could, for example, denote the ability to go to religious places, Haas (1999) clarifies that functional status is simply an objective assessment and as such is not the same as QoL, which has a large subjective component. Most researchers also agree that although an important component of, or influence on QoL, health is only a subset of the overall QoL (e.g. Haas, 1999). Prutkin and Feinstein (2002) put it clearly and bluntly: "a person's 'quality of life' is a state of mind, not a state of health, which is uniquely perceived by that person" (p. 79).

Despite the lack of agreement amongst the researchers, life satisfaction, and subjective well-being are related concepts that are sometimes used interchangeably with QoL (Dissart & Deller, 2000; Smith et al., 2004). WHO (1998), however, clearly states that QoL cannot be equated with terms such as health status, life satisfaction, well-being, life style, or mental state. Haas (1999) also argued against the practice of equating subjective well-being with QoL, as the later, in her conceptualization (described under Components of QoL), is a superset of the former. Life satisfaction, according to her, is only a subset of well-being and as such should not be used interchangeably with either well-being or QoL.

Stability of QoL
Several researchers have commented on the stability of life satisfaction or the sense of well-being (Felce & Perry, 1995; Hensel, 2001). They have argued that external circumstances such as stressful life events can temporarily lower or raise the satisfaction level of the person, but over a period of time, individuals fall back to their base level. Hence, life satisfaction in younger age is the best predictor of life satisfaction in old age (Bowling, 2005). Hepner (2003) postulated that life quality would show similar stability. After loss of a spouse or after a chronic illness, for example, QoL would drop sharply but even in the absence of any intervention, it would rise again. She attributed such stability to the change in the expectation of the person, who slowly adjusts to the new life experience. Researchers agree that the changing expectations of a person plays an important role in influencing QoL, and is a reason why older adults or chronically ill people often exhibit improved QoL (Carr & Higginson, 2001).

The Theoretical Models of QoL
Several researchers have commented on the lack of theoretical basis for QoL despite its popularity in multiple disciplines (Hyde et al., 2003; Grewal et al., 2004). Felce and

Perry (1995) conceived of QoL as a combination of external life conditions and internal satisfaction with them mediated by the values of the person. They postulated that people attach different weights to various conditions based on their aspirations, goals and expectations. Since the value system and the worldview of people are so important in determining their QoL, rather than an exhaustive review of various theoretical models found in the literature, this section will focus on specialized models for older adults and ethnic migrants as old-age and late life immigration are the two defining characteristics of the population under study.

QoL of older adults. Using an international collaborative approach, a study was conducted in 22 centers across the world to understand whether the generic QoL instruments from WHO (WHOQOL-100 and WHOQOL-BREF) are adequate for the older adult population (Power, Quinn, Schmidt, & The WHOQOL-OLD Group, 2005). The result was a 24-item, six-facet supplementary module, WHOQOL-OLD, that can be administered in conjunction with either the short or the long form of the generic instrument. Sensory abilities; autonomy; past, present, and future activities; social participation; death and dying; and intimacy are the six facets in the new instrument with four questions each.

In a series of articles, Higgs, Hyde, Wiggins, Blane, and colleagues presented a model of QoL in early old age based on the theory of human need that identifies (a) control, (b) autonomy, (c) self-realization, and (d) pleasure as the four domains of QoL (e.g. Higgs, Hyde, Wiggins, & Blane, 2003, Wiggins et al., 2008). The researchers posit that both control and autonomy signify freedom required to fully participate in the society. Pleasure denotes the amount of enjoyment the individual derives from this freedom, and self-realization captures the reflexive nature of human life. The factors that influence QoL are categorized under (a) legacy of the life-course, which includes health, housing, age, finance, and other environmental factors; (b) social capital, which stands for people's perception of safety, trust, and quality of their neighborhoods and community; (c) social networks that includes both the frequency and quality of the interactions; and (d) recent life events, which takes into account bereavement and other stressful events (Wiggins et al., 2004).

QoL models for ethnic immigrants. Recognizing that older ethnic minority immigrants face unique challenges related to migration as well as their age that are not taken into account in most QoL models, Brockmann (2002) presented a model that is specifically suited for such migrants to European countries. She identified political and legal context, identity or a sense of belonging, social support, and material resources as the four key domains that affect the QoL for older minority migrants. The last two factors, the support network, and wealth and income, were two of the six factors identified in another study that conducted in-depth interviews of seniors from different ethnic groups in the U.K., and identified key issues that influence the QoL of older adults (Grewal et al., 2004). The other four factors were health, free time and ability to enjoy it, independence, and a sense of value that came from having a role. The researchers reported that although the six factors were consistent across ethnic groups, the manner in which they affected QoL varied across different ethnic groups.

QoL and Asian Indians

Nandi (1980) questioned whether the concerns of Asian Americans were suitably addressed by the multitude of quality indicators that were being used in various governmental programs and academic studies. He argued that such social indicators reflect the values of their creators, and not necessarily the concerns of Asian Americans. Therefore, purely Western models of QoL should not be applied while studying ethnic minority populations. As a result, new, innovative methods are needed to understand and measure the life quality of ethnic minorities like Indians. Since then researchers have examined life satisfaction of seniors (Kalavar, 1998), multiple aspects of their life quality (Mui, 2003; Mui & Shibusawa, 2008; Ryan et al., 2003), their positive and negative affect, and depression (e.g. Diwan, 2008; Diwan et al., 2004). However, as stated in Chapter 1, older adults of AI descent have been underrepresented in academic research.

The disciplinary orientation or the lens through which QoL of AI senior immigrants was evaluated in this study was the systemic perspective. With a plethora of definitions and interpretations found in the literature, this study focused on how environmental factors affected psychological well-being of Indian seniors. Recognizing that late-life immigration has impacted QoL of these older adults, who are immersed in their Indian cultural heritage, and find it very difficult to adapt or change in their old age, this study examined (a) the influence of political and legal context on their lives; (b) how their sense of autonomy and control have been impacted; and (c) how lack of social support in the new land has resulted in their isolation. That is, the factors identified by both the Brockmann (2002) model and the Grewal et al. (2004) study as well as those identified in recent literature on Indians seniors in the U.S. (discussed later in this chapter) were studied.

The Political and the Legal Context

In his proposed model for QoL of older, ethnic migrants, Brockmann (2002) emphasized the crucial role that political and legal contexts play in their lives. Policies of the host nation impact the social inclusion and exclusion of the immigrants, their social, political and civic rights, access to the welfare programs, and the degree of equality they have with the indigenous population (Brockmann, 2002; Torres-Gil & Treas, 2009). Equally important is the political setting and the rules and regulations of the home country, as they not only form the background in which the immigrant leaves the country, but also affect his or her ongoing relation with the parent country. Further, according to therapists of AI origin, the mental health of immigrants is deeply impacted by political issues such as the prejudices, overt or covert discrimination and racism by the natives, visa issues and the delay in bringing families to the U.S., worries and anxieties related to remaining legal and the huge financial cost associated with it, and the colonial history of India (Khanna et al., 2009). Moreover, analysis of California Health Interview Survey data from 2003 and 2005 showed that discrimination negatively affected HRQoL amongst Asian ethnic groups, including South Asians (Gee & Ponce, 2010).

Immigration Policies of the United States
Within the political and legal framework, the immigration policy of the host country deeply influences both the number of immigrants from a particular region and the quality of their lives. The Immigration Act of 1965 is exemplary in this regard. By opening the floodgates for the arrival of immigrants from non-European countries, it changed the very demographics of the United States, a consequence that was never envisaged by its proponents (Center for Immigration Studies, 1995; Daniels, 2007; Ludden, 2006). Realizing the monumental significance of this law, the United States Department of State included "The Immigration Act of 1965: Intended and Unintended Consequences" authored by Roger Daniels in their publication, *Historians on America*, a book that selected eleven significant events or developments that changed the course of this nation's history (America.gov: Engaging the World, n.d.).

Pre-1965 scenario. Prior to 1965, the immigration policy of the U.S. was restrictive and exclusionary toward Asians. For example, the 1882 Chinese Exclusion Act barred the entry of the Chinese while the 1907 Gentlemen's Agreement prohibited the Japanese and the Koreans from entering this country (Center for Immigration Studies, 1995; Nandi, 1980). The success of Indian farmers in California resulted in the 1913 California Alien Land

Law, which prohibited immigrants from owning land (Rangaswamy, 2007; Ruggiero, 2006). "Asiatic Barred Zone" was created by the 1917 Immigration Act to specifically prevent Asian immigration from other countries such as India. Interestingly, prior to this, AIs were regarded as White, and were even allowed citizenship (Mui & Shibusawa, 2008).

In 1923, however, in the landmark case of U.S. v. Bhagat Singh Thind, the Supreme Court ruled that although AIs were Caucasians, they were ineligible for citizenship as they were not "free white persons" in the popular sense of the word (Mui & Shibusawa, 2008; Ruggiero, 2006; Sutherland, 1923/2006). This was a dramatic reversal of the earlier judgment in the case of U.S. v. Balsara in 1910, where the court had found Indians eligible for citizenship, as they were Caucasians (Rangaswamy, 2007). The 1923 decision was also used to annul the citizenship of Indians who were already naturalized (Ruggiero, 2006). Disillusioned and frustrated, approximately 3,000 AIs chose to return to India between 1920 and 1940 (Rangaswamy, 2007).

The national immigration quotas were launched through the 1921 Quota Act, and the 1924 Immigration Act. World War II, however, became a turning point for the immigration policies towards Indians (Hess, 1982/2006). Decades of intense efforts for civil rights by Indian activists led to the Luce-Celler Act of 1946, which paved the way for AIs to become citizens. An annual quota of 100 was also established through the Indian quota-immigration bill passed in the same year (Hess, 1982/2006). Although the 1952 Immigration and Nationality Act abolished the Asian exclusion, it kept the quota system based on the country of origin. It also laid the foundation of the current preference system of immigration by giving preferential treatment to immigrants with education or special skills, and to the families of existing immigrants (Center for Immigration Studies, 1995).

The immigration and naturalization act of 1965. In an attempt to remove racism from their immigration policy and to be more egalitarian (Ludden, 2006; Rangaswamy, 2000), the Hart-Celler Act of 1965 abolished the national quotas, and heralded hemispheric ceilings—170,000 visas for the Eastern and 120,000 for the Western Hemisphere (Daniels, 2007). An annual upper limit of 20,000 visas for each country in the Eastern Hemisphere was also set while the countries in the Western Hemisphere remained exempt from such limits (Center for Immigration Studies, 1995).

A crucial aspect of the act was that for the first time, family reunification became the cornerstone of the United States immigration policy, as higher preference was given to the families of U.S. citizens and permanent residents compared to immigration aspirants with special job skills. Further, the spouses, parents, and minor children, that is, the immediate relatives of the U.S. citizens were exempt from the country-based quota or the hemispheric ceiling. This resulted in "chain migration," a phenomenon in which the relatives of recent immigrants form the bulk of new immigrants, who in turn sponsor their families, triggering a chain of migration (Daniels, 2007; Ludden, 2006; Reimers, 2006). As many siblings were sponsored on the basis of the 1965 act, it also became popular as "brothers and sisters act" (Reimers, 2006, p. 77).

Post-1965 regulations: Embracing the diversity. The mono-cultural homogeneity ideal of 1920s was further abandoned in favor of cultural diversity (Daniels, 2007) when the 1976 and 1978 Amendments to Immigration and Nationality Act first imposed a per-country limit of 20,000 on the nations in the Western Hemisphere, and then consolidated the hemispheric ceilings for an annual worldwide quota of 290,000 immigrants (Center for Immigration Studies, 1995). The immigration policy was further liberalized when the 1990 Immigration Act more than doubled the annual quota to 700,000. Although family reunification remained the guiding principle, the employment-based immigration limit was also significantly increased. Further, the new law had special provision for allowing immigrants from "under-represented" countries to improve the diversity of incoming population (Center for Immigration Studies, 1995).

The immigration structure essentially remains the same 45 years later as most permanent visas are allocated under the family reunification act, and only 20% are given for employment-based categories (Batalova, 2009). In 2007 for example, out of the 1.1 million green cards issued, 66% went to family-based, 15% to employment-based, and 20% to miscellaneous categories, such as refugees, asylum seekers, and green card diversity lottery winners (Batalova, 2009).

Social Security and Welfare

Various social insurance programs, such as social security and Medicare as well as the welfare schemes such as Supplementary Security Income (SSI) and Medicaid, make a major impact on the lives of elderly immigrants (Burr et al., 2009). As the cost of health care is extremely high in the United States, it is imperative for aging seniors to have some form of health insurance. Immigrants are also entitled to several other public assistance programs. However, the policies and laws of the country have changed significantly in the last few decades, thereby deeply affecting the lives of senior immigrants. This section will examine some of the major laws, reforms, and their impact.

The Older Americans Act (OAA) of 1965. Although the Social Security Act that provided insurance and other benefits for older adults was passed as far back as 1935, the Older Americans Act of 1965 took the effort several steps forward by creating the Administration on Aging (AOA) within the Department of Health, Education and Welfare, and paving the way for establishing State Units on Aging (AOA, 2010). Various amendments since then have resulted in national nutrition program, multipurpose senior centers, community service employment grant program for low-income people aged 55 years or more, subsidized housing for the elderly, in-home services, food stamps, prevention of elder abuse, and outreach efforts for the eligible individuals including minorities (AOA, 2009). The National Institute on Aging was established in 1974 with the mission to conduct research and training activities related to aging, and in 1990, age discrimination in employment was made illegal. The latest amendments were in 2006 when emphasis was laid on evidence based prevention programs (AOA, 2009).

The Medicare act of 1965, SSI, Medicaid, and other benefits. From the point of view of legislative reforms for immigrants, 1965 became a key year as the Congress passed the Medicare Act in the same year. Used by 95% of the aged (Majmundar, 2003), Medicare is the federal government's health insurance program for older adults aged 65 years or more, and some disabled individuals. Noncitizen immigrants however, are only eligible after they have been resident in the U.S. for at least five years (Majmundar, 2003). As a result, AI parents must find alternative methods of health care when they first arrive in the country. Further, even after they become eligible, they have to pay a high premium, since they have not worked in the U.S. for 10 years (40 quarters), a condition required for zero premium (Majmundar, 2003).

Passed in 1972 and effective since 1974, SSI is a federal program that provides cash assistance to the older adults, and individuals with blindness or other disabilities (Social Security Online, n.d.). In the 1980s, there was a growing concern that SSI was not being used by non-White minority groups, which resulted in an outreach program that even placed advertisements in ethnic media (Lamb, 2009a). A dramatic 379% increase in the number of immigrants who enlisted for SSI between 1982 and 1994, however, resulted in a growing perception in early 1990s that immigrants were "gaming the system" (e.g. Torres-Gil & Treas, 2009) by first agreeing to financially support their parents while bringing them under the

Family Reunification Act but later enrolling them in SSI or food stamp programs (Lamb, 2009a; Torres-Gil & Treas, 2009). This heralded a serious public debate since articles such as "America as a deluxe retirement home" by Rector and Lauber were published in 1995 (Lamb, 2009a). Eventually, the Congress passed the Welfare Reform Act of 1996, which seriously curtailed the eligibility of immigrants to most public assistance programs.

Also established in 1965, Medicaid is a joint federal and state government program that provides health-care for people with limited financial resources. Although there are broad federal guidelines, each state establishes its own eligibility criteria, types and cost of services that they provide (U.S. Department of Health & Human Services, 2011; Majmundar, 2003). As a result, some states such as California offer medical assistance to immigrant seniors, while other states might refuse. Further, the number of years the immigrant elderly must wait before they become eligible for services also differs across the country. Several states have even given a different name to Medicaid; for example, in California, it is called Medi-Cal.

In addition, California cash assistance program for immigrants (CAPI), subsidized lunches, and transportation services for the seniors are just a few of the other benefits that are available to immigrants (Majmundar, 2003). However, the eligibility criteria are complex, and due to language and other barriers such as the lack of "Americanizing influence of school" (Treas, 2009), seniors are often unaware or unable to avail them.

The 1996 Welfare Reform Act and the 1996 Immigration Act. In the Congressional hearing of 1996, when Robert Rector of the Heritage Foundation expressed "The U.S. welfare system had inappropriately 'become a form of deluxe retirement home' for elderly immigrants 'from the third world' (U.S. Congress, Senate 1997:109)" (Lamb, 2009a, p. 256), he was only echoing the sentiment of a large section of Americans. In senate hearings in 1997, Senator Alan Simpson clarified the position further:

> 'Immigrants should be able to earn their way into our generous network of social support, but we should no longer permit unfettered access to welfare by newcomers who have not worked in our country and who have not contributed to these taxpayer-supported assistance programs, such as SSI' (U.S. Congress, Senate 1997:2) (Lamb, 2009a, p. 264).

The perception that immigrants were taking advantage of the welfare system was so strong that some Americans such as Daniel Stein, director of the Federation for American Immigration Reform, took a more hardened view: "the system should not allow immigrants to bring elderly parents here over the age of fifty-five as a general rule" (Lamb, 2009a, p. 265). Prominent amongst those who supported immigrants was Senator Edward Kennedy, who held the opinion that the right to be with their children and grandchildren should be accorded not just to the wealthiest Americans but to everyone, including the immigrants (Lamb, 2009a).

The major change that the 1996 welfare reform act called the Personal Responsibility and Work Opportunity Reconciliation Act (PRWORA) brought was that the immigrants who are permanent residents but not citizens are no longer eligible for SSI and a host of other welfare programs unless they have worked for at least a decade in the United States (Burr et al., 2009; Majmundar, 2003; Torres-Gil & Treas, 2009). Further immigration reforms put more onus on the sponsoring citizens and their spouses to bear the expenses of the immigrants they were sponsoring. Although entitled to Medicare, aged immigrants must now wait for a minimum period of five years before they can avail it.

The two laws of 1996 further tilted the social policies of the U.S. against immigrants and have thereby increased the elder care burden of the families (e.g. Batalova, 2009). Further, the power of the States has been increased in PRWORA so that they determine the eligibility of noncitizen immigrants to various benefits, resulting in wide variation in immigrant entitlements across the country (Burr et al., 2009).

Impact of the American Politico-Legal Context

On October 3, 1965, at the signing ceremony of the 1965 immigration bill, President Lyndon Johnson stated, "This bill we sign today is not a revolutionary bill. It does not affect the lives of millions. It will not restructure the shape of our daily lives" (Center for Immigration Studies, 1995, para.1). History, however, has proved him wrong on every count. The bill has not only impacted millions of lives, it has also changed the very demographics of the United States.

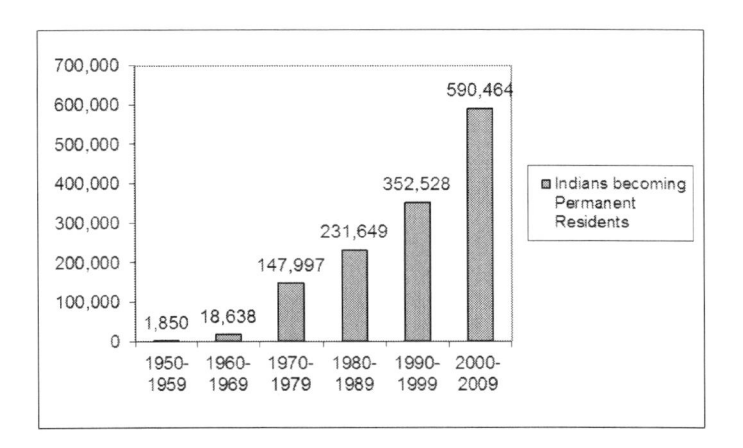

Figure 3. Number of Indians Obtaining Permanent Resident Status in the U.S. in each decade from 1950 to 2009. Adapted from Department of Homeland Security, 2010, *Yearbook of immigration statistics: 2009: Table 2: Persons obtaining legal permanent resident status by region and selected country of last residence: Fiscal years 1820 to 2009*. Copyright 2010 by the Department of Homeland Security.

The number of Asian immigrants, including Indians, surged in the wake of the act. Skilled professionals such as engineers, doctors, and scientists came to fill a gap in the labor market of the country (Rangaswamy, 2000). Young, mostly talented Indian students arrived in search of quality education and continued to stay beyond their university days to follow the American dream.

From a mere 1,850 individuals from India who obtained permanent residence in the decade 1950-1959, the figure jumped ten times to 18,638 in the period 1960-1969 (Department of Homeland Security, 2010). Another almost tenfold increase took place between 1970 and 1979, when 147,997 AIs became permanent residents.

By 1980, AI population in the United States was large enough for the Bureau of Census to agree to reclassify them. Whereas the 1970 census form required that Indians select "other" option and then write-in their race, "Asian Indian" was introduced as a race category in 1980 for the decennial census (Lal, 2006; Rangaswamy, 2007; Ruggles, Alexander, Genadek, Goeken, Schroeder, & Sobek, 2010). The next two decades saw steady increase to 231,649 in 1980-1989, and 352,528 in 1990-1999. Between 2000 and 2009, as many as 590, 464 Indians obtained legal permanent residence (Department of Homeland Security, 2010), which indicates that the upward immigration trend continues (Figure 3).

A look at the total number of legal immigrants shows that 2,499,268 individuals took permanent residence in the decade 1950-1959, and the count rose to 10,299,430 for the period 2000-2009 (Department of Homeland Security, 2010). That is, not just the absolute number but also the percentage share of AI immigrants changed from a negligible 0.07% to 5.7% (Department of Homeland Security, 2010). The figures are even more significant when the total number of Asians obtaining permanent residency are considered. In the decade 1950-59, only 5.4% of 2.5 million, that is, 135,844 Asians, became legal residents whereas in the decade 2000-2009, the numbers rose to 3,470,835 Asians, which is 33.7% of all legal immigrants

(Department of Homeland Security, 2010). Thus, the 1965 immigration reforms have resulted in major racial diversification of the United States.

Indian Laws that Influence QoL of Expatriates

Not just the laws of the host country U.S. but also those of the parent country impact the lives of the immigrants. For example, rupee, the Indian currency, was heavily regulated till recently, and assets in India could not be transferred abroad as they were controlled through the Foreign Exchange Regulation Act (FERA) of 1947 and 1973 (Gopinath, 2005). In June 2000, however, the act was repealed and was replaced by Foreign Exchange Management Act (FEMA) passed by Indian parliament in 1999 (NRI Realty News, n.d.; Reserve Bank of India, n.d.). In FERA, 1973, severe restrictions existed on all foreign currency transactions (Gopinath, 2005; Indian Export Import Portal, n.d.), and Indians were only allowed to purchase a very small amount of foreign currency while leaving the country. This implied that even if seniors coming to the United States were wealthy in India, and had assets or income, they could not bring it with them to this country.

Further, the exchange rate, which currently hovers between Rupees 45 to 55 for a dollar (Exchange-rates.org, n.d.), does not reflect the buying power of the rupee in India. Moreover, it reduces the value of Indian assets substantially when considered in terms of dollar (Kalavar & Van Willigen, 2005). As a result, the immigrant seniors must completely depend on their children or the state to support them financially (Burr et al., 2009; Kalavar & Van Willigen, 2005), a situation that causes grief for many, "Elder Indian Americans thus express feelings of discomfort and humiliation in having to ask for *everything* from their children, even any little bit of pocket money to ride the bus," (Lamb, 2009a, p. 215)

The Asian Indians in the United States

As discussed in the previous section, AIs started relocating to the U.S. in significant numbers only after the 1965 immigration reforms. Unlike the usual perception about the immigrants, most of these post-1965 Indian immigrants belonged to middle or upper class, urban professional community in India, who emigrated to advance their career with better job or higher education rather than to escape political persecution or poverty (Rangaswamy, 2007). They, however, are not a homogeneous population, and vary considerably based on the language spoken at home, food-habits, educational background, socioeconomic status, religion, and other practices (Durvasula & Mylvaganam, 1994; Miltiades, 2002; Nandan, 2005).

Further, Indian immigrants include those who migrated not directly from India but from another country where they or their ancestors had settled such as former British colonies in Africa, U.K., Canada, and Pacific Islands (Rangaswamy, 2007). Such members of the Indian diaspora who settled in a specific country, such as Fiji, have also adopted some of the culture of the host country (Nandan, 2007). Rangaswamy (2000) captured the diversity of AIs succinctly in the extract below:

> On the one hand, it is dominated by a highly educated elite of professionals who have six-figure incomes, live in sprawling suburban homes, drive late-model luxury cars, and send their children to Ivy League schools. They were followed in the 1980s by lesser-skilled relatives who moved into nonprofessional fields such as retail trade, food, and service industries. At the other end of the spectrum are the still-struggling newer arrivals who lack English language skills, need basic job training, and remain on the fringes of society. The number of Indians living below the poverty line increased in the 1980s and

1990s, adding to the economic stratification within the community. (p. 2)

Despite such differences in socioeconomic status, the AI community in the United States is considered to be one of the most successful communities in the country, judging from the prevalent norms of the American society. According to the U.S. Census Bureau (2008a), 69% of AIs over 25 years of age have a bachelor's degree, compared to only 27% of all Americans, and 36% Indians have a graduate or professional degree, as opposed to 10% of all Americans. Not just in education but also in median household income, AIs are ahead of the general American population with the median income of $78,315 versus $48,200 in 2006 (U.S. Census Bureau, 2007, 2008a).

With more than 35,000 physicians, AIs make up almost 6% of all doctors in the U.S., and more than 5,000 Indians are on the faculty of various universities (Rangaswamy, 2007). Many are amongst the most influential names in the computer industry, and several have been featured amongst the richest according to Forbes and Fortune magazines.

Whether it is the field of creative writing or entertainment, AIs in the United States have left their mark. Moreover, Indian children have had spectacular success in the Spelling Bee Championship by winning five times between 1998 and 2006 and by claiming the top four places in 2005 (Rangaswamy, 2007). Not surprisingly, therefore, Indian community has earned the title of "model minority." Nevertheless, as several investigators assert, that is only one side of the story, and one which deprives many struggling members of the community from the assistance they require (Rangaswamy, 2000; 2007). According to the 2000 Census reports, 7% of AIs were below the poverty line (Rangaswamy, 2007).

Waves of Asian Indian Immigrants

A number of scholars have classified Indian immigrants based on the year they entered in the United States. In *Coming to America: The East Indians* (Ruggiero, 2006), three waves of Indian immigrants have been identified: (a) those who arrived prior to 1946; (b) those who came after the passage of the 1946 Luce-Celler Act but before the 1965 immigration reforms; and (c) post-1965 arrivals. Different investigators have further subdivided the 45 years since 1965 in different ways. Based on her research and the literature, Nandan (2007) identifies three waves of post-1965 AI immigrants with distinct needs and values.

1. First Wave (1965-1975): The first wave of AI immigrants was predominantly that of young adult men who arrived as students soon after the 1965 Immigration Act took effect. They pursued the American dream, adopted the culture and the citizenship of this country to become successful bicultural individuals. With second-generation adult children, and third-generation grandchildren, their ties with India are reduced, and they are able to navigate American health system well (Nandan, 2007).

2. Second Wave (1976-1985): Those who arrived between 1976 and 1985 were mostly adult men who came either in search of a job or as students according to Nandan (2007). Such immigrants often brought their families along, and in many cases their wives were also well-educated professionals who pursued their careers in this country of immigrants. In addition, diaspora Indians settled in different parts of the world also arrived during this period. Although bicultural and comfortable with American health system, these second wave of immigrants have closer ties with the country of origin (Nandan, 2007).

3. Third wave (1990 onwards): Those who came in the wake of the 1990 Immigration Act are categorized as the third wave of immigrants comprising mostly of the parents, siblings and other family members of citizens and permanent residents of

AI descent (Nandan, 2007). Less educated than earlier immigrants, these recent immigrants find it difficult to acculturate, and are isolated and alienated from the mainstream American society and its healthcare system.

Interestingly, the period between 1986 and 1989 is missing from the analysis by Nandan (2007). Similar to Nandan's approach, Rangaswamy (2000) postulates two waves of AIs: (a) pre-1980 immigrants, comprising mostly of those who arrived for education or employment; and (b) post-1980 immigrants, a majority of who came under family reunification category. In the years since the publication of her book, however, the trend has reversed again. Even though the number of AIs arriving under employment category had dwindled in 1980s and were overtaken by those coming under family reunification, the numbers surged again so that between 2001 and 2004, more than 50% of AI immigrants arrived for employment (Rangaswamy, 2007).

Asian Indians in Silicon Valley

With the advent of the information age in the 1990s, a demand for information technology (IT) workers was created (Rangaswamy, 2007). Taking full advantage of this need, Indian educational system geared itself to produce graduates who had skills in demand, and a large number of them immigrated under special H1B Visa in the late 1990s and 2000s (Rangaswamy, 2007). Many of them were headed to the Silicon Valley, the epicenter of computer and IT innovations (Hans, 2002; Shankar, 2003). In 2000, a McKinsey report ranked the SF Bay Area as number one leader for worker's productivity and in knowledge intensive industries such as bioscience, environmental technology, telecommunication, multimedia, computers, and electronics (Mendonca, Nichols, Rajgopal, 2000).

The contributions of AIs in the rise of the Silicon Valley have not gone unnoticed (Rangaswamy, 2007; Ruggiero, 2006; Weisman, 2005). The innovative, risk-taking, and entrepreneurial abilities, as well as the hard work of Indians, received favorable media coverage and attention from academia. Not only did AI scientists and engineers play a key role in the innovations in the field of telecommunication and computer technology but 10% of the start-up companies in the technology sector in late 1990s were founded by Indian entrepreneurs (Ruggiero, 2006). This became feasible as Indians who had worked for many years for large corporations used their saved earnings to start companies during the internet boom and made fortunes (Rangaswamy, 2007). The fortunes did reverse and many lost heavily when the internet bubble finally burst in 2000 but the Silicon Valley remained dominated by Indian engineers and entrepreneurs.

Notwithstanding the rise and fall of technology sector, since 1990, AI population has steadily increased in the Valley. As shown in Table 1, the total AI population in Santa Clara County has increased from 20,000 in 1990 to over 120,000 in 2010. Alameda County has seen a similar growth from 15,000 in 1990 to 78,000 in 2010 (U.S. Census Bureau: American Fact Finder, 1990, 2011). Part of this growth is because many Indians have chosen to bring their parents to the U.S. despite the high cost of supporting them.

From Brain-Drain to Reverse Brain-Drain

The contribution made to the American economy by ethnic minority individuals, who were highly educated and skilled prior to their arrival is often ignored in the United States. Nevertheless in India, since early 1970s, the phenomenon of "brain-drain" has been discussed in intellectual circles as large numbers of engineers, scientists and doctors from top institutions in India migrated in large numbers to the U.S. (Rangaswamy, 2007).

According to the head of a premier research institute in India, at least 10,000 of the brightest Indian minds immigrated and contributed at least $10 billion to the U.S. economy through their productivity (Rangaswamy, 2000). Considering that this was an estimate prior to 2000, the numbers would be even higher as of now. Since higher education is heavily subsidized by government funds in India, the issue was hotly debated till in recent years, the well-established Indian Americans started showing their gratitude to their institutes and country by donating large funds, forging collaborations, and helping in bringing investments and jobs to India.

The global realities four decades after 1965, however, have taken a 180-degree turn. Many well-educated Indians, especially in the technology sector working in places like Silicon Valley or Route 128, the high-tech zone of Boston, are choosing to return home (Weisman, 2005/2006). Moreover, the number of those aspiring to come to the U.S. has reduced (Rangaswamy, 2007). With India emerging as a center for business process outsourcing and software development, opportunities are available for jobseekers as well as job-providers, which is giving rise to fears of reverse brain drain, "Some business leaders are worried that the immigrant Indian entrepreneurs who helped fuel the U.S. technology boom might now start companies in India, and take whole classes of jobs with them" (Weisman, 2005/2006, p. 123).

While acknowledging that attracting foreign talent has been the lifeblood of the innovative industry of the Silicon Valley, which makes up 16% of the state's revenue from the personal income tax even though it houses only 7% of the state population, the 2010 Index of Silicon Valley report warns that this source of foreign talent is drying up, and that the region is at risk economically unless innovative steps are taken (JVSVN & SVCF, 2010).

A large and growing domestic market, a pool of skilled software professionals, and continuous supply of qualified new graduates as well as availability of consumer goods, luxury items, and American lifestyle within India are some of the advantages that lure the returning expatriates. Responsibility for the aging parents and a desire to shield the children from American culture and raise them in India are some of the personal reasons behind the return (Weisman, 2005/2006). Indians whose parents have also relocated to the U.S., however, do not consider returning as they are able to take care of their parents here. Thus, by bringing parents, Indian families build roots in this country.

Diversity within the Asian Indian Older Adults

The AI older adults residing permanently in the United States are not a monolithic population (e.g. Diwan, 2008; Mui & Shibusawa, 2008). Rather, considerable diversity exists amongst them in terms of socio-demographic variables such as educational background, socioeconomic status, language proficiency, religious or spiritual beliefs, acculturation status, self-assessed identity, immigration status, living arrangements, characteristics of social network, and patterns of interaction (Diwan & Jonnalagadda, 2001; Nandan, 2007).

As mentioned in Chapter 1, literature on Indian older adults categorizes them as (a) early immigrants, who came as students or job-seekers, and (b) recent or late immigrants, who were sponsored by their adult children (e.g. NIAASC, n.d.; Prasad, 2009, 2010). Although there are some common concerns, the issues that are important to these two populations are essentially different.

Whereas early immigrants have assimilated in the mainstream and are concerned about retirement housing, financial planning and intergenerational conflict with their second-generation children and third-generation grandchildren, recent immigrants remain isolated and are struggling with language barrier, lack of transportation, difficulty in adjusting to the new way of life in the U.S., financial dependence on children, and loss of traditional authority and decision-making role that they had in India (NIAASC, n.d.; Prasad, 2010). Additionally, "single seniors," which include those who are widowed, unmarried, or divorced, form the third emerging category of seniors (Prasad, 2009, 2010). Acceptance within the community and their families is an issue these seniors battle with, in addition to the lack of companionship.

In a way, the words "early" and "recent" are misleading as many parents who came as dependents of their children have now been living in this country for 20 or 30 years. "Early" stands for those who came at a relatively younger age while "late" indicates migration at a relatively later or older age.

Family-sponsored seniors: Characteristics of population under study. The seniors who arrived to reunite with their adult children belong to this category. Literature refers to them as "recent or late immigrants" (e.g. Prasad, 2009). The current study focuses on these family-sponsored older adults. Their major characteristics are (a) old age and associated physical limitations; (b) late-life immigration and related acculturation issues; and (c) dependence on their adult children for transportation, finance, communication, and interaction.

Although immigrating to a distant land is stressful at any age, the problem is intensified manifold for seniors (Akhtar, 1999; Mui & Shibusawa, 2008; Nandan, 2005). Considering migration as cumulative trauma the effect of which runs deep and lasts for a long time, Grinberg and Grinberg (1989) likened it to birth trauma because of the feeling of helplessness it invokes. Further, since the protection of familiar culture is lost, and the boundaries are blurred, migration could lead to ego disintegration or even dissolution according to the authors.

Categorizing the elderly as a special-risk population amongst the general population of immigrants and refugees, Carlin (1990) identified a long list of issues they face including isolation from former friends coupled with difficulties in making new ones, guilt at leaving people behind, limits on their independence, not having anything useful to do, feeling unneeded and unappreciated, acculturation of their children and grandchildren leading to loss of traditional values, disapproval of the family, fear of dying in unfamiliar surroundings, and depression.

Barriers and perceived needs. Literature on the needs of elderly immigrants is scarce; nevertheless, evidence so far suggests that senior immigrants from Asia lack knowledge of the social services that are available (Kalavar, 2003; Mui & Shibusawa, 2008; Prasad, 2010). In fact, information about the eligibility for Medicare and Medicaid as well as help in applying for them is one of the most desired services for Asian older adults (Trang, 2009).

Housing, transportation, interpretation services during medical appointments, and senior centers are some of the needs voiced by Chinese, Vietnamese, and Korean elderly immigrant communities (Trang, 2009). The need for a regular meeting place and social activities for seniors was also voiced (Diwan & Jonnalagadda, 2001; Jonnalagadda, Diwan, & Desai, 2002).

In a study with 132 South Asian seniors, lack of independent income, access to transportation, proficiency in English, and no opportunity to interact with mainstream society were identified as barriers whereas their problems ranged from poverty and poor health to isolation and boredom (Rangaswamy, 2000). Adherence to the traditional Indian way of life, lack of knowledge of American history and culture, inability to adapt to the lives of their children and grandchildren who are far more Americanized, and lack of social network outside the family are some of the other issues that Indian seniors struggle with (NIAASC, n.d.; Prasad, 2009, 2010).

The Asian Indian Cultural Value System

Describing the Indian culture and capturing its nuances is beyond the scope of this book. This section, therefore, will focus on only those aspects of Indian culture that are affected, interrupted, or discontinued due to migration, thereby significantly affecting the life quality of seniors. Since considerable diversity exists amongst Indians in terms of language, religion, rituals, clothing, diet preferences, and other cultural aspects (Durvasula & Mylvaganam, 1994; Miltiades, 2002; Nandan, 2005), this section will present the views held by the majority of Indians. The philosophical values and practices of Hinduism will be discussed as more than 80% Indians are Hindus (e.g. Miltiades, 2002), and many aspects of Indian culture beyond religion have become intertwined with Hinduism (e.g. Mehta, R., 2005).

It is important to examine these cultural values since research evidence suggests that recent immigrants such as parents coming to unite with their families are more likely to retain the values of the country of origin compared to individuals who have been living in the U.S. for a significant period (Nandan, 2005). Further, retention of ethnic values and aspects of culture that conflict with dominant culture as well as higher assimilation and acculturation of their children increases the vulnerability of older Asian immigrants to depression or other mental health concerns (Diwan, 2008; Khanna et al., 2009; Markides et al., 2009; Mui & Kang, 2006).

It is equally important, however, to recognize that within-group differences amongst AIs are large, and that individuals may not fit the norm (Khanna et al., 2009), or they may even acculturate differently in different dimensions of life (Nandan, 2005). For example, they may adapt physically but continue holding on to their native values at social, emotional, and spiritual levels (Nandan, 2005).

Individualistic Versus Collectivistic Culture

Like other Eastern cultures, Indian society follows the collectivistic model rather than the individualistic Western model (e.g. Kalavar & Van Willigen, 2005). Family is the most important in-group; filial piety is important and individuals are expected to sacrifice self-interest for the good of the community (Durvasula & Mylvaganam, 1994; Gill, 2008; Khanna et al., 2009; Nandi, 1980). Further, the family structure is hierarchical and patriarchal (e.g., Sue & Sue, 2008) where men occupy the position of power and women are expected to adhere to the "rule of three obedience" (Mui & Shibusawa, 2008). That is, in childhood women must obey their fathers, after marriage their husbands, and as widows their sons.

Further, whereas American culture emphasizes differentiation of the self, the traditional joint family culture of India values and fosters dependency (Khanna et al., 2009; Miltiades, 2002). Women, in particular, are taught to rely on the wisdom and strength of their fathers, brothers, husbands, nephews, and other men in their lives. As young girls, they are repeatedly told that they are weak and their salvation lies in obeying and accepting the wishes of men. Young boys, in contrast, are taught that they are strong and have the ability to solve whatever life hands them. They should, therefore, protect the women in their lives while following in their fathers' footsteps and obeying the older men in the family. Since they rely less on themselves and more on their families, Indians are even called "dividuals" (Militades, 2002). Researchers warn that judging by the Western standards, this can be incorrectly interpreted as unhealthy enmeshment or pathological dependency (Durvasula & Mylvaganam, 1994; Khanna et al., 2009).

Disruption in the family hierarchy and power structure. Literature suggests that immigration disrupts the existing family homeostasis and creates new systemic issues as the entrenched family hierarchy and its power structure are destroyed (Beckerman & Corbett, 2008). Researchers and practitioners specifically discuss the cases where children and adolescents are forced to act as the translators and language brokers for their parents, thereby gaining a position of power within the family (Beckerman & Corbett, 2008; Mui & Shibusawa, 2008; Sue & Sue, 2008). Similar challenges exist in immigrant families with elderly grandparents who become dependent on their adult children, resulting in a demotion of their status (Kalavar & Van Willigen, 2005).

Acculturative dissonance amongst family members. It is not uncommon that different members of a family are at different levels of acculturation (Khanna et al., 2009; Nandan, 2005; Portes, & Rumbaut, 2006; Sue & Sue, 2008). Several studies have explored the overt and covert intergenerational struggle in a family when the school going children assimilate faster and adopt the American values of their peers in stark contrast to their first-generation parents, who find it much more difficult to give up their traditional cultural identity or values (Beckerman & Corbett, 2008; Khanna et al., 2009; Langit, 2007).

The perception that their children and grandchildren are discarding the cultural values and are not following the family traditions is a major source of frustration and unhappiness for Asian elders, resulting in depression and low life satisfaction (Mui & Cross, 2003b; Mui & Shibusawa, 2008). While studying intergenerational conflict amongst Filipino families, Langit (2007) reported that although second generation children were not openly oppositional, they "regarded conflict with their parents as something imminent," (p. 98) and to be expected.

The cultural differences become more pronounced if grandparents are part of the household since they are more home-bound and have relatively fewer opportunities to interact with Americans (Nandan, 2005; Treas, 2009). The seniors, therefore, continue to adhere to Indian values they grew up with, while their adult children and grandchildren acculturate albeit at different rates. The households thus become multicultural with each generation holding a different set of values (Kalavar & Van Willigen, 2005) resulting in conflicts, misunderstanding and miscommunication (Sue & Sue, 2008). Further, the inability of grandchildren to understand or speak the native language adds to the communication gulf between the generations thereby increasing the sense of isolation that the elders feel (e.g., Kalavar & Van Willigen, 2005).

It is important for older adults to look back at their life with satisfaction, or in other words successfully resolve the eighth psychosocial stage of integrity as proposed by Erikson

(Cloninger, 2008). Passing on their culture and tradition to their descendants, and having good communication with them is a way of accomplishing that, but acculturative dissonance thwarts this process which may lead to worsening mental health for elderly immigrants.

Perspectives on Aging

Hindu culture divides the course of a human life into four stages of 25 years each (e.g. Kalavar, 1998; Miltiades, 2002). The first 25 years fall under *Brahmacharyashram* and are supposed to be devoted to studies, while the next 25 are in the purview of family life or *Grihasthashram*. At age 50, people enter *Vanaprasthashram*, when they are supposed to start withdrawing from the family responsibilities, social bonds, and material pursuit of the earlier years in order to prepare themselves for completely renouncing the world at age 75, the period of *Sanyasashram*. That is, the ideal for the older adults is to gradually disengage themselves from their societal duties and family bonds, and eventually abandon them completely to focus on their spiritual growth.

This worldview on aging seems to be remarkably similar to the *disengagement theory* of aging put forward by Cumming and Henry, which also advocates withdrawal from activities and social roles gradually so that the person is protected from the fear and trauma associated with dying, and the eventual death results in least impact on society (Bowling, 2005).

On the other side of the pole is the *activity theory* to which the American culture subscribes, where for higher life satisfaction and sense of well-being, the older adults are expected to continue social engagement and activities of the earlier years for as long as possible (Bowling, 2005; Kalavar, 1998; Kalavar & Van Willigen, 2005).

The *continuity theory* is the third social theory on aging according to which the individual continuously grows and adapts to the external circumstances and realities of life while maintaining a consistency in their inner self-concept and societal roles, relationships and activities (Bowling, 2005). In many ways, the continuity theory is more applicable to elderly immigrants, who are forced to change cultural norms and adopt new roles and ways of living in the new land.

Wisdom and privilege. In Indian culture, the elderly command respect (Kalavar, 1998; Lamb, 2009a; Miltiades, 2002; Nandan, 2007; Nandi, 1980; Rangaswamy, 2000). They are the head of the families, who are consulted before any major family decision is taken. Old age is equated with wisdom, experience, and social and emotional stability, which is in stark contrast to the American culture, where the old age is associated with lack of productivity, and older adults are regarded as liabilities (Kalavar, 1998; Lamb, 2009a; Miltiades, 2002; Nandan, 2007; Nandi, 1980; Rangaswamy, 2000).

Emphasizing that older individuals are targets of negative stereotypes, *ageism* and discrimination not just from general public but also from mental health professionals, Sue and Sue (2008) point out that American society believes that elders "have declining physical and mental capabilities, have grown rigid and inflexible, are incapable of learning new skills, are crotchety and irritable, and should step aside for the benefit of the young" (p. 60). Moreover, there is a perception that "their lives are worth less than their younger counterparts" (p. 60). Many elders, unfortunately, internalize such ageist norms, lose self-esteem and start believing that their mental faculties will decline (Sue & Sue, 2008).

For Indian seniors migrating late in life, such negative attitudes towards the elderly is a major cultural shock. They arrive expecting respect and obedience that old age deserves in Indian tradition because of the knowledge, wisdom and experience of the elderly. What they receive, however, is often a condescending attitude from their children and grandchildren. They learn that in this country, they are totally dependent on the next generation for things that they had in abundance back home, such as transportation, a social circle, and independence. Suddenly, from being assets, they realize, they have turned into liabilities for their families.

An interesting historical perspective in this context was provided by Fischer, who claimed that the founding years of the United States, the period between 1607 and 1780, was characterized by gerontophilia or the love for the elderly (Kalavar, 1998). That however, changed dramatically during the period 1780-1820, when gerontophobia replaced the earlier reverence and heralded the culture of youth (Kalavar, 1998).

Responsibility for the Elderly

The traditional family structure in India is that of a patriarchal, joint-family (e.g. Lamb, 2009a; Nandi, 1980), where the elderly parents and the families of all their sons live together. Although with industrialization and modernization in India, nuclear families are becoming a norm, studies have reported that more than 80% of older adults in India still live in extended families (Lamb, 2009b; Miltiades, 2002), and expect their sons to provide for them.

The responsibility for the aging parents thus resides with the sons, who have a moral duty to look after the financial, medical, and emotional needs of the parents (Kalavar, 1998; Nandi, 1980; Rangaswamy, 2000). When that is not feasible, the brothers, nephews, and other relatives are supposed to take over. Although traditionally, parents did not even drink water in their daughters' homes, in modern context where people have far fewer children than before, the distinction between sons and daughters is rapidly reducing. Studies have even reported that parents nowadays find their daughters more reliable than their sons and depend more on them (Miltiades, 2002).

The younger generation, thus, is obligated to care for the aged (Kalavar, 1998; Miltiades, 2002; Nandi, 1980; Rangaswamy, 2000), and by doing so, they pay back some of the "debt" that they owe to their parents for giving birth to them and raising them (Lamb, 2009a; Miltiades, 2002). This sentiment was echoed by the participants in Nandi's (1980) study, who had clearly expressed that not just material but also the emotional needs of parents must be borne by the children, and that even sending the parents to nursing homes was akin to shirking this responsibility.

The same cultural norm is also deeply rooted in the parents who expect to be provided for, "To have prosperous sons abroad and not be able to live with them was considered the ultimate indignity in old age. All the immigrants in the focus group took it for granted that their sons would look after them" (Rangaswamy, 2000, p. 198).

The 2007 senior citizens bill in India. The discussion regarding the responsibility for the older adults in the Indian context would not be complete without looking into the Maintenance and Welfare of Parents and Senior Citizens Bill introduced in the Indian parliament in 2007. Discussing the need for the legislation, the bill emphasized that traditionally the elders were cared for by the family but:

> in recent times, society is witnessing a gradual but definite withering of the joint family system, as a result of which a large number of parents are not being maintained by their children, as was the normal social practice. Consequently, the elders are now exposed to emotional neglect and to lack of physical and financial support . . . . with their dwindling financial resources and weakening health, parents are often being perceived as burden, even while living within the family . . . . Unfortunately, the time has come when the moral obligation of children to look after their parents in their old age has to be backed by a legal obligation" (Government of India: Ministry of Social Justice And Empowerment, 2007, p. 2)

Thus, the intra-family tension and lack of adequate care for the elderly is slowly but steadily becoming a problem not just amongst Indian diaspora but in the subcontinent itself.

Role reversal, unrecognized contribution. Lamb (2009b) discussed the two goals for old age traditionally recognized by Hindus: (a) focus on spiritual awareness, which requires withdrawal from worldly ties in preparation for impending death, and (b) fulfillment associated with living in a multi-generational joint family where they are served by younger members of the family. In contemporary Indian society, however, the focus is on the second goal while the detachment and spirituality have taken a back seat, which is often regarded as an influence of Westernization (Lamb, 2009b).

Traditionally, as discussed earlier, the elderly parents are served and their materialistic as well as medical needs are taken care of by the family members (Kalavar, 1998; Nandi, 1980). The intergenerational reciprocity pattern is that parents provide for their children, and in return, the adult children take care of them in their advanced years (Lamb, 2009a, 2009b). However, the cycle is broken once these older adults immigrate to Western countries.

Caught into the race for success, and demands from their children, the adult immigrants, often called the *sandwich generation* (Lamb, 2009a), find it very difficult to cook, clean or serve the aging parents. Moreover, while the adult children go out to work, the seniors must pitch in by cooking, cleaning, and babysitting (e.g. Kalavar & Van Willigen, 2005; Rangaswamy, 2000). That is, the older adults often discover that their expected roles are reversed, and their status is reduced (e.g. Kalavar, 1998, 2003). Instead of being served, they are now serving their children, who are the decision makers.

This leads to frustration and dissatisfaction as can be heard in the voice of Mrs. M, a research participant, "In olden days, we youngsters had to compromise. Today, elderly people have to compromise" (Kalavar & Van Willigen, 2005, p.220). This reversal of traditional roles is not unique to Indian families; rather, most Asian communities report similar intergenerational conflict (e.g. Mui & Shibusawa, 2008).

Perhaps what seniors find more hurtful is that their contribution to the success of their adult children is not recognized or appreciated by the community. Whether directly in the form of babysitting, housekeeping, cooking, and helping out with the family business, or indirectly as transmitters of culture, tradition, rituals and language, older adults have played a significant role in the success story of Indian Americans (Rangaswamy, 2000). Yet, the entire credit is given to the education and hard work of the adult children ignoring the fact that without the support of their parents, first in India, and later in the United States, they may not have succeeded. Further, the elders have enriched the community life by participating in the religious and cultural events and celebrations.

Spirituality and Religion

Religion and spirituality play a fundamental role in the lives of Indians (e.g. Gill, 2008, Ryan et al., 2003), and act as a source of strength and resilience in the face of adversity (Khanna et al., 2009). This is particularly true for older adults as prayers, meditation, and rituals are often an important part of their daily activities regardless of their faith (Nandan, 2005).

Jeste and Vahia (2008) compared how wisdom is conceptualized in Western cultures with how it is described in the Hindu holy text, *Bhagavad Gita*. Whereas both East and West value knowledge, insight, compassion, societal good, and emotional regulation, striking differences include how Gita emphasizes control over desires, self-contentedness, and the need to renounce materialistic and physical pleasures. Further, passion is valued in Western society, both for relationships and work, whereas Hinduism lays emphasis on detachment in professional work as well as relations (e.g. Prasad, 1995). Thus, what is valued in one culture is a liability in another.

Role of karma. In Hindu philosophy, the notion of *karma*, which is duty to the society, or selfless service (Jeste & Vahia, 2008) plays an important role. Individuals are expected to perform their duty without worrying about the results as outcomes are not in their control (e.g. Chokkanathan, 2009; Prasad, 1995). Rather, God, or the higher power, decides what eventually happens, but people's karmas stay with them. That is, Hindus believe that their current lives, the positives and the negatives, are the results of their past good or bad actions, either in this life or in previous lives (e.g. Gill, 2008; Lai & Surood, 2008).

On one hand, this provides meaning in life at a spiritual level and gives emotional strength for coping in adverse situations (Chandra, Satyanarayana, Satishchandra, Satish, & Kumar, 2009). On the other hand, it encourages people to accept their lives and dissuades them from seeking help especially for psychological issues such as depression (Lai & Surood, 2008).

Hinduism has also been compared to psychotherapy because of its inherent healing practices, such as yoga, meditation, and prayer (e.g. Mehta, R., 2005). Watts (1975) argued that though psychotherapy is usually practiced with disturbed individuals whereas Hinduism and Buddhism are practiced by ordinary individuals, their objective of changing feelings and consciousness of individuals is the same.

Another interesting point Watts made is that Hinduism and Buddhism cannot be classified as "religions, philosophies, sciences, or even mythologies, or again as amalgamation of all four, because departmentalization is foreign to them even in so basic a form as the separation of the spiritual and the material (p. 7). Wig (1999) made a similar observation that dwelling on dichotomies including that of the body and the mind is a European concept whereas the Indian tradition takes a more holistic view, thereby accepting and integrating opposing viewpoints. He called for synthesizing science with spirituality for better mental health of people. A similar example of such merger can be seen in the Western culture in the way the Twelve Steps (Gorski, 1989) have become a part of Alcoholics Anonymous.

Stigma of Mental Health

Similar to other Eastern cultures, Indian culture emphasizes the need to keep family matters private. As a result, in crisis, people seek help from within the extended family rather than from outside professionals (e.g. Gill, 2008). The literature on the resulting underutilization of psychological services amongst Indians suggests that Indians tend to use traditional healing methods such as astrologers, *Ayurveda*, folk and spiritual healers (Durvasula & Mylvaganam, 1994; Mehta, R, 2005).

Mental health issues are particularly hidden from the society, and seeking help from professionals is taboo since that is considered to bring shame and disgrace to the family (e.g. Durvasula & Mylvaganam, 1994; Lai & Surood, 2008; Patel, 2005). Fear of racial discrimination was cited as another reason for not seeking help from professionals in the literature (e.g. Mehta, R., 2005).

Major Studies Relevant to this Research

This section summarizes studies that are most relevant to the present research. They have either been conducted exclusively on AI older adults, or such seniors form a subgroup of the population researched. Although most of them do not directly study QoL, related physical and mental health issues including acculturation, depression, subjective well-being, and life-satisfaction are the subjects of the studies.

Age-Neutral Studies on Asian Indians

Although the age group for the studies included in this section is not exclusively that of older adults, the research topic is closely related to the present study, and seniors are included amongst the participants.

An early study on the QoL of Asians. One of the earliest studies on the QoL of Asians was a qualitative study conducted in a mid-sized community near Chicago (Nandi, 1980). Forty-five Asians, including 10 Indians, 10 Pakistanis, nine Koreans, eight Chinese, and eight Filipinos were interviewed in depth to gain an insight on their lives in a Mediopolis (middle-sized community), and their perceptions and feelings about America. Although the age of the participants ranged between 21 and 60, only three of them—one Indian, one Pakistani, and one Filipino—fell into the age category of 51-60.

The respondents shared their views on the quality of their housing, neighborhood community, work-place, family lives, and their interactions and friendship patterns with Americans as well as individuals from their own ethnic communities. The social and cultural continuities and discontinuities experienced by these first-generation immigrants, and their identities and traditional values were also explored in-depth (Nandi, 1980). The interviewees admitted experiencing a covert rather than an overt discrimination. Their interactions with Americans was limited and restricted to the work lives. On the question of caring for their elderly, the researchers reported that the participants were against nursing homes, and believed that it is the duty of the children to take care of their parents (Nandi, 1980).

A study on ethnic identity and acculturation in SF Bay Area. Hans (2002) studied the effect of acculturative stress on the mental health of Indians living in the SF Bay Area. She investigated whether acculturative stress can be predicted by demographic variables such as age, education, gender, immigration, marital, and socioeconomic status, and other psychosocial variables such as ethnic identity, and sense of coherence. She found that lower education, lower sense of coherence, lower incomes, and lower acculturation level led to higher psychological distress. Although the participants in this study were not exclusively older adults, the study is significant for this research as it explored ethnic identity and acculturation issues of AI individuals in the geographic region of the Silicon Valley.

Studies with AI Older Adults in the United States

As mentioned in the introduction, research on the AI immigrant gerontological population in the United States is scarce (e.g. Nandan, 2005; Mui, Nguyen, Kang, & Domanski, 2006). However, in the last 10-15 years, several studies on this population have been conducted. The literature reveals that some researchers have carried out multiple studies on the perceived needs, behaviors, issues, and coping resources for the AI seniors. This section is devoted to the work of such seminal authors in this field.

A landmark study in New York. The largest and most comprehensive study involving elderly AIs was sponsored by the Asian American Federation of New York (AAFNY). Using area probability sampling in New York based on 1990 census data, 407 foreign born Asians, 65 years or older, who immigrated in middle to late age were surveyed between February and May 2000 (Ryan et al., 2003). Six different ethnic groups, including 105 Chinese, 100 Indians, 100 Koreans, 52 Filipinos, 25 Japanese, and 25 Vietnamese were interviewed in depth on multiple dimensions of their lives including physical and mental health, QoL, financial status, language proficiency, the quality of care they receive, and their social service needs.

With the goal of establishing "a benchmark for measuring and evaluating changes in the quality of life and care of Asian American elders in New York city and other urban areas" (Ryan,

2003, p. 2), the study explored how acculturation and immigration experience influenced the mental health, formal and informal support networks, and service needs of these individuals.

The study confirmed that Asian American older adults do not form a homogeneous group; rather, considerable diversity exists in their educational and financial backgrounds, English language ability, reason for migration, immigration status, religion and importance of religion in their lives, health insurance, and other governmental support (Mui et al., 2006). A high rate of depressive symptoms of almost 40% was reported by the participants, which is significantly higher than the prevalence rate found in American older adults (Mui & Kang, 2006). Acculturation stress including perceived cultural gap with adult children, poor self-rated health, and stressful life events predicted depression for this sample.

A surprising result, which is contrary to other studies, was that longer rather than shorter length of residence in the U.S. was associated with depression (Mui & Kang, 2006). However, similar results were also reported by Diwan and Jonnalagadda (2001) for AI elderly, which indicates that for some Asian immigrants, physical and mental health deteriorates rather than improves as they continue to stay in this country. Further, 43% variance in general life satisfaction amongst the study participants was explained by five factors—depression, low satisfaction with family, lack of a confidant, living with others, and not considering religion as important (Mui & Cross, 2003b). The study also showed a healthy tendency of providing and receiving mutual assistance between parents and their adult children.

Early studies in Washington, D.C. and Chicago areas. A study that comes quite close to the present study demographically but for which the field-work was conducted more than 20 years ago during 1989-90, is by Kalavar (1998). Drawn from the Washington D.C metropolitan area, all 50 participants were English-speaking, at least 60 years old, and permanent residents or citizens for at least two years.

Through surveys and semi-structured interview consisting of both open and close-ended questions, the study examined the effect of various sociodemographic and domain variables on the life satisfaction of these individuals. She found that women and individuals who immigrated to join their families were less satisfied compared to men and those who came in pursuit of better careers (Kalavar, 1998). Age, marital status, education, employment, and duration of stay in this country had no significant impact on the life satisfaction. Self-assessed health was an important predictor of life satisfaction while finance, living arrangement, transportation, number of friends and frequency of interactions also contributed to the variance in life satisfaction. Further the life-satisfaction levels of Indians were comparable to American older adults.

Asian Human Services surveyed 132 elderly South Asians in Chicago area in 1993, and identified lack of independent income, lack of access to transportation, inability to speak in English, and no opportunity to interact with mainstream society as barriers (Rangaswamy, 2000). Poverty, poor health on one hand and alienation and boredom on the other, were some of the issues identified. A focus group was also conducted, where six out of eight seniors expressed that because of better social support and independence, they would have preferred living in India (Rangaswamy).

Studies in the tri-state area of New York, New Jersey, and Connecticut. Nandan (2005) used a naturalistic, case study, in-depth interview approach to study the adaptation to the American culture of 50-74 year old Indians, who had immigrated between 1950 and 1990. The study focused on comparing the adaptation experience of those who arrived as young adults and have been living in the U.S. for several decades with that of people who migrated as older adults.

Chosen from the tri-state area on the East Coast, an ethnic hub of South Asians, the participants reported adjusting well to this country physically but many were struggling in the social, emotional, and spiritual spheres (Nandan, 2005). Those who were financially and socially well-off in the country of origin but migrated to be with their spouses could not successfully adapt while those who were socially and financially insecure before migration adjusted much better.

Although many participants with strong family ties in India desired to return permanently, they expressed their inability to do so because their children and grandchildren are well-settled in the U.S. Interestingly, all the respondents came from middle to upper-middle class backgrounds with comfortable lifestyles, which contributed to their successful adaptation. However, the journey to the financial security was smooth for some participants and rather rough for others (Nandan, 2005).

In telephone interviews with hundred senior Indian immigrants living in New York or New Jersey, Kalavar (2003) found that family reunification was the main motive behind their relocation in late life. The mean age when these older adults emigrated was 66 years and most of them lived with their adult children.

Although their household income was much higher, the individual annual income for 95% of them was $6,500 or less. Lack of health insurance was one of the concerns expressed by the participants as only 66% of them had coverage. Higher income and lower age predicted higher self-reported health ratings while lower education was associated with higher acculturative stress. Language barrier, lack of opportunities for social interaction and access to transportation led to isolation, which emerged as the main theme of their lives in the U.S.

Purposive sampling was used to select three women and two men aged between 63 and 75 years out of these 100 participants for open-ended, life-history interviews (Kalavar & Van Willigen, 2005). The researchers explored their worldviews on wide-ranging subjects such as cultural values, family relationships, acculturation experience, and intergenerational conflicts. Change in the power structure of the family, role reversal with and financial dependence on adult children leading to new role for older adults as cooks, cleaners, and child-care providers, shifting value-system including lack of respect for seniors in the U.S., language and transportation barriers, social isolation, and loneliness were some of the issues identified by the participants.

The disparity between their expectations and reality was evident especially when the seniors described themselves as babysitters, cooks, or cleaners. Some respondents emphasized that health care is easier or more affordable in India, which directly contrasts the perceptions of others.

The narratives also demonstrated the overarching fear of seniors that they might become a burden on their families, and their wish for a healthy, peaceful end. Some participants lamented that Indian culture is being debased or ignored by the younger generation in the immigrant, ethnic community, which heightened their sense of isolation (Kalavar & Van Willigen, 2005). Lack of corruption, and minimal bureaucracy in the U.S. was appreciated by all, a finding that is corroborated by other studies (e.g. Kalavar, 1998).

Studies in Atlanta. A group of researchers used telephone interviews of 226 English-speaking AI individuals, 50 years or older, residing in metropolitan Atlanta area, who have been living in the U.S. for a minimum of five years (Diwan & Jonnalagadda, 2001). Starting with the premise that social integration acts as a protective factor for physical and emotional well-being, they examined the relation between perceived social support and the presence of chronic health conditions. The researchers found that poor health status was associated with older age, women, higher Body Mass Index, perception of lower social support, not having family nearby, and longer stay in the U.S. (Diwan & Jonnalagadda, 2001; Jonnalagadda & Diwan, 2005). The study also reported that temples and other places of worship play a significant role in this community, and that frequency of visit to such places approached significance in explaining the health status of the participants (Diwan & Jonnalagadda, 2001).

Researching the correlation between health behaviors and self-rated health for this sample, Jonnalagadda and Diwan (2005) discovered that more physical activity was associated with younger age, bicultural or American identity, and longer residence in the U.S., while the higher fat intake was associated with higher income, bicultural or American identity, and depression. Examining the coping resources, the study reported that negative affect was predicted by female gender and stressful life events while satisfaction with friendships and a bicultural or American identity predicted positive affect (Diwan et al., 2004). Higher religiosity and greater mastery (perceived control) were also significant in predicting lower negative affect.

A second sample of 114 Gujarati-speaking individuals was introduced to study how the social networks of the two study groups differed and whether they influenced the rate of depression (Diwan, 2008). Although the sociodemographic characteristics of the two samples were different, the rate of depressive symptoms did not change.

The non-English-speaking sample was older in age and less educated, had higher ethnic identity, and poorer self-rated health, was in the U.S. for shorter duration, had less friends nearby, was living with children, was more dependent on family for social interaction, and attended more religious events. For both the groups, poor health and traditional ethnic identity were predictors of higher depression. In addition, perceived dissatisfaction with child-relationship acted as a predictor of higher depressive symptoms in the Gujarati-speaking sample (Diwan, 2008).

Jonnalagadda et al. (2002) reported that 253 English-speaking and 114 non-English-speaking individuals participated in surveys with open-ended questions. In addition, three focus groups with English-speaking participants were also conducted.

The researchers documented the needs perceived by the participants, which included social, cultural and religious activities, information seminars for retirement housing and chronic diseases, transportation, medical aid, and mental health support services. Language, food, religion, and music were identified as important factors that affect the QoL of this community.

Gaps in the Literature

Despite these efforts by a few researchers, as discussed in Chapter 1, AI older adults remain very much under-represented in the academic research. Nandi's study (1980) provided a good insight in the QoL of South Asians, but only one Indian participant above age 50 was present. All the studies on Indian seniors described above included self-sponsored, first-generation immigrants, who, as clarified earlier, are culturally very different from family-sponsored seniors despite belonging to the same age-group. Further, none of the studies have targeted AI seniors living in the SF Bay Area thereby indicating a major gap in the literature, and a dire need to study this population. Moreover, none of the studies focused on the impact of political and legal context on the lives of AI seniors. Brockmann (2002) identified it as a key factor for European migrant population but her focus was on first-generation immigrant workers who had migrated to Europe several decades ago and were now approaching retirement; that is, she focused on early immigrants of Europe, not the family-sponsored, late-life immigrants, who are the focus of the present study.

Factors Affecting Quality of Life

As discussed earlier, old-age, late-life immigration, and culture shock characterize the study population. Because of the abstract nature of the QoL concept and due to its multidimensional aspects, a large number of interdependent factors and several variables or facets within each factor influence the QoL of these seniors. First, there are issues that are common to all older adults, such as physical health, financial condition, and access to transportation. Next come the factors associated with late life immigration, which include identity and acculturation issues. Various studies have documented the effect of different factors on QoL or related concepts such as life satisfaction, happiness and psychological well-being, which will be examined in this section.

Identity or Sense of Belonging

Who are they? And where do they belong—to the country they came from or to their adopted country? These are issues that always plague many of the first-generation immigrants, and affect their mental health as well as coping behavior (Gill, 2008). It is no surprise, therefore, that most of the dissertation studies on South Asians in general or Indians in particular, deal with the identity issue (e.g. Das Gupta, 1999; Deepak, 2004; Gupta-Carlson, 2007; Han, 2007; Rudrappa, 2001; Sen, 2002; Verma, 2004). Identity is also one of the four main factors in the QoL model devised specifically for older ethnic immigrants (Brockmann, 2002).

Sense of belonging and identity are broad umbrella terms that encompass the entire acculturation issues that the immigrants battle with. In the United States, AIs have struggled in defining who they are. In a 1980 study of Indians in New York City, they described themselves variously as Indian, Indo-Aryan, Aryan, Caucasian, Asian, Oriental, Mongol, and Dravidian (Lal, 2006). Tracing the history of how the term "Asian Indian" evolved, Lal explains that although in Britain, Indians are grouped together with Africans and Caribbeans as "blacks," Indians in the U.S. found it derogatory. Organized activism on their part eventually led to the Census Bureau's acquiescence to reclassifying them as AIs in the 1980 census (Rangaswamy, 2007; Ruggles et al., 2010).

Literature on ethnic identity suggests that it could be both a resource and a challenge. Some studies have reported that higher self-assessed ethnic Indian identity is associated with depression (Diwan, 2008; Lai & Surood, 2008; Mehta, 1998) whereas in other studies ethnic identity was not found significant in predicting psychological distress (Hans, 2002). In another study, rejection of Indian identity, food, and culture associated with assimilation attitude was found predictive of psychological stress whereas rejection of American identity and culture indicative of separation attitude led to psychosomatic stress (Krishnan & Berry, 1992). Further, lower QoL for some ethnic minorities compared to the White majority has been reported by a number of studies (Smith et al., 2004).

Acculturation. The life quality of immigrant older adults is inherently linked to their acculturation experience. Under acculturation lies language proficiency and acceptance in the new culture as well as any perceived gap of original culture with the new one, length of residence within the U.S., the reason for immigrating, and a host of other issues.

Like QoL, acculturation is a nebulous construct that researchers have conceptualized and operationalized in many different ways. While offering a multidimensional definition, Mehta (1998) commented on the limitation of one-dimensional conceptualization used in several studies. For example, Diwan and Jonnalagadda (2001) assessed acculturation through a single variable—the length of residence in the United States—and Diwan (2008) used ethnic identity as a single measure of acculturation. Proficiency in English is another variable that is sometimes used as a proxy for acculturation (Mui & Shibusawa, 2008).

Racism and prejudice. Acceptance by the host community goes a long way towards successful adaptation of the newcomer (e.g. Mehta, 1998). The perception of being rejected by Americans on the other hand, stultifies the acculturation process, and could even result in ethnic withdrawal. Scholars from diverse disciplines have also commented on the invisible "glass ceiling" that separates all Asians from rising to higher political, executive, and managerial positions (e.g. Lal, 2006).

For elderly immigrants, opportunities to mix with the natives are low as they neither work nor go to school, the two places where immigrants usually interact with Americans (Treas, 2009). Confined within the four walls of their home, the feeling of being an outsider grows in the older adults, which is further aggravated when they hear the reports of overt or covert racism. Although most studies have reported only covert discrimination at work places and in society, violent incidents of racism have also been reported.

Organized racism occurred in 1980s when several Indians were assaulted and murdered by "dot busters," a group of young White men (Lal, 2006). The dot referred to the *bindi* (colored spot) used by Hindu women on their forehead. More recently, the terrorist attacks of 9/11 have instigated fresh acts of racial violence against South Asians, and in particular against Sikhs, who wear turbans and keep beards (Melwani, 2006). Ranging from physical assaults to verbal abuse, threats, anti-immigrant sentiments such as "go back where you came from," and bias crimes affect not just blue collar workers but also the elite: "Racists do not differentiate between rich and poor immigrants, they are driven – like raging bulls – solely by color" (Melwani, 2006, p. 106).

On the positive side, such acts have resulted in fostering solidarity amongst immigrants, and the advent of human rights and advocacy groups that speak out against the injustice (Melwani, 2006).

In stark contrast to racism is the view held by some scholars that adjustment to the new culture is not just the responsibility of the immigrant but also of the host community (Mullins, 1990; Santamaria & Palma, 2008). Mullins (1990) prescribes that social service providers should receive training in cultural competence, and that the administrators should make every effort to recruit employees from within the immigrant community. Studies have also reported that racism, or the perception of being discriminated because of skin color or ethnicity, adversely affects the mental health of immigrants (e.g. Gill, 2008; Khanna et al., 2009)

Acculturation strategies. Adjustment, reaction, and withdrawal from the host culture are the three adaptation strategies that individuals employ during acculturation (Berry, 1990). Based on whether newcomers see merit in associating with the host community, or in maintaining their ethnic identity and ties with the original culture, Berry proposed a model that has four outcomes. First is *assimilation*, in which the individual becomes immersed in the dominant culture discarding his or her parent culture including language, social networks, food, and entertainment. *Integration* is the second option where the newcomer accepts aspects of both the original and the host culture. The term *bicultural* has also been used in the literature for this method of acculturation (e.g. Mehta, 1998).

Krishnan and Berry (1992) found that Indians overwhelmingly adopted integration strategy, and attributed it to the sample chosen, which was highly educated. Similar results were reported by Hans (2002): 92.1% of her 101 participants drawn from the SF Bay Area were bicultural. Further, studies have reported that integration is the preferred strategy of AI population (Gill, 2008), and is associated with lower acculturative stress leading to less psychological distress and better mental health (Hans, 2002; Krishnan & Berry, 1992; Mehta, 1998). Similar results have been reported by other immigrant groups such as Filipino American (Langit, 2007).

The third acculturative strategy is *separation* in which the immigrant withdraws completely from the dominant culture in favor of his or her traditional customs. *Marginalization* is the last strategy; it occurs when the individual is disillusioned with both the dominant and the parent culture, and withdraws from both.

Krishnan and Berry (1992) associated both separation and marginalization with older age, lack of fluency in English, retaining Indian citizenship, shorter stay in the U.S., and a desire to return to India. Such immigrants socialized mostly within their own community, used Indian languages, and ate Indian food while rejecting American culture. Berry's model has been used widely in the literature, and examining it from the framework of senior Indian immigrants, separation and marginalization seem to be the only options for most of them because they have limited opportunity to interact with the Americans (Treas, 2009). However, most AI seniors seem to embrace Indian culture, which indicates that separation is likely to be the most common strategy for this group. Further, irrespective of the strategy adopted, the dilemma of choosing between retaining or discarding cultural values results in internal conflicts and mental distress (Gill, 2008).

Reason for coming to the United States. The reason behind coming to the United States has been found to be an important factor in determining acculturative stress (Krishnan & Berry, 1992), and emotional well-being of immigrants (Akhtar, 1999). Compared to those who came for career enhancement or other reasons, older adults who relocated simply for family reunification reported less life satisfaction (Kalavar, 1998). Further, some seniors, who immigrated mainly to sponsor their adult children, reported frustration and depression as the years spent while waiting for the visas depleted their financial resources and social contacts in India thereby closing their return migration path (Nandan, 2007; Rangaswamy, 2000).

Length of residence in the U.S. and age at the time of immigration. Length of residence in the U.S. has been used by investigators as a proxy measure for acculturation (Diwan & Jonnalagadda, 2001) but the evidence is contradictory on how the mental and physical health is affected by the time spent in this country. Longer stay was associated with lesser acculturative stress in some studies (Hans, 2002) while other studies associated it with higher acculturative stress (Mui & Kang, 2006), depression (Mui & Shibusawa, 2008), and poorer health (Diwan & Jonnalagadda, 2001). Yet other studies did not find the length of residence significant (Diwan, 2008). Mui and Shibusawa (2008) postulated that a side-effect of longer residence is that children and grandchildren are more Americanized, which increases the cultural gap that aging parents perceive thereby exacerbating their depression.

Age at the time of immigration is another important factor in determining QoL, especially the financial well-being of the immigrants (Burr et al., 2009). Relocating at a younger age gives the immigrant time to learn English and customs of the country while offering them an opportunity to work here. Employment has a two-fold benefit: it adds to the income as well as improves their eligibility for most of the social welfare programs (Burr et al., 2009). Most AI seniors 65 and above, however, have immigrated late in life with 79.1% immigrating after age 40, and 43% after age 60, according to the 2000 census data (Mui & Shibusawa, 2008). As a result, very few seniors have any opportunity to work in the U.S., and the majority remains dependent on their children.

Language proficiency. Scholars assert that by the third generation, immigrants speak fluent English and lose touch with their native languages: "The United States is indeed a veritable 'cemetery of languages' in which the most varied linguistic backgrounds—from German to Italian; from Chinese to Spanish—have disappeared into a monolingual world in the course of two or three generations" (Portes & Rumbaut, 2006, p. 348). First-generation Asian immigrants, however, particularly the older adults, show a strong preference towards not only retaining their language but also perpetuating it by passing on the legacy (Mui & Shibusawa, 2008).

In studies conducted among Polish, Albanian, Arab, Mexican, Puerto Rican, White, and Black Americans in Detroit, immigrant parents strongly endorsed the view that by being bilingual and maintaining their heritage culture, their children would have more pride in who they are, would be more tolerant towards other racial and ethnic groups, and would have better chance at securing jobs (Lambert & Taylor, 1990). Even Black and White communities were pro-multiculturalism as opposed to assimilation in Detroit but in Miami, Blacks and Whites favored that immigrants should use English, and adopt the American way of life, thus signaling that host communities across the country vary in their attitude towards immigrants. Immigrant groups (Cuban, Nicaraguan, and Haitian), however, continued to be in favor of maintaining their heritage culture and language (Lambert & Taylor, 1990). Nevertheless, immigration scholars admit that there is a strong push towards forced assimilation in the U.S. (Portes & Rumbaut, 2006).

Among AI older adults, proficiency in English was associated with less acculturative stress in several studies (Kalavar, 2003; Krishnan & Berry, 1992). Regarded as a personal resource, elders with knowledge of English are more likely to provide help to their children, and have higher life satisfaction (Mui & Shibusawa, 2008). On the flip side, a language barrier was cited as a cause of isolation (Kalavar, 2003), lack of awareness about public benefits (e.g. Diwan, 2008; Mui & Shibusawa, 2008), and inability to utilize public transportation (Prasad, 2010; Rangaswamy, 2000). Along with food, music, and religion, own native language also emerged as an important factor that affects life quality in focus groups of AI seniors (Jonnalagadda et al., 2002).

Advocating the need for linguistically appropriate health care, Mui and Shibusawa (2008) argued that not having medically trained interpreters not only goes against the spirit of the Civil Rights Act of 1964 but it is also a form of discrimination against non-English-speaking clients. Further, using children and grandchildren as interpreters can result in miscommunication due to inadequate medical knowledge and improper translation as well as can undermine the authority of the elderly, thereby disturbing the power structure of the family. Language proficiency was also used as a factor while operationalizing life-stress in the AAFNY study, where the researchers argued that the stress-level of Asian American seniors is increased because they find it difficult to interact with the mainstream culture and access formal services due to the language barrier (Mui & Shibusawa, 2008).

Perceived cultural gap. A number of researchers (Akhtar; 1999; Kalavar & Van Willigen, 2005) have emphasized that the magnitude of cultural difference between the adopted and the home country on multiple dimensions, such as food, clothing, language, music, political ideologies, and entertainment, is a strong indicator of how the immigrant feels. That is, migrating from Canada or England to the United States is not likely to be as stressful as coming from India.

Brockmann (2002) posited that ethnic withdrawal could result from a sense of belonging to the country of origin, and perceived cultural gap with host culture. Perceived acculturation gap between the elders and their adult children was also found to be a source of low life satisfaction (Mui & Shibusawa, 2008), and depression for the elderly (Mui & Kang, 2006; Mui & Shibusawa, 2008). This link between psychological health and cultural differences has also been endorsed by other studies (Farver, Bhadha, & Narang, 2002; Hans, 2002; Patel, 2005).

Autonomy and Independence

Immigration often results in a loss of perceived control, and hence plays an important role in life quality of immigrants in general (Akhtar, 1999), and seniors in particular. It is, therefore, not surprising that six out of eight participants of a focus group of immigrant parents stated that remaining in India would have been better for them as it offered "better social life" and "independent living" (Rangaswamy, 2000). Independence also emerged as one of the major factors influencing QoL in a study with different ethnic groups in England (Grewal et al., 2004). In the landmark AAFNY study, having to depend on others emerged as a serious problem for Asian elders (29.9%) in general and Indian seniors (53%) in particular (Mui & Cross, 2003b). Loss of autonomy can be felt in many different spheres of life such as economic dependence, communication dependence because of the language barrier, and transportation dependence due to lack of affordable and accessible public transportation. Further, poor health could lead to reliance on others for performing activities of daily living while emotional dependence on adult children could stem from a sense of isolation in the new culture.

Sense of self-efficacy in the new culture. Also referred to as *mastery* or sense of control over one's life, *self-efficacy* refers to how competent one feels in dealing with his or her life circumstances (Bandura, 1977; 1994), and is an important component of successful aging (Bowling, 2005). It is positively correlated with self-esteem and influences a person's motivations, actions, behavior, and well-being. It also affects physical and mental health as well as social resources of a person, and is in turn impacted by the socioeconomic status of the person.

Self-efficacy usually rises from adolescence to middle age and falls in old age (Bowling, 2005). Performance accomplishment or success, observational learning, social persuasion, and interpretation of physiological state are the four main sources of efficacy (Bandura, 1977; 1994). It gains importance, because when asked about the factors that bring quality to their lives, 27% of the 999 participants surveyed, and 69% of the 80 interviewed in-depth chose autonomy, independence, or control over life as one of the factors (Bowling, 2005).

Emphasizing that mastery is concerned with controlling only those circumstances that are important to people rather than all circumstances per se, Pearlin, Nguyen, Schieman, and

Milkie (2007) argued that it is not a personality trait; rather, it can change if critical experience changes. They examined the roots of mastery in seniors 65 or older, and found that it is important to take into account the *life-course perspective* as race, gender, perceived discrimination in education and job, early exposure to stressors, and periods of economic hardships cumulatively impact the current mastery. Researchers investigating QoL have supported this view, and agreed that the reserves of older adults depend on historical events as well as their life experiences (Bowling, 2005; Mui & Shibusawa, 2008).

The colonial history of India followed by its partition and the subsequent wars fought with China and Pakistan, have left lasting impressions that have shaped the lives of AI seniors. Further, immigration in late life disturbs the normal transition processes associated with aging (Mui & Shibusawa, 2008). Whereas Asian seniors are normally expected to disengage from responsibilities and adjust to physical limitations imposed by old age, those who immigrate are forced to adapt, which impacts their psychological well-being (Mui & Shibusawa, 2008). For psychological continuity amidst a sea of changes therefore, Akhtar (1999) stressed the importance of continuing one's profession after immigration. For older adults relocating after retirement, however, that road is not open.

While past events indirectly influence the level of current mastery in older adults, recent stressors such as bereavement losses, functional limitations, care-giving, and economic hardships have a direct impact (Pearlin et al., 2007). As age advances, relationship losses due to deaths of family members and friends mount, leaving the elderly psychologically vulnerable. Research data also indicates that larger numbers of stressful events lead to increased depression (Mui & Shibusawa, 2008), whereas higher mastery is linked to reduced depression (Chokkanathan, 2009), a feeling of well-being, and improved health (Jonnalagadda & Diwan, 2005).

In the AAFNY study, receiving more assistance from children was predictive of more depression, which led the researchers to postulate that this is perceived as a loss of dignity, self-worth, and authority over children by the parents (Mui & Shibusawa, 2008). However, when parents assisted their children or grandchildren, it improved their sense of efficacy, thereby improving their life satisfaction.

Access to transportation. In gerontology research, access to transportation has been a consistent concern of the elderly, and some studies (Kalavar, 2003) have cited transportation barrier as a cause of isolation. Despite this, very few studies investigating the effect of access to transportation on AI seniors could be located.

In one study, restricted access to transportation was significantly correlated with life satisfaction but after controlling for self-assessed health, the significance disappeared, which led the researcher to speculate that health is a better predictor compared to the access to transportation (Kalavar, 1998). Transportation also emerged as one of the unmet needs of Asian Americans and an area where the seniors needed more assistance (Mui & Cross, 2003a). Among the barriers to transportation access, lack of English proficiency was cited as a cause in several studies (e.g. Rangaswamy, 2000).

According to the Americans with Disabilities Act (ADA) of 1990, not only do public transit agencies have to ensure that their vehicles are usable by people with disabilities but they must also provide paratransit services for people who are unable to travel by regular buses and trains (U.S. Department of Justice, n.d.). Either the inability to board a vehicle without assistance, or the incapacity to reach the bus and train stops qualifies a person for ADA paratransit service (City of Fremont Human Services, 2009).

In the SF Bay Area, several agencies such as Outreach (Outreach, n.d.) and East Bay Paratransit offer curb-to-curb or door-to-door services to eligible residents provided the rides are reserved 24 hours in advance. Some agencies also offer same day booking albeit at higher prices. The convenience offered by such services has made them popular amongst many AI seniors, who commute to senior centers or go to their doctor's appointments using this mode of transportation.

Financial dependence. The economic status of a person has been associated with QoL in several studies (Smith et al., 2004; Bowling, 2005). In one study, poor people reported much lower QoL compared to others on a ratio of 2:1 (Smith et al., 2004) while in another study, the need to have adequate finances for quality in their lives was mentioned by 73% of 80 participants interviewed in-depth, and 33% of 999 surveyed (Bowling, 2005). Further, more money was one of the most common responses when older adults were asked to name one thing that would improve their life quality (Bowling, 2005). Among Indians, lower incomes were associated with higher acculturative stress (Hans, 2002), less satisfaction with life (Kalavar, 1998), and experience of prejudice and discrimination (Kalavar, 2003; Rangaswamy, 2000). Moreover, even though more years in the United States usually predicted higher incomes for other age-groups, it was not so for older adults (Hans, 2002).

Burr et al. (2009) point out that the financial status particularly affects the well-being of older immigrants in addition to making a deep impact on governmental policies, programs, and the U.S. economy in general. In order to meet the basic living costs associated with food, housing, and medical needs, the older immigrants need substantial funds for which they must either depend on their sponsoring children or on the wealth they accumulated in their country of origin. This is so because government benefits are linked to the citizenship status (Burr et al., 2009) and as described under the politico-legal context, immigrants cannot become citizens for at least five years even after receiving their green card.

In addition, even if the seniors had assets or received pensions in their home country, due to the foreign exchange regulation act of India, they were unable to bring it in this country until as recently as 2000 when the old act was replaced by a new foreign exchange management act (Reserve Bank of India, n.d.). Moreover, the exchange rate, which hovers between 45-55 rupees to a dollar, make the rupee savings insignificant in dollar terms. Therefore, the older adults are completely dependent on either their children or the state.

Based on the 2004-2006 American community survey conducted by the U.S. Census Bureau, the median household income for AI immigrants aged 65 or more was almost $84,000 compared to the median household income of nearly $34,000 for the general American population aged 65 or more (Burr et al., 2009). However, the median personal income of these elderly Indians was only $8,149 compared to $16,655 for general population. Thus, one is likely to jump to wrong conclusions if only household income is considered (Burr et al., 2009; Kalavar, 2003). In reality, AI seniors, who have relocated in late life have very low independent income, and are totally dependent on their children. Further, significant within-group differences exist as 6.9% of elderly Indian immigrants live below the poverty line (Burr et al., 2009).

It is also important to note that Medicaid coverage has been used as a proxy variable for measuring financial resources in several studies (Mui & Shibusawa, 2008) because Asian seniors are often uncomfortable in divulging income data, and the eligibility for Medicaid depends on means testing based on federal guidelines on poverty.

Dependence for interaction and communication: Language barrier. The importance of having proficiency in English was examined in detail under acculturation. Of relevance here is to emphasize how language barrier makes the elderly immigrants dependent on their children for human interaction and communication. On one hand, lack of fluency in English isolates them from the mainstream culture so that they are unable to either utilize public resources or socialize with anyone outside their community (Sue & Sue, 2008). On the other hand is the frustration the elders feel over the lack of native language ability in their grandchildren, which increases the gulf between the two generations, and causes further isolation.

Political and Legal Context: Citizenship Status

As discussed in an earlier section, the political and legal contexts of the host and home country significantly affect the QoL of immigrants, and it was one of the four factors that Brockmann (2002) identified in her QoL model for older ethnic migrants of Europe. Much of the influence is abstract in nature and cannot be operationalized or concretely measured. However, citizenship status of the immigrant senior is one attribute that can be determined and the vital role that it plays on the QoL can be examined.

As described earlier, since late 1990s, welfare laws have seen major modifications so that noncitizens are no longer entitled to most social benefits, including health insurance like Medicare and Medicaid, in a majority of states (e.g. Mui & Shibusawa, 2008; Torres-Gil & Treas, 2009). Research data indicates that this could be a source of substantial stress and anxiety for elderly immigrants, thereby affecting their QoL negatively. Mr. R, a 71-year old man with no health insurance, for example,

> repeatedly pointed out the financial risk this involves for his son as the cost of health care in the United States is very steep . . . . Mr. R also stressed that if he had immigrated prior to August of 1996, he would have health coverage . . . . He repeatedly expressed his fear of being a financial burden on his family, and said he would return to India "at the first sign of failing health." . . . . "The care there is at an affordable cost. My son can always remit the money for my care. It will be cheaper than caring for me here." (Kalavar & Van Willigen, 2005, p. 221)

"Too many medical bills" was also identified as a serious problem by 37% Indians in the AAFNY study (Mui & Cross, 2003b). Taking the citizenship exam, which tests the knowledge of American history and English language skills, is essential for receiving public benefits but can become a source of considerable mental anguish for older adult immigrants. Trang (2009), for example, reported the story of an old Vietnamese woman who almost had a stroke after she was interviewed by an immigration officer. Lack of proficiency in English, therefore, becomes a deterrent, and many who are eligible do not apply for citizenship (Mui & Shibusawa, 2008).

The prejudice and discrimination associated with lack of citizenship, and to be treated as "second class citizens" despite holding citizenship are major mental health concerns according to therapists who have been counseling AI clients (Khanna et al., 2009). Further with no health insurance for noncitizens, the financial burden of care-giving falls exclusively on adult children (Nandan, 2007; Gupta & Pillai, 2002), who in some cases, have no option but to send their parents back to India where health care is more affordable (Nandan, 2007).

Citizenship is sometimes tied to ethnic identity and acculturation attitude as in the study conducted by Krishnan and Berry (1992), who reported that assimilated individuals are more likely to be American citizens rather than permanent residents whereas those with separation or marginalization strategy continue to hold Indian citizenships, and self-identify as Indians rather than Asian Americans.

Utilization of public resources. Four major means-tested federal programs are available for older adults in the United States (a) SSI, (b) Temporary assistance to Needy Families (TANF) which can be availed by only those seniors who care for minors, (c) Medicaid, and (d) Food stamp program (Burr et al., 2009). As discussed earlier, the eligibility depends on the citizenship status, and other factors such as work history in the U.S., the year of immigration, and the state in which the immigrant resides as different states have different rules to determine the eligibility (Burr et al., 2009).

Several U.K. based studies assert that the knowledge about both means-tested and non-means-tested public resources among South Asians is poor (Moffat & Mackintosh, 2009) resulting in low utilization of available resources. Similar concerns have been raised in the U.S. for Asian senior immigrants (Mui & Shibusawa, 2008; NIAASC, n.d.; Prasad, 2010). Compared to the general population, immigrants use less than 50% of health-care resources, and due to the fear that they may be denied citizenship or be deported, even documented immigrants are wary of seeking services (Sue & Sue, 2008).

Asserting that Asian Americans are underrepresented in non-means-tested AOA programs designed to serve the low income group, Mui and Shibusawa (2008) cite studies that show that in 2003, nursing-home care or at-home care constituted 41% of Medicaid cost but Asian Americans rarely use such services. The AAFNY study examined in detail the percentage of Asian seniors who use community based, in-home and health services, and predisposing, enabling and need factors that predict such use.

Longer stay in the U.S., and having Medicare and Medicaid, were consistently associated with more service utilization while number of medical conditions, poor perceived health, older age, female gender, stressful life events and a number of other factors contributed to a lesser extent (Mui & Shibusawa, 2008).

Social Capital, Support Network, and Isolation

The link between social capital and mental health has been amply demonstrated in the literature as evident from the comprehensive review published by Whitley and McKenzie (2005). The authors emphasized that though the research so far on the impact of social capital has focused more on physical health rather than mental health, social capital could play a significant role in the community psychiatry.

In the article, "Social Capital and Mental Health," Henderson and Whiteford (2003) point out that the underlying hypothesis for this association is that mental disorders are inversely proportional to the social capital of a person; that is, the higher the social capital, the lower is the incidence of mental disorders. Further, it is also hypothesized that in supportive environments, the duration of a mental-health episode will be shorter.

Accordingly, through in-depth interviews, Bhattacharya (2008) linked the depleted social capital of the adult male Indian immigrants to acculturative stress, and disorders such as depression and substance abuse. It is, therefore, not surprising that relationship with family is reported as one of the most important factors for life-quality by research participants irrespective of their age (Smith et al., 2004), and the relationship between various QoL constructs and social support is one of the most researched topics.

Social support was identified as one of the factors in the QoL model of older ethnic minority immigrants (Brockmann, 2002). Further, Grewal et al. (2004) regarded it as a key factor influencing the life quality of various ethnic groups.

The joint family structure prevalent in India acts as an informal support network (e.g. Chandra et al., 2009), and the structure continues to be preserved in many Indian households with immigrant parents. Despite that, isolation emerged as the number one problem that AI seniors face in open-ended interviews about life in the United States, and limited opportunities for social interaction was cited as one of the causes (Kalavar, 2003). Other scholars corroborate that loneliness and isolation are major issues for this demographic group (Prasad, 2010, Rangaswamy, 2000). Further, since Indians usually socialize within their ethnic community (Nandan, 2005; Nandi, 1980), leaving behind their extended family members in India is another reason that enhances the feeling of isolation.

Literature review suggests that the relation between social contact and mental health is equivocal, as some studies have found negative correlation between them; rather, it is the degree of closeness that people feel in their relationships, or the perception of social support that matters the most (Gauntlett, 2009; Low, 2005; Smith et al., 2004).

Personal social capital (including social activities, number of social contacts, and the perception of support) as well as external social capital (comprising of the quality of neighborhood, safety, available community facilities, and transportation) were found to be predictors of better QoL in Bowling's (2005) study. Smith et al. (2004), however, reported that the neighborhood and community did not directly affect the QoL but the sense of loneliness significantly lowered it. By researching the patterns of social integration, Diwan (2008) reported that the type of social network differed amongst English-speaking and non-English-speaking AI older adults; nevertheless, that had no bearing on the prevalence of depression.

According to 81% participants in the Bowling (2005) study, good social relationships provided quality to their lives. Further, 96% of the respondents interviewed in depth considered social relationships important for better QoL, and it was one of the top two things selected as the single most important aspect of QoL (Bowling, 2005). In Kalavar's (1998) study, number of friends and the frequency of interaction with them increased life satisfaction, but no such evidence was found for the interaction with the family. This led her to suggest that Indian seniors are possibly not as well cared for as is expected by the cultural norm.

Refueling: Access to AI culture. Having a connection with the culture that the immigrant has grown up with, having friends in similar situations, having access to ethnic community centers, or even having ethnic television channels could have a bearing on the QoL perceived by the individual. Likening it to emotional refueling that a child in symbiotic relation with the mother needs, Akhtar (1999) argued that separation from the motherland triggers similar emotions in immigrants, which requires similar reinforcement of intrapsychic connection with the country left behind, "Visiting ethnic marketplaces, celebrating one's original festivals, watching ethnic television shows, and attending services at religious centers that are operated by those from one's country of origin are among the activities that offer the immigrant an ethnopsychic rejuvenation" (Akhtar, 1999, p. 10).

Such refueling could be in the form of (a) *extramural refueling*, which signifies direct connection through phone calls to relatives and friends, or visits to the country of origin; and (b) *intramural refueling*, which includes support in the host country from own ethnic community, family, and friends, who have also immigrated (Akhtar, 1999).

Extramural refueling. Burr and colleagues (2009) assert that for elderly immigrants, the country of origin impacts multiple dimensions of their well-being. Indians, however, differ widely in their connection with the homeland (Nandan, 2005). Some seniors feel, "If it is my choice, I would go back to India.... My heart is always there" (p. 191) while others are well-settled in their adopted country unable to think of returning permanently. Yet others would like to return but would not do so leaving their children and grandchildren in this country.

According to Rangaswamy (2007), so many Indians harbor the myth that they would retire in their homeland that many jokingly say that NRI refers to "Non-Returning Indians" rather than the official term "Non-Resident Indians." People who have strong bonds with extended family and friends in India but relocate to reunite with their families often experience emotional suffocation, especially when they first migrate (Nandan, 2005). The lack of avenues to emotionally express themselves is reflected in the voice of the following respondent:

> "My emotional well-being . . . initially, when I came to live permanently with my son, was suppressed to the

maximum. I feel that I had to recoil myself which gave me suffocation... may be the blood pressure was a result of that. Having an outlet is very difficult for Indian people because we have no social standing here, especially my family, we are the only family here so there is no one to share with anybody . . . But, I feel that I have everything today." (Nandan, 2005, p. 191)

Indians are sometimes called transnationals, as they try to remain connected to their birth-place (Gill, 2008). Due to advances in computer technology such as cell phones and emails, and dropping prices of air travel and telecommunication, immigrants are now able to keep closer touch with their home country (Rangaswamy, 2007; Torres-Gil & Treas, 2009). Some seniors, especially those from higher socioeconomic backgrounds, go a step further and travel between East and West spending 3-6 months in India every year.

Intramural refueling. Intramural refueling has become easier as the availability of ethnic goods and services in the U.S. has grown dramatically in the last decade. By 1990s, the number of Indians had reached a critical mass plus the second generation Indians, now in their adolescent or young-adult years, started showing interest in Indian music and movies, which spurred the growth of music and video stores (Rangaswamy, 2007). Soon afterwards, the telecommunication industry went through a revolution creating a market for phone cards. Meanwhile in India, the cable and satellite television channels grew exponentially, and a couple of them became available in the United States.

By the middle of the first decade of 2000, however, viewers in the U.S. had access to a much larger number of television channels that catered to different audiences. The choice now included regional languages, news, spiritual, and business channels in addition to regular entertainment channels. Among older adults, particularly those visiting from India, religious or spiritual channels were quite popular. Further, as the ethnic population in the Bay Area grew in the last decade, public libraries started catering to their diverse customers by carrying ethnic DVDs and music in addition to books in native languages.

Role of ethnic organizations. "It is only natural that when traditional networks of association that exist in the home country are no longer available for immigrants in a foreign land, they will form new associations to replace the old ones," (p. 217) said Rangaswamy (2000), thereby, encapsulating both the need for ethnic organizations and the important role they can play in the lives of ethnic minorities. Based on literature review, Mui and Shibusawa (2008) concluded that connection with own community is more important for members of collectivistic cultures such as Asians so that compared to other minorities, Asian Americans are more likely to belong to their nationality groups.

In a comprehensive review, Raj (2004) discussed the role that ethnic networks and organizations have played in shaping the lives of Indian diaspora in North America. Not only have the organizations given a collective voice to Indians to forge a diasporic identity and combat discrimination, but they have also provided fertile ground for building social capital through networking. Further, they have helped in uplifting Indian image and improving both political and business ties between the U.S. and India (Raj, 2004). This demonstrates that in the new land surrounded by new realities and challenges, the minorities build institutions that are not replicas of what was available in their homeland. Instead, the new organizations reflect "the immigrants' need to forge an identity that draws from both Old and New World influences, at first for themselves and later for their children" (Rangaswamy, 2000, p. 217).

Regional and linguistic organizations such as Telugu, Bengali and Rajasthan associations along with religious and cultural institutions have promoted intra-ethnic networking and group cohesion by providing socialization opportunities. Unlike in

India, temples have served as centers for not just religious rituals but also for charitable, social, cultural, and educational activities (Raj, 2004). For children, they are the venues where they learn their languages and traditions, whereas for adults such associations offer an opportunity to give back to the community and educate children so that the culture is carried to the next generation (e.g. Gill, 2008). Older adults play a significant role in this cultural transmission, and several studies have commented on the positive influence of religious institutions in the lives of the elderly (e.g. Diwan & Jonnalagadda, 2001).

The current programs for AI seniors. Although there is a scarcity of culture-specific programs for elderly immigrants, yet, the beginnings have been made. Based in New York state, the National Indo-American Association for Senior Citizens (NIAASC) was founded in 1999 specifically to address the issues of Indian seniors in the aftermath of 1996 Welfare reforms. Acting as an information, referral and advocacy agency, NIAASC's mission is to improve the well-being and QoL of AI older adults (NIAASC, 2010). Building awareness about the seniors' issues through workshops, seminars, and conferences, advocating at the local, state, and national level, collaborating with various public and private provider agencies, and disseminating information to the seniors are the main objectives of NIAASC.

Amongst local organizations, the India Community Center (ICC) in Milpitas, California has programs for seniors in Milpitas, Cupertino, and Fremont locations several days a week (India Community Center, n.d.). Ranging from open discussions, poetry, music, theater, knitting, card-playing, dancing and yoga to celebrating cultural festivals and computer classes, the programs cater to both physical and mental health of older adults providing them ample opportunities to socialize with their age cohorts. Subsidized lunches are also available several times a week. Based on personal communication with several members who come regularly, ICC seems to be filling a vacuum in their lives created by late immigration thereby impacting their QoL in multifarious ways.

The seniors in Fremont have several associations, such as Indian Seniors Association of Fremont (INSAF), that meet at different locations. The Community Ambassador Program for Seniors (CAPS), an initiative of the City of Fremont Human Services Department, and the Tri-City Elder Coalition, made possible through a grant from the Robert Wood Johnson Foundation, is exemplary in terms of innovative community involvement (CAPS Services, n.d.; Tri-City Elder Coalition, n.d.).

Already a recipient of a national multicultural aging award given by American Society on Aging, and sponsored by the American Association of Retired Persons (AARP), the CAPS program partners with 12 different ethnic, faith-based and other minority organizations to provide culturally competent services to seniors and their families in their own languages (CAPS Services, n.d.). More than 100 volunteers in diverse communities have been trained to help seniors with information about a wide range of local resources and services such as social security, financial and legal aid, transportation, housing, health, and immigration.

Faced with the demographic reality of the tri-city (Fremont, Newark, and Union City) in 2005, where no ethnic group was in majority, 47% of the population was foreign-born, 50% residents were Asians, and 57% population spoke a non-English language at home, the Tri-City Elder Coalition and City of Fremont devised this innovative program, Pathways to Positive Aging, to improve the QoL of seniors and their families (CAPS Demographics and History, n.d.; Tri-City Elder Coalition, n.d.). The CAPS program has published *The How-To Guide for Immigrant Seniors* (City of Fremont Human Services, 2009), a resource book that helps elderly immigrants in familiarizing themselves with the rules and regulations associated with insurance, taxes, transportation, housing, banking, citizenship, employment, medical, and legal services.

In Santa Clara County, the Council on Aging Silicon Valley (2009) has published a similar resource guide, albeit it is not geared towards immigrants. In late 2011, however, the Senior Peer Advocate (SPA) program has been launched in Santa Clara County by the Health Trust and its partners (Health Trust, 2011). Funded by the Council on Aging, the SPA program has been modeled after the CAPS program, and it provides similar services.

Religiosity, role of religious organizations. Although not a focus of this study, religion and spirituality have been cited as foundational for the worldview of first-generation Indians (Khanna et al., 2009). Daily prayers, worship, meditation, and rituals are an important part of the lives of many elderly Indians irrespective of their religious faith (Nandan, 2005). A growing body of evidence suggests that religion and spirituality are positively correlated with happiness and well-being, even though there is some evidence that this relation is not significant (Gauntlett, 2009).

Lower level of religiosity was associated with more depression and less life satisfaction in the AAFNY study (Mui & Shibusawa, 2008), and the frequency of visits to places of worship approached significance in predicting the health status of AI seniors in the Atlanta study (Diwan & Jonnalagadda, 2001).

Religiosity provides the inner strength in adverse conditions, and fosters community building amongst immigrants (Khanna et al., 2009). As a result, religious and spiritual centers play a key role in the lives of AI seniors. They serve as the meeting ground of like-minded people, and satisfy the need of the expatriates to remain connected with their faith. Temples, *gurudwaras,* and mosques are places where the diaspora can practice rituals, and celebrate religious and cultural festivals, some of which might seem too bizarre for the dominant culture. Studies, however, have emphasized that culturally appropriate behavior and practices should not be pathologized (Khanna et al., 2009).

Marital status and living arrangement. Being married and living together has been correlated with higher QoL (Smith et al., 2004), and lower acculturative stress (Hans, 2002). Nevertheless, contrary to other studies, Kalavar (1998) reported that AI seniors living alone had higher life satisfaction compared to married persons: Her study, however, had only two participants living alone; hence, no generalization can be made. Living in a good home and neighborhood was mentioned by 37% of older adults surveyed, and 96% of those interviewed in-depth, as a factor that attributed quality to their lives (Bowling, 2005).

In the AAFNY study, those who lived alone were more satisfied with life, which directly contrasts the common assumption that Asian parents prefer living with their family (Mui & Shibusawa, 2008). One possible explanation offered by the researchers was that living alone increases the autonomy and independence of the seniors, which has already been linked to higher life satisfaction. Among AI seniors, three participants living in seniors' housing were found to be less satisfied with life compared to one person living with non-relatives (Kalavar, 1998) but the numbers are too small to draw any conclusion.

Having a Role or Meaning in Life

In a qualitative study of older adults from multiple ethnic groups conducted in the U.K, having a role that gave an opportunity to feel useful emerged as one of the most important attributes of QoL (Grewal et al., 2004). In family settings, the role was sought through parenting of grandchildren, teaching them cultural values, caring for partners, and being the decision-maker, or managing the finances of the household.

Volunteering for a cause or in a religious setting provided a role in the community, whereas paid work when possible was another avenue to feel useful (Grewal et al., 2004). Research evidence has associated volunteering with better physical health, higher life expectancy and a feeling of being productive, all of which enhance happiness, life- satisfaction, and the sense of well-being (Guantlett, 2009). Not feeling useful, on the other hand, has been correlated with higher depression, disability, mortality, and lower levels of physical activity, social interaction, and healthy behavior (Guantlett, 2009).

Consistent with this finding, in Bowling (2005) study, 80% of people interviewed in-depth and 60% of those surveyed mentioned that having social roles and activities gave their lives quality. The AAFNY study reported that when elderly parents assisted their children, it raised their life satisfaction scores (Mui & Shibusawa, 2008), which can be interpreted in terms of seniors finding a concrete role by assisting.

Health

Research evidence shows that immigrants, in general, live longer and have healthier habits compared to natives (Markides et al., 2009). The authors attribute this partly to "immigrant advantage," which refers to selective migration of healthier people from relatively higher socioeconomic backgrounds in the sending country, a view supported by other scholars (Rangaswamy, 2007). Despite this advantage and the evidence of better mental health amongst younger immigrants, older Asian immigrants report worse mental health (Markides et al., 2009).

While acknowledging that Asian Americans as a group report lower levels of heart disease, cancer, and stroke, the three leading causes of mortality, Mui and Shibusawa (2008) argued that this could also be due to the unwillingness of Asian elders to seek medical services, thereby remaining uninformed about their disease condition or under-reporting.

South Asians, however, have four times higher risk of heart diseases than the general population, according to SAHC (SAHC CAD Statistics, n.d.). Emphasizing that Coronary Artery Disease (CAD) is a global epidemic among this population, the Center asserts that CAD strikes South Asians at a younger age, and is often fatal so that 50% of heart attacks are before the age of 50, and 25% are even before the age of 40.

Physical health. The relation between physical health and life quality or surrogate constructs seems to be one of the most researched subjects. Bowling (2005) reported good health and functional status to be predictors of better QoL while Kalavar (1998) found that AI seniors with poor health scored lower in life satisfaction. Further, poor perceived health was found to be the strongest predictor of depression in the AAFNY study (Mui & Shibusawa, 2008).

The magnitude of influence that health exerts on QoL, however, depends on the population characteristics. Developers of WHOQOL-100 reported that the physical domain is the largest contributor to overall QoL for the sample of ill people, whereas for healthy individuals, the environmental factors contribute the most (WHO, 1998). Further, as physical limitations arise with advancing age, health becomes more important to people (Bowling, 2005).

For people aged 85 or more, health and functional capacity become the most important determinant of QoL, and in a 2001 study of participants with age in the range of 55-95 years, 34% of the variance in QoL was explained by the self-reported health (Smith et al., 2004). Further, when asked to specify the single-most important attribute of QoL, 37% respondents in Bowling's (2005) study selected good health, making it one of the top two desired items along with social relationships. Moreover, better health and physical mobility was also selected as the single thing that would improve QoL by the maximum number of respondents.

Amongst the predictors of poor health according to the literature, are perception of lower social support, distance with family members, female gender, older age, and higher body mass index whereas healthy behavior including more physical activity is associated with bicultural or American identity, longer stay in the U.S. and young age (Diwan & Jonnalagadda, 2001;

Jonnalagadda & Diwan, 2005). Ample evidence also supports that regular physical exercise improves both physical and mental health.

An interesting but confounding result reported in the context of physical health is the "disability paradox," whereby socially-isolated patients with limited financial support but significant disabilities including difficulties in performing daily activities, have reported excellent or very good QoL (Carr & Higginson, 2001). This has led researchers to conclude that the QoL is not static; rather, it changes, and chronic illness affects it in an unexpected manner.

Since perceptions are important, another interesting finding is that several AI seniors with chronic health conditions attributed them to their age as well as the lifestyle in America: "I had blood pressure . . . . That is the gift this country has given me for whatever reason." (Nandan, 2005, p. 193)

Yoga and pranayam. Until recently, yoga was known chiefly as a form of physical exercise or postures. Millions, however, rediscovered *pranayam*, the breathing exercise component of yoga, through television in India and other countries. *Patanjali Yogpeeth,* an institution devoted to research in yoga and *Ayurveda*, played a significant role in this revolution, and it claims that yoga is a holistic medical science, which improves physical, mental, and spiritual health (Balkrishna, 2007).

Meanwhile, with body-mind connection firmly established in the literature (Harvard Health Publications, 2009; Zittel, Lawrence, & Wodarski, 2002), researchers have started to quantifiably measure the long suspected health benefits of yoga, especially its breathing techniques. Citing various studies that relate activation of the parasympathetic nervous system to deep, slow breathing, Burke and Marconett (2008) discuss the positive psycho-physiological effects of alternate-nostril and other breathing exercises. Citing an increasing number of randomized controlled trials that demonstrate the positive effects of yoga, the Harvard Mental Health letter reports, "For many patients dealing with depression, anxiety, or stress, yoga may be a very appealing way to better manage symptoms" (Harvard Health Publications, 2009, p. 5).

The positive effects of yoga have been researched on diverse, chronic diseases, including breast or ovarian cancer (Danhauer, Tooze, Farmer, Campbell, McQuellon, Barrett, et al., 2008), fibromyalgia (da Silva, Lorenzi-Filho, & Lage, 2007), HIV/AIDS (Brazier, Mulkins, & Verhoef, 2006), chronic low-back pain (Tekur, Singphow, Nagendra, & Raghuram, 2008), cardiovascular disease and diabetes mellitus (Bijlani, Vempati, Yadav, Ray, Gupta, Sharma, et al., 2005), heart attacks (Shannahoff-Khalsa, Sramek, Kennel, & Jamieson, 2004), diarrhea-predominant irritable-bowel syndrome (Taneja, Deepak, Poojary, Acharya, Pandey, & Sharma, 2004), dyspnea (Donesky-Cuenco, Nguyen, Paul, & Carrieri-Kohlman, 2009), obesity, hypertension, blood sugar, and cholesterol (Gokal, Shillito, & Maharaj, 2007), and stress, anxiety, PTSD, depression, and substance abuse (Brown & Gerbarg, 2005).

Along with the results of various clinical trials, Balkrishna (2007) presents testimonials and supporting factual evidence of cure from people suffering from incurable diseases including cancer, HIV, heart diseases, hepatitis B and C, pancreatitis, arthritis, diabetes, hypertension, kidney or gall bladder stones, leucoderma, hyper- or hypothyroidism, epilepsy, paralysis, depression, migraine, and asthma.

Believed to be practiced in India for thousands of years, *Ashtang Yog* (eight-limbed yoga) was codified in a short, approximately 200 line verse form in *Yogasutra* by Sage Patanjali (Ramdev, 2008). The eight limbs or principles are self-restraint, discipline, *asana* or yoga postures, *pranayams*, control over the sense organs, concentration, meditation, and transcendental meditation (Ramdev, n.d.). Thus, yogic posture is only a small part of yoga, a synecdoche that is so popular that it hides the true meaning and power of yoga. The focus, however, is gradually shifting from postures to breathing techniques, and technology, especially television is playing an important role in it. As the viewers of *pranayam* based intervention experienced personal benefits, *Patanjali Yogpeeth* grew dramatically with their support. Whether or not their claim that yoga is a holistic medical science is accepted, based on research evidence and testimonials, it seems that yoga can play a much bigger role in improving QoL.

Mental health. Depression, depressive syndrome, or symptoms of depression have been shown to be correlated with QoL in a number of studies (Hepner, 2003). Combined with the fact that almost 25% of suicides amongst the elderly are related to depression (Mui & Kang, 2006), and that there is a high prevalence of depression amongst Asian senior immigrants (Mui & Kang, 2006; Mui & Shibusawa, 2008), no study of life quality can be complete without looking at research on depression. Amongst the predictors of depression are poor self-rated health (Diwan, 2008; Mui & Kang, 2006), stressful life-events (Mui & Kang, 2006), perceived cultural gap, and splitting of house-hold with adult children (Mui & Kang, 2006), dissatisfaction in relationship with children (Diwan, 2008), female gender (Diwan, 2008), and lower education (Diwan, 2008).

The pain felt by the elderly at their social exclusion affects mental health, and is reflected in the desire for "greater tolerance of the aged by the younger generation" (Bowling, 2005, p. 82) expressed by a respondent as the single thing that would improve QoL of older adults. Further, when asked what brings quality to their lives, 38% of the participants surveyed, and 96% of those interviewed in-depth in Bowling (2005) study mentioned psychological well-being as an important factor.

Anxiety, loneliness, and personality characteristics. Personality characteristics such as optimism were found to be a predictor of higher QoL (Bowling, 2005) as well as higher life expectancy. In Berlin Aging Study, for example, 516 seniors aged between 70 and 103 years were assessed for positive and negative affect as well as subjective well-being during 1990-1993. By 1996 only 50% of the participants had survived, and statistical analysis showed a clear link between positive affect and longevity, and between negative affect and mortality risk (Gauntlett, 2009). In the AAFNY study, anxiety was identified as a source of stress by 33.6% Asian seniors but amongst Indians the rate was as high as 46% (Mui & Cross, 2003b). Loneliness also emerged as a problem for 14.1% Indians.

Discrepancy between expectation and reality. Expectations of people play a major role in how they assess their life quality and psychological well-being. The same objective circumstances can make one person really happy and content while they might throw another person with different expectations in deep discontent, frustration, anger, or depression.

As a result, Carr and Higginson (2001) define QoL as "the extent to which hopes and ambitions are matched by experience" (p. 1358) or the "appraisal of one's current state against some ideal" (p.1358) while others suggest that the magnitude of discrepancy, or the gap between expectation and experience, can explain the difference in QoL (Bowling, 2005; Hepner, 2003). Yet other investigators have reported that the downward social comparisons of self with others less well-off leads to higher self-rated QoL (Bowling, 2005).

Researchers point out that elderly AI parents expect better life and closeness with family members but do not anticipate the struggles awaiting them in the new country (Gill, 2008), which significantly adds to their dissatisfaction with life in the U.S. For example, Mrs. M., a research participant in Kalavar and Van Willigen's (2005) study, was the daughter of a wealthy family married in another affluent family, which gave her a luxurious life style in India:

> The house was full of people who provided different types of services, gardening, cooking, cleaning, etc . . . .

She never envisaged that in her old age she would be living as a dependent in her son's family, cooking and cleaning for them (p. 220).

Another major unexpected change for AI seniors is the loss of authority and the necessity to defer to the wishes of children and grandchildren while their expectation was just the contrary (Kalavar & Van Willigen, 2005). This demotion of status within the family structure is a major cause of grief for AI older adults (e.g. Prasad, 2010).

Demographic Variables
There is contradictory evidence on how much influence the various demographic factors have on the QoL. Analysis of the literature, according to Gauntlett (2009), shows that if basic needs are met then happiness is unrelated to age, race, culture, marital status, income, and education but the results from other studies differ.

Age. In gerontology research, aging is sometimes viewed as a "leveling experience" that eradicates the divisions and inequalities due to race or ethnicity (Kalavar, 1998). The old age, however, spans several decades and the geriatric literature emphasizes the heterogeneity within older adults. There is no consensus on the age at which a person is considered an older adult (Gauntlett, 2009; WHO, n.d.).

According to the glossary of terms published by WHO Centre for Health Development, people aged 60-74 are considered as the *"young old,"* and those between 75 and 84 are known as the *"old old"* or simply old people while those aged 85 and above are categorized as the *"oldest old"* (2004). Another similar concept is that of the third and the fourth age. When Peter Laslett divided human life into four ages, he envisioned the *third age* as the time when people are healthy, relatively free from responsibilities, and have energy to pursue their interests (Wiggins et al., 2004). In contrast, the *fourth age* was a period of waning health and dependence on others.

Contradictory findings on how age impacts QoL have been reported in the literature (Low, 2005). Some studies suggest that within the older adult population, QoL deteriorates with advancing age as the challenges related to health, functioning, and bereavements steadily increase (Bowling, 2005). Worse mental health was also reported for old-old Asians compared to young-old Asians (Mui & Shibusawa, 2008).

In a study with 999 participants in Britain aged 65 or more, 71% of those aged between 65 and 69 reported their QoL as either "so good that it could not be better" or "very good" but the percentage decreased with age, and was reduced to 32% for seniors aged above 80 years (Bowling, 2005). An interesting finding in this context is that older adults often report lower level of happiness but higher level of satisfaction compared to the young (Bowling, 2005; Campbell et al., 1976) but for very old people, life satisfaction reduces as health and relationship losses mount (Bowling, 2005). Gauntlett (2009), however, cites studies that show that happiness increases with age.

Education level. Lower level of education amongst immigrants has been associated with higher acculturative stress, and hence more psychological distress (e.g. Diwan, 2008; Hans, 2002; Kalavar, 2003). Higher education opens the door for better jobs resulting in more economic stability, which could be a reason why less education was found to be a predictor of psychosomatic stress symptoms (Krishnan & Berry, 1992).

Gender. Whether gender affects the life satisfaction or well-being of a person has not been clearly established as investigators have found contradictory evidence (Low, 2005). Researchers have discussed the importance of studying the gender difference in the light of radically different upbringing and status accorded to the males and females in the predominantly patriarchal Indian culture (Chandra et al., 2009;

Kalavar, 1998). In addition to continued subordination, denial of rights to education, employment and inheritance, and enforced subservience (Kalavar, 1998), the responsibility of preserving the marriage lies predominantly with the women (Chandra et al., 2009).

Kalavar (1998) found that AI women were less optimistic about their current lives and were less satisfied in general. She attributed her findings to the lack of employment and education, which would have imparted better coping strategies to the women. Other studies have reported higher psychosomatic stress (Krishnan & Berry, 1992), poorer health condition or physical functioning (Diwan & Jonnalagadda, 2001; Mui & Shibusawa, 2008), and higher levels of depression amongst women (Diwan, 2008; Lai & Surood, 2008).

Summary

A theme that emerges based on the literature review is that people value the most what they have lost, or what is not available to them (Bowling, 2005). Thus, for example, sick or older adults having health issues consider health of paramount importance, those who are divorced or widowed value social relationships, and individuals with low financial resources believe that more money would improve their QoL (Bowling, 2005).

Lack of autonomy and the need to depend on children leading to lack of status and authority over them is a major source of frustration for AI older adults immigrating in late-life. Further, the direct and the indirect contribution made by the parents in the success of Indian community is neither recognized nor understood:

> This success has usually been attributed to the high educational levels of the immigrants themselves, their professional skills, and their solid family values, but the fact is that many of the immigrants could not have done it without the presence in the United States and the

> active cooperation of their elderly parents. (Rangaswamy, 2000, p. 195)

As a result, despite the material comfort and proximity with children that the United States offers, for many seniors, the reality seems to be what Kalavar and Van Willigen (2005) expressed in a nutshell: "Older Indians have limited incomes and no employment history, as a result in many ways, India is a better place to be sick and die." (p. 228)

CHAPTER THREE: METHODOLOGY

In this chapter, the research design and methodology including the population studied, instruments used, and the data collection and analysis methods, will be described. Both quantitative and qualitative methods were used, with a focus on descriptive quantitative methods due to the exploratory nature of this study. Likert-type scale questions as well as open-ended questions were employed in self-administered or interviewer-assisted format in this study. To explore various aspects of QoL as reviewed in previous chapters, published instruments and a psychosocial questionnaire designed by this author were used. The established instruments include a QoL instrument, WHOQOL-BREF (WHO, 1998), a mastery scale (Pearlin & Schooler, 1978), PHQ-9 (assessing level of depression; Pfizer Inc., n.d.), and GAD-7 (assessing level of anxiety; Pfizer Inc., n.d.). The author-designed questionnaire will also be described in a later section of this chapter.

Purpose of the Study and the Research Questions

As described in Chapter 1, the main purpose of the study was to gain an insight into the lives and mental health of AI older adults living in the SF Bay Area who have immigrated to the U.S. to be with their adult children and grandchildren. The objective of the study was to understand the concerns and social-service needs of such AI seniors. Specifically, how late-life immigration has influenced their life quality was examined. The research questions and hypotheses were described in Chapter 1.

Selection of Participants

The target population for this study was AI seniors, who are at least 60 years of age and have immigrated to the U.S. to be with the families of their adult children.

The background of potential participants and reason for immigrating to the U.S. were explored during the screening process. To be included in this study, the participants met the following criteria: (a) Sixty years or older; (b) India as the country of origin; (c) Family reunification as the primary cause of immigration; and (d) Permanent residents (green-card holders) or U.S. citizens living in this country for at least one year.

As described in the procedures section, the participants were recruited through email groups and flyers, and the selected participants were provided with the informed consent forms. Only those who signed the informed consent were allowed to participate in the study.

Instrumentation

This section describes the published instruments used in this study as well as the rationale and design of the author-designed survey.

The Deficiencies of the Standard Instruments

A major problem in selecting instruments for this study was the standard instruments' lack of cross-cultural and content validity for the AI population, "the measures of quality of life, happiness, and even mental health, are themselves biased and are neither culture nor class-free measures" (Liu, 1980,

Foreword in Nandi, 1980). For example, several researchers have questioned the applicability of SF-36, a widely used instrument, for Asian and other populations (e.g. Haroon et al., 2007; Hawthorne, Herrman, & Murphy, 2006). Nandi (1980) aptly described the issue:

> The concept of quality of life is so bound by time, class, ideology, and values that there is a general lack of consensus about what conditions are desirable and what are not, and to what extent. Further, all aspirations and desires are learned in a particular social context under certain assumptions. (p.13)

Thus, lack of consensus, and the domain and culture-specific nature of life quality, influenced the selection of instruments for this study. As Andrews and Withey (1976) attested, "The notion of measuring the quality of life could include the measurement of practically anything of interest to anybody. And, no doubt, everybody could find arguments supporting the selection of whichever set of indicators happened to be his choice." (p. 6)

Further, as Kreitler and Kreitler (2006) attested, the efforts to standardize the QoL instruments aiming at applying them to wider populations have led to the omission of important content areas relevant to QoL. Moreover, most standard instruments were designed for people with health issues hence they focus on diseases and physical health aspect of QoL. As a result, these instruments may lack construct and content validity for assessing QoL of healthy people or individuals affected by such psychosocial factors as immigration, unemployment, and loss of relationships through death or separation (Kreitler & Kreitler, 2006). The inadequacy of available instruments to assess QoL of immigrants who are older adults and belong to ethnic minority groups was also highlighted by Brockmann (2002).

With the limitations of the standard instruments and the research objectives in mind, the researcher evaluated different

QoL instruments. The 60-item Multidimensional Quality of Life (MQOL; Kreitler & Kreitler, 2006) was not chosen because three essential aspects of this study (culture of the clients, their immigration experience, and their old age) were not assessed. The Quality of Life Inventory (Frisch, 1994) was also not selected for the same reasons although it aims at assessing numerous aspects of QoL (health, self-esteem, goals-and-values, money, work, play, learning, creativity, helping attitude, love, friends, children, relatives, home, neighborhood, and community).

The Chosen Instruments

The instruments used for this study were (a) World Health Organization Quality of Life Brief version (WHOQOL-BREF), (b) Mastery scale (Pearlin & Schooler, 1978), (c) PHQ-9, the mood scale of the Brief Patient Health Questionnaire (BPHQ), and (d) Generalized Anxiety Disorder (GAD-7) assessment instrument. In addition, a psychosocial questionnaire developed for this study was used.

WHOQOL-BREF. The WHOQOL-BREF is a 26-item instrument for measuring QoL. It was derived from the WHOQOL-100, a World Health Organization initiative for which focus groups and field trials were conducted simultaneously in 15 countries (WHO, 1998). Intending to introduce a humanistic element into contemporary health care, and to reduce the focus on a medical model that focuses only on eradication of disease and associated symptoms, the WHO model takes a comprehensive and multidimensional view of QoL (WHO, 1996). It gives four domain scores: (a) physical health, (b) psychological, (c) social relationships, and (d) environmental.

The 26-item BREF version takes one item from each of the 24 facets in the WHOQOL-100 in addition to two global self-report items on respondents' overall QoL and satisfaction with health (WHO, 1997, 1998). The environmental, physical, psychological, and social domains contain eight, seven, six, and three items respectively. Because the respondent is asked to assess his or her level of satisfaction with the different aspects of life in 10 of the 26 items of the WHOQOL-BREF, Hawthorne et al. (2006) opined that it can be considered a life satisfaction scale. The authors also pointed out that inclusion of environmental domain makes the WHOQOL unique compared to other HRQoL instruments that ignore this important dimension. Most instruments include only physical and psychological domains and some incorporate social domain but none take into account the environmental well-being (Hawthorne et al.).

Various studies on the psychometric properties of the WHOQOL-BREF show that the instrument has good content validity and discriminant validity as well as test-retest reliability and internal consistency, with Cronbach alpha values ranging between 0.66 and 0.84 (WHO, 1998; Hawthorne et al., 2006). Multiple regression analysis showed that all four domains contributed significantly to the overall QoL score.

The contribution of the physical health domain was the highest and that of social relationships was the lowest in explaining the variance (WHO, 1998). The high correlation between the WHOQOL-BREF and the WHOQOL-100 domain scores, ranging from 0.89 for social relationships to 0.95 for physical health (WHO, 1998), further supports that WHOQOL-BREF is a reliable alternative to the WHOQOL-100. Preliminary population norms for WHOQOL-BREF were calculated for different age-groups, gender, and health status (Hawthorne et al., 2006). The norms reported for general category were: physical health (M = 73.5, SD = 18.1), psychological health (M = 70.6, SD = 14.0), social relationships (M = 71.5, SD = 18.2), and environmental health (M = 75.1, SD = 13.0).

From the very beginning, the WHOQOL was simultaneously developed in English and in the language of each field center, and was intended to be cross-culturally applicable (WHO, 1996; 1998). As it was developed through international collaboration, it has gained significant popularity, and is widely applied in studies across different countries and cultures including India (e.g. Haroon et al., 2007; Aggarwal et al., 2010).

The psychometric properties of Hindi versions of the WHOQOL-100 and the WHOQOL-BREF, developed in Delhi, India, were reported to be satisfactory (Saxena et al., 1998). While evaluating the cross-linguistic equivalence between Hindi and English versions, Saxena et al. suggested some equivalence but also raised concerns about the applicability of giving a different language version of instrument to people raised in another culture even if the participants are proficient in that language (Saxena, Quinn, Sharan, Naresh, Yuantao-Hao, & Power, 2005).

Further, by examining the item discriminatory power of different items of the WHOQOL-BREF from an Item Response Model perspective, Lin and Yao (2009) reported that items of a general nature had higher discriminatory power in assessing QoL compared to items that were so specific that they were applicable to only a subset of population. For example, "how would you rate your quality of life" performed the best, whereas the questions assessing the pain or the need for medication were the worst performers (Lin & Yao, 2009).

Pearlin and Schooler mastery scale. Developed in 1978, Pearlin and Schooler's mastery scale contains seven items that assess the level of control an individual perceives to have over his or her life. Each item is measured on a 4-point Likert-type scale with options strongly agree (1), agree (2), disagree (3), and strongly disagree (4). The range for possible scores, therefore, is 7 to 28, with higher scores indicating better perception of control.

Likening mastery to Bandura's concept of self-efficacy, Pearlin et al. (2007) emphasized that mastery refers to controlling only those circumstances that are important to the person rather than exerting control over all circumstances. As opposed to fatalism, where one believes that circumstances are beyond one's control and are either too difficult to change or in the hands of a higher power, mastery implies the belief that with effort they can be altered to suit personal needs.

The mastery scale has become one of the most commonly utilized instruments for measuring personal control beliefs in recent health research (University of California San Francisco [UCSF] MacArthur Research Network, 2008; Seeman, 2008). It shows satisfactory psychometric properties (Peralin & Schooler, 1978; Pearlin, Lieberman, Menaghan, & Mullan, 1981), and acceptable internal reliability and construct validity (as cited in UCSF MacArthur Research Network, 2008). Pearlin and Radabaugh (1976) established the norms by categorizing the raw scores (a) 4-17 as the limited mastery group; (b) 18-23 as the moderate mastery group; and (c) 24-28 as the heightened mastery group. These norms have been used by other studies (Elliott, Trier, & Stein, 1986). The mastery scale has been used in research on AI older adults both in India (Chokkanathan, 2009), and in the U.S. (e.g. Jonnalagadda & Diwan, 2005).

The PHQ-9: Mood scale of the BPHQ. Derived from Primary Care Evaluation of Mental Disorders (PRIME-MD), Mood scale (PHQ-9) of the BPHQ is a 9-item self-report instrument that assesses the presence of depressive symptoms in both clinical and general population (Martin, Rief, Klaiberg, & Braehler, 2006). It allows one to calculate the severity of depression by assigning scores of 0, 1, 2, and 3, to the responses "not at all," "several days," "more than half the days," and "nearly every day," respectively. The total possible score of the PHQ-9, the sum of scores for nine items, ranges from 0, signifying absence of depressive symptoms, to 27, indicating severe depressive symptoms. The cut-off scores for mild, moderate, moderately severe, and severe depression are 5, 10, 15, and 20 (Pfizer Inc., n.d.).

The criterion and construct validity of the PHQ-9, and its utility in diagnosing depression have been established (Spitzer, Kroenke, & Williams, 1999). In addition, the PHQ-9 performed comparably to the longer, clinician-administered original instrument PRIME-MD (Spitzer et al., 1999). The instrument was also found valid for general population in diagnosing both major depression and the sub-threshold depressive disorders (Martin et al., 2006). Studies have also been conducted to evaluate the applicability of the PHQ-9 in different settings such as older adults in primary care (Phelan, Williams, Meeker, Bonn, Frederick, LoGerfo, et al., 2010). For Indians, a modified version of the PHQ-9 called the PHQ-12, was also proposed with comparable psychometric properties (Poongothai, Pradeepa, Ganesan, & Mohan, 2009). The entire BPHQ, including the mood scale, has been translated in major Indian languages and has been standardized for each language (Kochhar, Rajadhyaksha, & Suvarna, 2007).

GAD-7 anxiety assessment instrument. The GAD-7 is a brief 7-item instrument that assesses generalized anxiety disorder and determines its severity (Spitzer, Kroenke, Williams, & Löwe, 2006). Response categories of "not at all," "several days," "more than half the days," and "nearly every day" are assigned scores of 0, 1, 2 and 3, respectively. The cumulative score is computed and ranges between 0 and 21 (Pfizer Inc., n.d.). The cut-point scores of 5, 10, and 15 indicate mild, moderate and severe anxiety. Although the instrument is specifically designed to assess for GAD, other anxiety disorders including panic, social anxiety, and post-traumatic stress disorder can also be assessed, and a score of 10 or more signifies that further evaluation should be carried out (Pfizer Inc., n.d.).

The psychometric properties of the GAD-7 were studied, and Spitzer et al. (2006) reported good criterion, construct, factorial, and procedural validity and reliability in clinical settings. The instrument was later validated for the general population, and normative data was also generated (Löwe et al. 2008). Löwe et al. reported good construct validity, internal consistency with a Cronbach alpha value of 0.89, and a single-dimension factorial structure that did not vary with gender or age. Women reported higher mean anxiety scores as compared to men. For the studied sample in Germany, population norms were calculated for different age and gender combinations. A score of 10 or more was reported by approximately 5% of the participants, whereas approximately 1% reported scores of 15 or higher. Löwe et al. argued that the normative data can be generalized for other developed countries, particularly the United States. The GAD-7 has been translated in several Indian languages, and the different language versions are available at the Pfizer website (Pfizer – PHQ Screeners, n.d.).

Psychosocial Questionnaire

To address the issue that the standard instruments do not take into account various aspects of life likely to be important for AI seniors who have migrated late in life, a questionnaire aiming at assessing the psychosocial data of the participants was developed. The psychosocial questionnaire is designed based on the landmark AAFNY study (Ryan et al., 2003), the Kalavar (1998) study, and other studies reviewed in previous chapters.

A 5-point Likert-type scale is used for the response categories wherever possible. Apart from usual demographic data, the questionnaire is designed to explore various dimensions of life, the details of which will be discussed in this section. Several paired questions that explore the participants' lives before and after immigration were also devised similar to the approach used in the Kalavar (1998) study.

Language. As discussed in the literature review, lack of proficiency in English is a major barrier for Indian seniors because it limits their interaction outside their local community. Further, ability to use native language adds quality to their lives, according to a focus group of AI seniors (Jonnalagadda et al., 2002). In the AAFNY study (Cross, 2003), only 18% of 100 Indian older adults stated that they spoke English "very well" while 28% chose "somewhat well," 26% "not too well," and 28% "not at all." Further, 59% of Indians reported that they had needed help with language translation in the past year (Mui & Cross, 2003a). Therefore, four questions related to language were included in the survey.

Identity. How Indians identify themselves, their sense of belonging, and whether they consider India or United States as their home may relate to their level of acculturation and mental health, as discussed in the literature review. Hence, the psychosocial questionnaire contains two questions that explore the participants' identity.

Financial condition. The financial condition of Indian senior immigrants has been linked to their experience of loss of autonomy in hypothesis 2d and 2e of this study. As a result, five questions explore the participants' health insurance status, and the source and adequacy of their finances in the U.S. and in India. Kalavar's (1998) study also explored the adequacy of finances through 3-point response categories of "less than adequate for your needs," "adequate for your needs," and "more than adequate for your needs." The question of financial dependence was researched in the AAFNY study, which reported that amongst different Asian ethnic groups studied, at 72%, Indians were the most likely group to receive financial assistance from children (Mui & Cross, 2003a).

Transportation. Transportation has been linked to the sense of autonomy of AI older adults in hypothesis 2b and 2c of this study; hence, three questions assess the adequacy of access to transportation for Indian seniors before and after immigration. Similar to the Kalavar (1998) study, the usual method of transportation is also assessed. Moreover, another question explores the participants' access to para-transit services such as Outreach because that adds to the autonomy of the person. In the AAFNY study, Indian participants had admitted that they required transportation help and that they receive help from their children (Mui & Cross, 2003a).

Access to Indian culture: Refueling. The necessity and desire to stay connected with Indian culture, including festivals, food, language, and rituals for immigrants in general, and for older adults in particular, has been discussed in Chapter 2. Therefore, three aspects of the participants' access to Indian culture are measured.

First, four questions were added to understand the role that Indian books, television, movies, and music play in the lives of seniors. Second, one question was added to survey the places the participants visit or the organizations they belong to. Third, three questions were added to survey the participants' connection with India, their country of origin, indicated by (a) the frequency of using telephone or e-media (e.g., e-mail and instant messaging) to communicate with people in India, and (b) whether the participants still have family members in India.

Kalavar (1998) examined the senior's connection with India in great details. In her interview schedule, she requested the frequency of communication with each child, grandchild, sibling, cousin, nephew and niece left behind in India.

Importance of religion. The literature suggests that religion plays a very important role in the lives of Asian American elders (e.g. Gill, 2008, Ryan et al., 2003). Religion improves resiliency and acts as an anchoring force in the face of adversity (e.g. Khanna et al., 2009).

As a result, the question, "How important is religion/spirituality to you," derived from the AAFNY study (Cross, 2003) was added. In the AAFNY study, 42% Indian elders had found religion very important, and 49% had considered it somewhat important while only 9% had stated that it is not important.

Physical health. Regular physical exercise has been associated with better physical and mental health in literature. Therefore, two questions were added to survey the frequency and type of exercise the participants undertake. As discussed in Chapter 2, yoga and *pranayams* are becoming increasingly popular amongst Indians, hence these were included in the response options.

Overall QoL and expectation. Four questions were added to assess the participants' perception of their current life quality. Two questions compared QoL before and after immigration, and another two contrasted the expected life quality with the current QoL.

Isolation versus social support. As per the available literature, lack of social support and a growing feeling of isolation are two of the most common complaints of elderly Asian seniors (e.g. Kalavar, 2003; Prasad, 2010; Rangaswamy, 2000). Three questions, therefore, were included to explore feelings of isolation and lack of social support. Both the AAFNY study (Ryan et al., 2003) and Kalavar (1998) explored this aspect in detail.

Open-ended questions. Two open-ended questions were added to the questionnaire to identify any issues that have not been raised in the chosen instruments but are significant to the participant. Emphasizing the need to include such an open-ended approach in research design, Bowling (2005) clarifies the disadvantage of not doing so, "When lay people have not been consulted in the development of a questionnaire then the items within it will reflect the values and assumptions held by 'experts,' and research results will not necessarily reflect the perspectives of respondents" (p. 38). The questions were designed to allow the participants to share what is important to them:

1. Tell me about one or two most important things that may improve your QoL?
2. Is there anything else that you would like to tell me about your quality of life that we have not discussed so far?

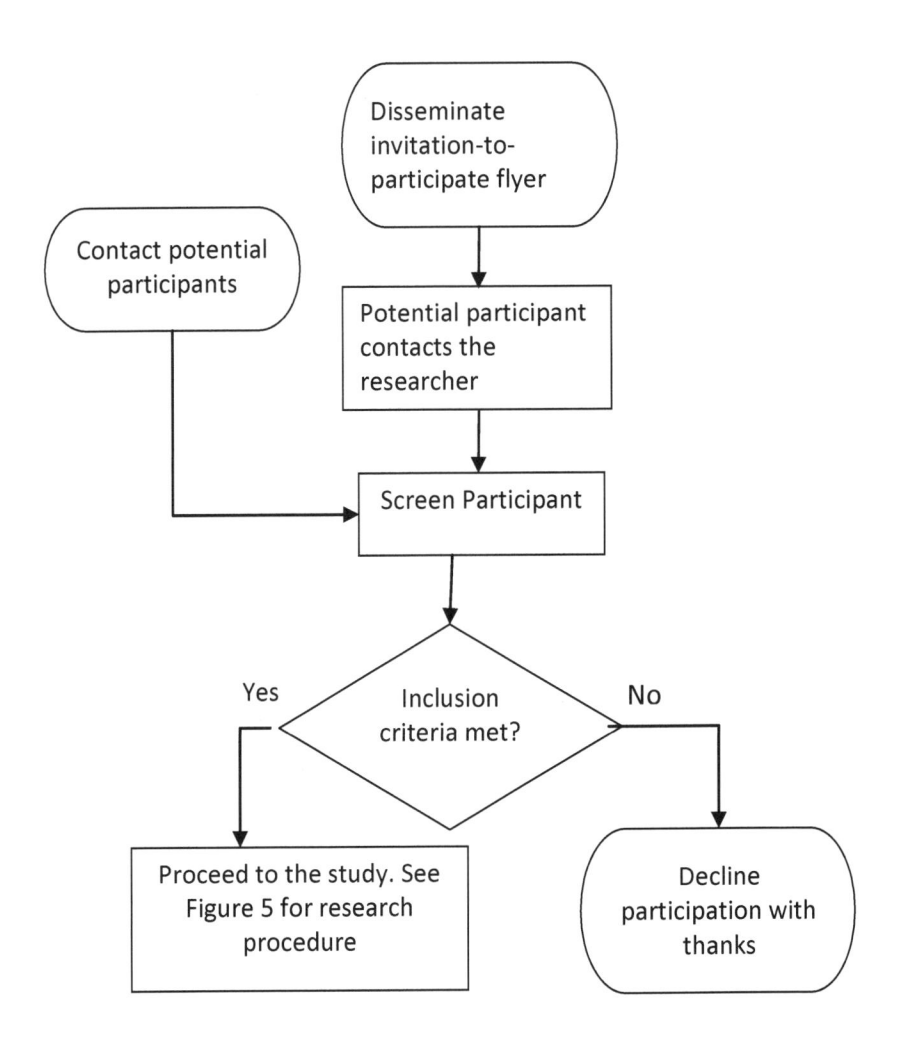

```
                    ┌─────────────────┐
                    │   Disseminate   │
                    │  invitation-to- │
                    │ participate flyer│
                    └────────┬────────┘
                             │
                             ▼
┌──────────────────┐  ┌─────────────────┐
│ Contact potential│  │Potential participant│
│   participants   │  │  contacts the   │
└────────┬─────────┘  │    researcher   │
         │            └────────┬────────┘
         │                     │
         └──────────►┌─────────▼────────┐
                    │ Screen Participant│
                    └────────┬─────────┘
                             │
                             ▼
              Yes       ╱ Inclusion ╲      No
         ┌────────────◄  criteria met? ►────────────┐
         │             ╲           ╱                │
         ▼                                          ▼
┌──────────────────┐                      ┌──────────────────┐
│Proceed to the study.│                   │     Decline      │
│See Figure 5 for  │                      │ participation with│
│research procedure│                      │      thanks      │
└──────────────────┘                      └──────────────────┘
```

Figure 4. Flowchart of Research Procedure: Identifying Participants.

Maximum flexibility in data collection can be achieved through this two-step approach, and a comprehensive understanding of QoL of the participants can be obtained. The closed-ended questions allowed easier analysis of the core variables that have already been identified, whereas the open-ended questions allowed newer themes to emerge. However, to reduce researcher bias, only those participants who can write their answers in English were asked to respond to these open-ended questions.

Procedures

In this section, the process for identifying and recruiting the participants, and the approach used to gather, secure, and analyze the data will be described. A short, introductory letter was used to introduce this study and to invite potential participants. This "invitation to participate" letter was circulated through various AI email-groups, flyers posted in community centers, and at AI cultural events in SF Bay Area.

The letter included the participation criteria, and the method by which potential participants may contact the researcher to participate in this study. Interested potential participants were screened, and those who met the inclusion criteria were selected. Those who did not qualify were declined participation with thanks. This process is shown through a flowchart in Figure 4.

The Study Setting

The researcher met the participants and administered the surveys in locations convenient to them such as (a) as a group in a community center or at a cultural event, or (b) individually at a mutually convenient location. For qualified participants, the study process is described in Figure 5.

Individuals who met the inclusion criteria were provided with the informed consent forms, and its key elements were reviewed with them in a language in which they were comfortable. After getting a verbal assurance from them that they have understood the key elements, they were asked to sign the consent forms. Those who did not give consent were excluded from the study.

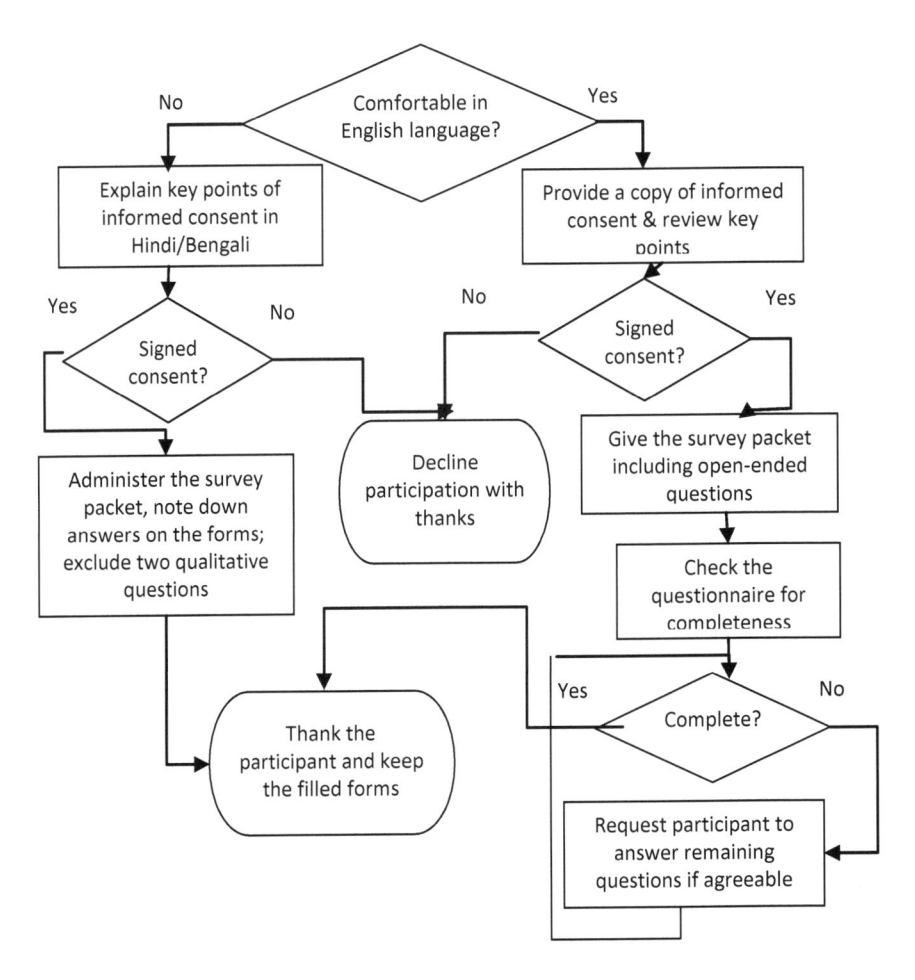

Figure 5. Flowchart of Study Procedure for Identified Participants. To check their comfort level with English, the participants were asked, "Do you feel comfortable enough in the English language to complete the questionnaire on your own or will you prefer that I walk you through the survey with explanations in Hindi/Bengali?"

Individuals who chose to fill the self-report surveys were also requested to write in their answers to the open-ended, qualitative questions. Some qualified participants needed assistance in filling out the English surveys of this study either due to the language barrier or because of poor eyesight. For these participants, the researcher administered the survey in the interview format recording their answers on a paper copy of the survey.

To overcome the language barrier, Hindi or Bengali was used as needed. No audio tapes were used, as that might have deterred AI older adults from participating in the study. In the interviewer-assisted format, the two qualitative questions were not asked to reduce the researcher bias, and to remove the need for audio taping.

The expected number of participants for this study was 50-100. A husband and a wife were allowed to participate separately in the study. The survey packet consisted of all the instruments discussed in the previous section. The sequence in which the instruments were filled out was (a) Psychosocial questionnaire, (b) WHOQOL-BREF, (c) mastery scale, (d) PHQ-9, and (e) GAD-7.

Data Analysis

SPSS version 19.0 (Statistical Package for the Social Sciences from IBM) software was used to analyze the data of this study. Several scores including (a) QoL scores consisting of an overall QoL score, overall health-satisfaction score, and four domain scores on physical, psychological, social and environmental domains; (b) Mastery score; (c) Depression-score on PHQ-9, and (d) Anxiety-score on GAD-7 were calculated and used in further analyses.

To understand different dimensions of the QoL of AI seniors, descriptive statistics were used in addition to chi-square analysis and Analysis of Variance (ANOVA). Graphs were used to illustrate the difference between groups pictorially such as the transportation and economic condition before and after migration from India. The open-ended questions in the psychosocial questionnaire were analyzed to identify new themes that may not have been considered by the various questionnaires used for this research. The results of the study will be presented in the next chapter.

Methodological Limitations

Because the study relied on structured interviews or survey responses, problems such as social desirability and agreeability to the interviewer (e.g. Campbell et al. 1976) common to all survey designs existed in this study. Further, the expected sample size of 50-100 did not provide sufficient power for a regression analysis. Moreover, most of the independent variables are nominal or ordinal, and they do not have normal distribution. Hence, the study relied on descriptive analyses in many cases.

CHAPTER FOUR: RESULTS

In this chapter, the results will be presented and each of the research questions and hypotheses will be examined. This study was conducted between July and October 2011 at different locations in the SF Bay Area. It received support from the AI senior community as the author visited various senior centers, cultural events, temples, and parks where seniors usually meet. Convenience sampling was used, and 109 seniors (63 men and 46 women) voluntarily participated in the study. Out of these 109 participants, 38 individuals filled out the questionnaire themselves while 71 chose the interview format. The interviews were conducted by the author in Hindi, English, and Bengali, depending on the preference of the participants.

Participant Characteristics

Approximately equal number of citizens ($n = 53$) and permanent residents ($n = 56$) participated in this study, as depicted in Table 2. More widowed women (43.5%) responded compared to widowed men (28.6%). Many participants were highly educated: 33% had post-graduate education while another 33% held a bachelor's degree.

Most participants ($n = 96$) were living with their children. Hinduism (80.7%) was the most dominant religion followed by Sikhism (12.8%), Jainism (4.6%), and Christianity (1.8%). The age of participants ranged between 61 and 92, with a mean of 74 and standard deviation of 7 (Table 3). Further, they had spent anywhere from 1 to 38 years in the United States with an average of 12.7 years.

Table 2

Demographic Profile of Participants

		Gender			
		Male	Female	Total (N = 109)	
		%	%	n	%
Immigration Status	U.S. citizen	49.2%	47.8%	53	48.6%
	Permanent resident	50.8%	52.2%	56	51.4%
Marital Status	Married	71.4%	56.5%	71	65.1%
	Widowed	28.6%	43.5%	38	34.9%
Education	Less than high school	7.9%	19.6%	14	12.8%
	High school	9.5%	17.4%	14	12.8%
	Some college	9.5%	6.5%	9	8.3%
	BS degree other than engineer or doctor	20.6%	28.3%	26	23.9%
	Engineer or doctor	15.9%	.0%	10	9.2%
	Post-graduate education	36.5%	28.3%	36	33.0%
Living Place	Child's home	87.3%	89.1%	96	88.1%
	Alone or with spouse in single Family home/rented unit	6.3%	4.3%	6	5.5%
	Relative's home	3.2%	.0%	2	1.8%
	Senior housing	3.2%	6.5%	5	4.6%
Religion	Hindu	77.8%	84.8%	88	80.7%
	Sikh	15.9%	8.7%	14	12.8%
	Jain	6.3%	2.2%	5	4.6%
	Christian	.0%	4.3%	2	1.8%

In terms of native language, which also denotes the originating state in India, the participants were very diverse (Table 4). However, the number of participants from various states differed widely. Almost one in four (23.9%) were Punjabis (natives of the state of Punjab); Gujaratis (natives of the state of

Gujarat) were a close second with 20.2%. The third highest numbers were Telugu-speaking individuals from the state of Andhra Pradesh, as those who chose Hindi as native language could have originated from several different states.

Table 3

Age, Number of Years in USA, QoL, Mastery, Depression, and GAD Scores

	n (N = 109)	Range Potential	Range Actual	M	SD
Age at the time of interview	109	≥60	61-92	74.39	7.221
Number of years in USA	107	≥1	1-38	12.72	8.710
WHOQOL: Overall QoL	109	1-5	1-5	3.68	.891
WHOQOL: Health Satisfaction	109	1-5	1-5	3.63	1.077
WHOQOL Domain 1: Physical Health	109	0-100	6-100	67.61	19.606
WHOQOL Domain2: Psychological Health	109	0-100	19-100	68.59	16.712
WHOQOL Domain3: Social Relationships	109	0-100	31-100	72.18	15.484
WHOQOL Domain4: Environmental	109	0-100	50-100	74.74	12.558
Mastery Score	109	7-28	7-28	17.83	5.891
PHQ9 Score	108	0-27	0-21	4.64	5.085
GAD7 Score	108	0-21	0-17	2.33	3.401

Research Question 1 (RQ1): QoL of AI Senior Immigrants

The first research question is: "What is the QoL of elderly AI immigrants who came to the United States to be with their adult children? Which psychosocial factors influence the QoL of such seniors living in the Silicon Valley?" This is the overarching or main question for this research. All other questions examine specific components of QoL, or factors that influence QoL, and as such can be considered as subquestions.

Table 4

Language Profile, Entertainment Preferences

		n	%
Native Language	Punjabi	26	23.9%
	Gujarati	22	20.2%
	Hindi	16	14.7%
	Telugu	10	9.2%
	Tamil	9	8.3%
	Marathi	9	8.3%
	Bengali	7	6.4%
	Marwari	4	3.7%
	Sindhi	2	1.8%
	Kashmiri	2	1.8%
	Konkani	1	.9%
	Kannada	1	.9%
Like reading Indian books, newspapers, etc.	Yes	100	92.6%
	No	8	7.4%
Like watching Indian movies and videos	Yes	96	89.7%
	No	11	10.3%
Indian TV is important	Strongly Disagree	2	1.9%
	Disagree	11	10.2%
	Neither Agree nor Disagree	9	8.3%
	Agree	35	32.4%
	Strongly Agree	51	47.2%
Number of Indian TV channels at home	Zero	24	22.2%
	One 1-2 Channels	23	21.3%
	Three 3-5 Channels	31	28.7%
	More than 5 Channels	30	27.8%

A number of sociodemographic variables were examined to answer RQ1 in addition to quantitatively looking at their life quality through established instruments. Table 3 presents the descriptive statistics for WHOQOL-BREF, mastery, PHQ-9 and GAD7 scores. For WHOQOL, the overall health satisfaction and QoL scores as well as the domain scores for physical health, psychological health, social relationships and environmental health are shown. Internal reliability for the published scales was examined, and the Cronbach's alpha was found to be 0.91 for WHOQOL-BREF, 0.87 for mastery scale, 0.82 for PHQ-9, and 0.84 for GAD7.

Table 5
Self-identification, Connection with India

		U.S. Citizen %	Permanent Resident %	Total n	Total %
Self-identification	Indian	77.4%	92.9%	93	85.3%
	Indo-American	11.3%	.0%	6	5.5%
	American	5.7%	.0%	3	2.8%
	Multiple identities chosen	5.7%	7.1%	7	6.4%
In your view, where is your home?	India	73.6%	91.1%	90	82.6%
	United States	20.8%	3.6%	13	11.9%
	India and United States	5.7%	5.4%	6	5.5%
How often do you go to India?	At least once a year	35.8%	57.1%	51	46.8%
	Once in 2 years	30.2%	19.6%	27	24.8%
	Once in 3-4 years	17.0%	19.6%	20	18.3%
	Less than once in 4 years	17.0%	3.6%	11	10.1%
How often do you have virtual communication with India?	Daily	28.3%	23.2%	28	25.7%
	Weekly	37.7%	50.0%	48	44.0%
	Once or twice a month	26.4%	19.6%	25	22.9%
	Less than once a month	7.5%	7.1%	8	7.3%
Family living in India	Yes	79.2%	81.8%	87	80.6%
	No	20.8%	18.2%	21	19.4%

Despite relocating to this country, participants have a strong identification with India. As shown in Table 5, 85.3% of the participants self-identified as Indians while 2.8% considered themselves Americans. Another 5.5% of the participants thought of themselves as Indo-Americans, while 6.4% selected multiple categories for self-identification.

Similarly, most participants (82.6%) considered India as their home country. Almost half (46.8%) visit India every year while another 24.8% visit once in 2 years. Most participants (80.6%) have families in India and stay connected through telephone, email or social media. A quarter of them communicate virtually on a daily basis while another 44% connect every week.

In addition to native language of participants, Table 4 depicts the entertainment preferences of the participants. Most participants stated that they liked reading Indian literature (92.6%) and watching Indian movies or videos (89.7%). Four out of five participants either strongly agreed or agreed that having Indian television at home is important to them ($M = 4.13$, $SD = 1.060$). Accordingly, 77.8% of the participants' homes have at least one Indian television channel, and more than 50% have three or more channels.

Further, when asked about the importance of religion or spirituality through the question, "Religion/spirituality is very important to me" (1 = Strongly disagree, 2 = Disagree, 3 = Neither agree nor disagree, 4 = Agree, 5 = Strongly agree), the participants responded with $M = 4.33$, and $SD = 1.037$, indicating religion and spirituality plays an important role in most AI seniors' lives.

In terms of the health insurance (Table 6), almost half (47.7%) of the participants have MediCare whereas 70.6% have Medi-Cal. Eleven persons (10.1%) reported having no health insurance, out of which 6.4% stated that they were eligible. Table 6 also depicts the frequency and type of exercise practiced by seniors. Almost 80% of the participants reported that they exercise in some form on a daily basis. Walking was the most common exercise with 92.5%, while more than 40% of the participants practice yoga and *pranayams*.

Table 6
Health Insurance, Exercise, Expected versus Actual QoL

		n	%
Health Insurance	Medicare	52	47.7%
	Medi-Cal	77	70.6%
	Yes-other	19	17.4%
	No health insurance but eligible	7	6.4%
	No health insurance	4	3.7%
Frequency of Exercise	6-7 Times a week	86	78.9%
	3-5 Times a week	14	12.8%
	1-2 Times a week	4	3.7%
	No	5	4.6%
Type of Exercise	Yoga	46	43.4%
	Pranayam	48	45.3%
	Walk	98	92.5%
	Exercise other	33	31.1%
Current life versus expected	Current life is much worse	18	16.5%
	Slightly worse	19	17.4%
	Same	52	47.7%
	Slightly better	9	8.3%
	Current life is much better	11	10.1%

Additionally, participants' expectation of their QoL was compared to their current lives through the following questions:

1. Before you immigrated, what was your expectation regarding what your quality of life in United States would be like? (1 = Very poor, 2 = Poor, 3 = Neither poor nor good, 4 = Good, 5 = Very good)
2. What is your current quality of life in United States? (1 = Very poor, 2 = Poor, 3 = Neither poor nor good, 4 = Good, 5 = Very good)

3. How does your current life compare to how you expect your life to be? (1 = Current life is much worse, 2 = Slightly worse, 3 = Same, 4 = Slightly better, 5 = Current life is much better)

Table 7
QoL: Expected versus Actual (N = 109)

	Very Poor	Poor	Neither Poor Nor Good	Good	Very Good
QoL expected in U.S. before immigration	1	1	34	52	21
QoL current	1	6	34	45	23

Based on the first two questions (Table 7), there was similarity between expectation ($M = 3.83$, $SD = 0.776$) and reality ($M = 3.76$, $SD = 0.881$). Chi-square analysis ($\chi^2 (16) = 38.104$, $p = .001$), however, confirmed that there was statistically significant difference between expected and current QoL.

Further, when asked to make a direct comparison (Question 3), 33.9% of the participants rated it as much worse or slightly worse compared to 18.4% who rated it as slightly or much better (Table 6). The mean was 2.78 whereas the standard deviation was 1.133. Qualitative themes to answers RQ1 will be presented in a later section.

Research Question2 (RQ2): Loss of Autonomy or Independence

The second question states: "How has the immigration influenced the self-reported autonomy or independence for the participants? Specifically, how has the immigration experience impacted their physical and social mobility, including access to transportation, finances, and social interaction?" This question has an associated hypothesis and several subhypotheses, each of which will be examined in this section.

Hypothesis 2 states that those AI seniors, who immigrate in late life to be with their adult children, will experience a loss of autonomy or independence. Loss of independence was operationalized using four variables (a) self-efficacy or mastery, (b) access to transportation, (c) financial dependence, and (d) language barrier. Corresponding to each variable, there is a hypothesis. The subsections below will examine each of the hypotheses.

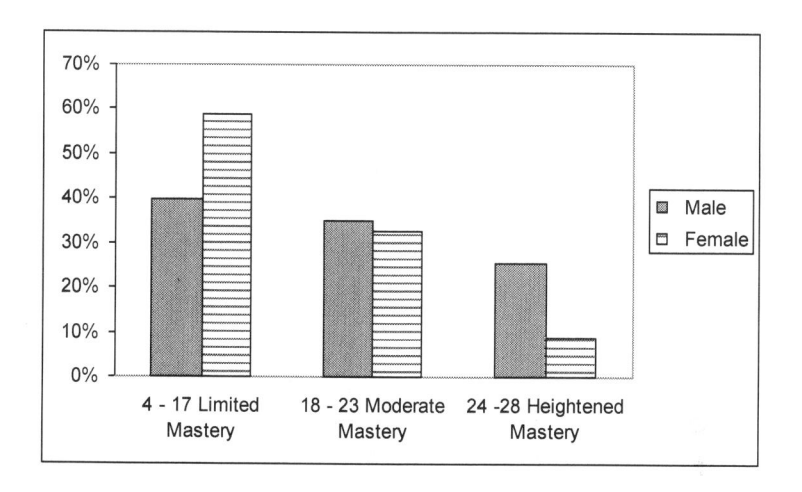

Figure 6. Self-reported Mastery scores by Gender

Hypothesis 2a: Self-efficacy or mastery. This study hypothesizes that the self-efficacy or mastery of the senior immigrants being studied will be low. Using the mastery scale (Pearlin & Schooler, 1978), it was indeed found that 47.7% seniors (39.7% men and 58.7% women) showed limited mastery (scores 4-17) while another 33.9% (34.9% men and 32.6% women) had moderate mastery (scores 18-23), and only 18.3% (25.4% men and 8.7% women) had heightened mastery (scores 24-28). Figure 6 depicts this graphically and also shows that men reported higher mastery compared to women. The mean score was 17.83 and the standard deviation was 5.89 (Table 3).

Table 8

Transportation in USA: Access and Satisfaction

		n	%
USA: Satisfaction with Transportation	Very dissatisfied	21	19.3%
	Dissatisfied	24	22.0%
	Neither satisfied nor dissatisfied	20	18.3%
	Satisfied	35	32.1%
	Very satisfied	9	8.3%
USA: "I have Access to Transportation"	Strongly disagree	48	44.4%
	Disagree	21	19.4%
	Neither agree nor disagree	3	2.8%
	Agree	29	26.9%
	Strongly agree	7	6.5%
Access to para-transit transportation	No	81	74.3%
	Yes-Outreach	23	21.1%
	Yes-Other	5	4.6%

Hypothesis 2b: Access to transportation. Hypothesis 2b states that Indian seniors will not be satisfied with their current access to transportation. Access to transportation was assessed using one question from WHOQOL-BREF and two questions of the psychosocial questionnaire designed for this study:

1. WHOQOL-BREF: 25(F23.3) How satisfied are you with your transport? (1 = Very dissatisfied, 2 = Dissatisfied, 3 = Neither satisfied nor dissatisfied, 4 = Satisfied, 5 = Very Satisfied)
2. I have access to transport that allows me to go wherever I want to go. (1 = Strongly disagree, 2 = Disagree, 3 = Neither agree nor disagree, 4 = Agree, 5 = Strongly agree)

3. Do you have access to transportation services like Outreach? (1 = No, 2 = Yes-Outreach, 2 = Yes-other)

Table 9
Most Common Mode of Transportation

		n	%
Most Common Mode of Transportation	Ride with family	45	41.7%
	Public transport	22	20.4%
	Self-drive	12	11.1%
	Outreach or similar para-transit service	11	10.2%
	Walk	3	2.8%
	Ride with others	2	1.9%
	Multiple methods	13	12%

Participants' responses are tabulated in Table 8, which shows that 19.3% were very dissatisfied, compared to 8.3%, who were very satisfied with transportation. However, when combined with dissatisfied and satisfied responses, almost equal numbers (41.3% versus 40.4%) were dissatisfied or satisfied.

When asked whether they had access to transportation that allowed them to go wherever they want to go, 44.4% of the participants strongly disagreed, compared to only 6.5% who strongly agreed. Further, three out of four participants did not have access to para-transit services.

In order to gain an understanding of how AI seniors usually commute, Table 9 tabulates the response to the question: "What is your most common mode of transportation?" As the table indicates, 41.7% of the participants depend mainly on their families while 20.4% take public transportation. Those who chose multiple modes of transports usually included ride with family as one option.

Hypothesis 2d: Financial condition. Hypothesis 2d proposes that AI senior immigrants will be financially dependent on their children or the government. This was assessed using the following question: "How do you meet your financial needs? Choose all that applies (1 = My and my spouse's personal income, 2 = Social Security, 3 = SSI or other assistance from state/federal government, 4 = Assistance from children, 5 = Other:_____)."

Table 10
Source of Finance

		n	%
Financially Independent	My and my spouse's personal income	7	6.4%
	Social Security	3	2.8%
	Personal income and Social Security	2	1.8%
	Total independent	12	11.0%
Financially Dependent	SSI or other assistance from state or federal government	12	11.0%
	Assistance from children	44	40.4%
	Multiple: Includes assistance from either government or children or both	41	37.5%
	Total dependent	97	88.9%

As social security is based on previous earnings, it was considered as personal income. Responses 1 and 2, therefore, indicated financial independence, whereas options 3, 4, and 5 signified financial dependence on children or the government. As shown in Table 10, 11% of the participants were financially independent, and the rest depended on either their children or the government or both, thereby supporting the hypothesis.

Table 11

Language Barrier and Proficiency

		n	%
Lack of English prevents access to services	Strongly disagree	24	22.0%
	Disagree	20	18.3%
	Neither agree nor disagree	10	9.2%
	Agree	30	27.5%
	Strongly agree	25	22.9%
I communicate very well in English	Strongly disagree	22	20.2%
	Disagree	12	11.0%
	Neither agree nor disagree	11	10.1%
	Agree	33	30.3%
	Strongly agree	31	28.4%
Language in which most comfortable	Native language	36	33.0%
	English	13	11.9%
	Other than native language or English	3	2.8%
	Multilingual including English	36	33.0%
	Multilingual but does not include English	21	19.3%

Hypothesis 2f: Dependency due to language barrier. For people who immigrate in middle to old age, language is a major barrier, as it limits their interactions with the general population. Hypothesis 2f states that AI older adults will experience a language barrier that would result in dependence for interaction or communication.

To test this hypothesis, the following question was used, "My ability to communicate in English prevents me from doing things or accessing services that I want (1 = Strongly disagree, 2 = Disagree, 3 = Neither agree nor disagree, 4 = Agree, 5 = Strongly agree)."

Scores of 4 or 5 indicate that the participant definitely perceives a language barrier. In addition, the language proficiency in English was ascertained using:

1. I communicate very well in English. (1 = Strongly disagree, 2 = Disagree, 3 = Neither agree nor disagree, 4 = Agree, 5 = Strongly agree)
2. Which language do you feel most comfortable communicating in? (native language, English, other: please specify: _____)

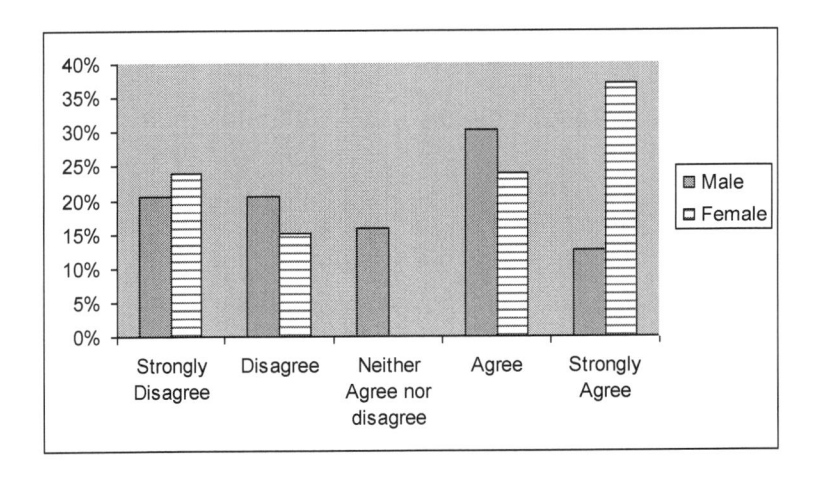

Figure 7. Response to: Lack of English prevents access to services

As shown in Table 11, half the participants (50.4%) either strongly agreed or agreed that their lack of proficiency in English prevents them from accessing services (M = 3.11, SD = 1.505) thereby supporting the hypothesis. However, when directly asked if they communicate very well in English (M = 3.36, SD = 1.500), 58.7% of the participants agreed or strongly agreed.

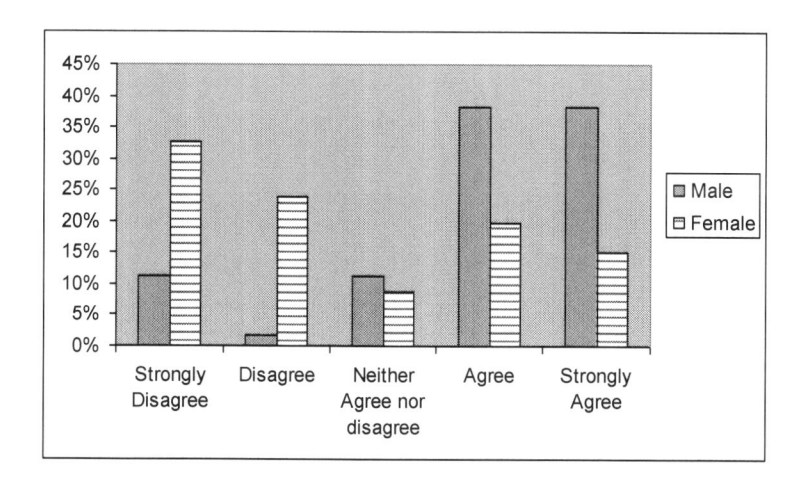

Figure 8. Response to: "I Communicate very well in English"

Figures 7 and 8 depict this graphically, and also highlight that women perceived a higher language barrier than men. While responding to the question of the language in which they are most comfortable communicating, many participants chose more than one language. However, in 55.1% cases, English was not among the languages chosen.

Hypothesis 2c and 2e: Comparison with situation in India. Because the study population has migrated to the U.S. at a mature age, they are likely to internally compare their current situation with the situation they left behind in their country of origin. Therefore, two hypotheses compare their lives in the U.S. and India.

To test hypothesis 2c, "AI older adults will have less access to transportation compared to when they were in India," the following three questions from the psychosocial questionnaire were used:

1. I have access to transport that allows me to go wherever I want to go. (1 = Strongly disagree, 2 = Disagree, 3 = Neither agree nor disagree, 4 = Agree, 5 = Strongly agree)

Table 12

Access to Transportation: U.S. versus India

	Strongly Disagree	Disagree	Neither Agree Nor Disagree	Agree	Strongly Agree
USA: Access to Transportation	44.4%	19.4%	2.8%	26.9%	6.5%
India: Access to Transportation Before Immigration	.9%	1.9%	.9%	20.4%	75.9%
India: Access to Transportation Now	.9%	6.5%	1.9%	21.3%	69.4%

2. Before I immigrated, I had access to transport that allowed me to go wherever I wanted to go. (1 = Strongly disagree, 2 = Disagree, 3 = Neither agree nor disagree, 4 = Agree, 5 = Strongly agree)
3. If I were currently living in India, I would have access to transport that would allow me to go wherever I want to go. (1 = Strongly disagree, 2 = Disagree, 3 = Neither agree nor disagree, 4 = Agree, 5 = Strongly agree)

Tabulated in Table 12, the results show that only 6.5% of the participants strongly agreed that they have access to transportation in the U.S. ($M = 2.31$, $SD = 1.432$) whereas the corresponding numbers for India were 75.9% before immigration ($M = 4.69$, $SD = 0.679$) and 69.4% now ($M = 4.52$, $SD = 0.891$).

Figure 9 graphically depicts the results. Chi-square analysis confirmed that the access to transportation in the U.S. is statistically significantly lower than what the participants had in India before migration: $\chi^2 (16) = 63.53$, $p < 0.001$.

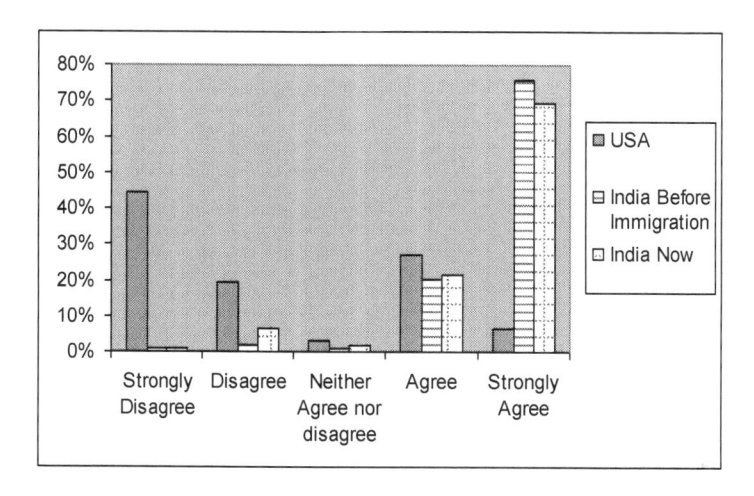

Asian Indian Older Adults in Silicon Valley 149

[Bar chart showing percentages for USA, India Before Immigration, and India Now across categories: Strongly Disagree, Disagree, Neither Agree nor disagree, Agree, Strongly Agree]

Figure 9 Access to Transportation: U.S. versus India. Response to: I have access to transport that allows me to go wherever I want to go

Further, if the participants were living in India now, their access to transportation would have been statistically significantly higher compared to what they have in the U.S. (χ^2 (16) = 35.207, p = .004).

Table 13
Finance: U.S. versus India

	Strongly Disagree	Disagree	Neither Agree Nor Disagree	Agree	Strongly Agree
US finance allows what I want to do	21.1%	21.1%	9.2%	37.6%	11.0%
India finance before allowed	.0%	7.3%	10.1%	27.5%	55.0%
India finance now will allow	.9%	15.6%	11.0%	28.4%	44.0%

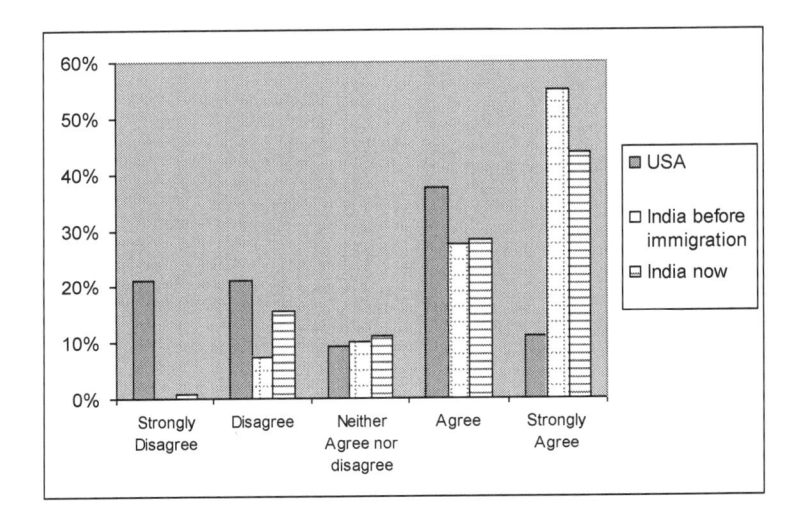

Figure 10. Finance U.S. versus India. Response to: My financial condition allows me to do the things that I want to do

To examine hypothesis 2e: "AI older adults will be more financially dependent compared to when they were in India," the following questions were used:

1. My financial condition allows me to do the things that I want to do (1 = Strongly disagree, 2 = Disagree, 3 = Neither agree nor disagree, 4 = Agree, 5 = Strongly agree)
2. Before I immigrated, my financial condition allowed me to do the things that I wanted to do (1 = strongly disagree, 2 = disagree, 3 = neither agree nor disagree, 4 = agree, 5 = strongly agree)
3. If I were currently living in India, my financial condition would have allowed me to do the things that I want to do (1 = Strongly disagree, 2 = Disagree, 3 = Neither agree nor disagree, 4 = Agree, 5 = Strongly agree)

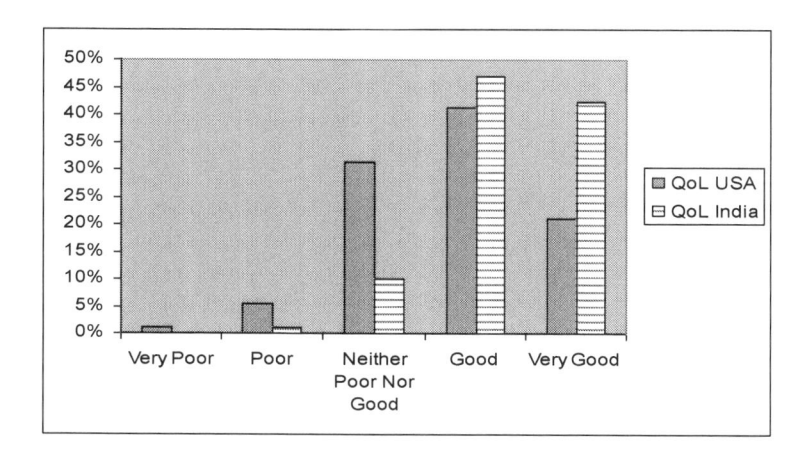

Figure 11. QoL: U.S. versus India

As shown in Table 13 and Figure 10, participants admitted having better financial condition in India before migration (M = 4.30, SD = 0.928) as well as now (M = 3.99, SD = 1.126) compared to that in the U.S. (M = 2.96, SD = 1.374). Chi-square analysis showed that the current financial condition in the U.S. is significantly worse than the condition in India before relocation (χ^2 (12) = 22.526, p = .032). Further, the comparison between their finances in the U.S. with their finances in India now yielded in χ^2 (16) = 32.442, p = .009, indicating that if the participants were living in India now, their economic condition would have been significant better than that in the U.S.

Table 14
QoL: U.S. versus India

	Very Poor	Poor	Neither Poor Nor Good	Good	Very Good
QoL USA current	.9%	5.5%	31.2%	41.3%	21.1%
QoL India	.0%	.9%	10.1%	46.8%	42.2%

Participants were also asked to rate their QoL in the U.S. and India on a 5-point Likert-type scale. The responses tabulated in Table 14 and graphed in Figure 11 show that the QoL in India ($M = 4.30$, $SD = 0.687$) was rated higher than that in the U.S. ($M = 3.76$, $SD = 0.881$). However, these differences were not statistically significant based on chi-square analysis: χ^2 (12) = 11.322, $p = .502$.

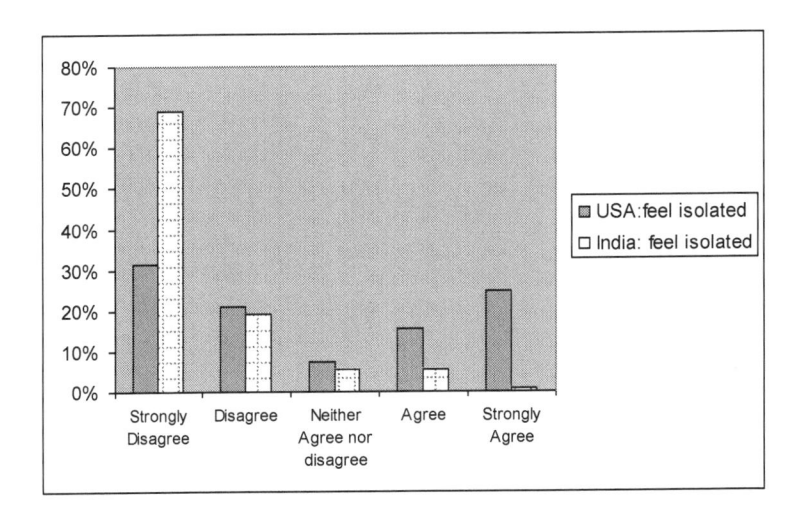

Figure 12. Feeling Isolated, Lonely, or Left out of Things: U.S. versus India

To understand how the participants' feelings of isolation have changed, two questions, "I feel isolated, lonely, or left out of things," and "Before immigrating, I felt isolated, lonely, or left out of things" were used with a 5-point Likert-type scale from "1 = Strongly disagree" to "5 = Strongly agree."

Participants reported feeling more isolated in the U.S. ($M = 2.82$, $SD = 1.611$) compared to India ($M = 1.50$, $SD = 0.899$). Shown in Table 15 and Figure 12, 31.2% of the participants strongly disagreed that they are isolated in the U.S. compared to 68.8% for India. Based on chi-square analysis, there was a statistically significant difference in the degree of isolation in the U.S. and India (χ^2 (16) = 68.341, $p < 0.001$).

Table 15
Social Support and Isolation: U.S. versus India

	Strongly Disagree	Disagree	Neither Agree Nor Disagree	Agree	Strongly Agree
USA: feel isolated	31.2%	21.1%	7.3%	15.6%	24.8%
India: feel isolated	68.8%	19.3%	5.5%	5.5%	.9%
Social support in USA is better than India	51.4%	17.4%	16.5%	12.8%	1.8%

When asked whether their social support in the U.S. is better than that in India ($M = 1.96$, $SD = 1.170$), 51.4% of the participants strongly disagreed compared to 1.8% who strongly agreed (see Table 15 and Figure 13).

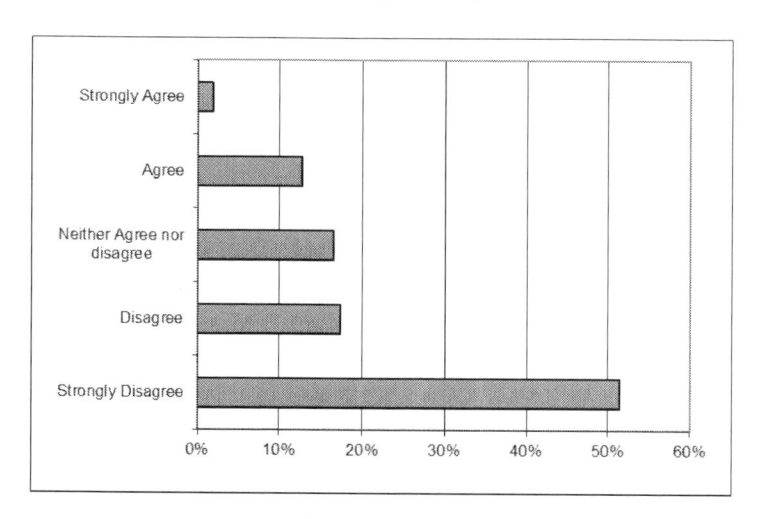

Figure 13. Social Support in the U.S. is Better than in India

Research Question 3 (RQ3): Political and Legal Context

The third research question was, "How does political and legal context of the United States influence the QoL of the participants? Specifically, does citizenship status impact their life quality?"

Hypothesis 3 proposed that AI seniors who are U.S. citizens will have a higher QoL compared to those who are not. To test this, ANOVA comparisons were made for various dimensions of QoL between citizens and noncitizens. The following conditions for conducting ANOVAs were examined: independent groups, homogeneity of variance, and interval scales for dependent variables. Because there are only two groups, no post-hoc comparison between groups was needed. As shown in Table 16, the citizenship status of the participants had a statistically significant effect on several different QoL dimensions:

1. Citizens have a statistically significantly higher QoL domain score for psychological health (M = 71.36, SD = 14.879) compared to permanent residents (M = 65.96, SD = 18.019). The results of the ANOVA analysis are $F(1, 107)$ = 2.886, p = .092.
2. For the environmental domain of QoL, the mean score of green-card holders was 71.55 (SD = 12.874), whereas the mean score for US citizens was higher at 78.11 (SD = 11.388). The difference was statistically significant based on ANOVA analysis: $F(1, 107)$ = 7.905, p = .006.
3. Whether their financial condition in the U.S. allows them to do what they want to do is statistically significantly ($F(1, 107)$ = 14.767, $p < 0.001$) higher for citizens (M = 3.45, SD = 1.324) compared to permanent residents (M = 2.50, SD = 1.265).
4. The feeling of isolation in the U.S. for citizens (M = 2.40, SD = 1.536) is statistically significantly ($F(1, 107)$ = 7.439, p = .007) lower compared to the isolation level of permanent residents (M = 3.21, SD = 1.592).

Table 16

ANOVA Analysis of QoL Dimensions by Citizenship Status

		Sum of Squares	df	Mean Square	F	Sig.
QoL Domain2: Psychological Health	Between Groups	792.305	1	792.305	2.886	.092
	Within Groups	29370.117	107	274.487		
	Total	30162.422	108			
QoL Domain4: Environmental	Between Groups	1171.647	1	1171.647	7.905	.006
	Within Groups	15859.160	107	148.216		
	Total	17030.807	108			
US Finance allows what I want to do	Between Groups	24.721	1	24.721	14.767	.000
	Within Groups	179.132	107	1.674		
	Total	203.853	108			
USA: feel isolated	Between Groups	18.222	1	18.222	7.439	.007
	Within Groups	262.108	107	2.450		
	Total	280.330	108			
How often goes to India	Between Groups	5.625	1	5.625	5.541	.020
	Within Groups	108.632	107	1.015		
	Total	114.257	108			
I communicate very well in English	Between Groups	6.242	1	6.242	2.820	.096
	Within Groups	236.804	107	2.213		
	Total	243.046	108			

5. The frequency of visits to India is statistically significantly ($F(1, 107) = 5.541$, $p = .020$) higher for green card holders compared to the citizens.

6. The self-reported English proficiency of citizens is statistically significantly ($F(1, 107) = 2.820$, $p = .096$) higher ($M = 3.60$, $SD = 1.485$) compared to that of permanent residents ($M = 3.13$, $SD = 1.490$).

Based on ANOVAs, there was no statistically significant difference between the depression ($p = .224$) and anxiety ($p = .329$) scores of citizens and permanent residents.

Research Question 4 (RQ4): Depression and Anxiety

Focusing on common mental health issues, the last research question is, "What is the prevalence of depression and generalized anxiety disorder in this population?" The PHQ-9 and GAD-7 were used to assess the participants for depressive and anxiety symptoms. Hypothesis 4 states that the prevalence of depressive symptoms and generalized anxiety disorder will be higher in participants compared to the general U.S. population.

Table 17
Depression and Anxiety Profiles

		n	%
PHQ9 Score	0 - 4 (None-Minimal)	69	63.9%
	5 - 9 (Mild)	23	21.3%
	10 - 14 (Moderate)	10	9.3%
	15 - 19 (Moderately Severe)	4	3.7%
	20+ (Severe)	2	1.9%
GAD7 Score	0 - 4 (None)	88	81.5%
	5 - 9 (Mild)	13	12.0%
	10 - 14 (Moderate)	6	5.6%
	15+ (Severe)	1	.9%

The PHQ9 score of the participants ranged between 0 and 21 with a mean of 4.64 and standard deviation of 5.085 (Table 3). Further, 14.9% of the participants had PHQ9 score of 10 or higher indicating at least moderate depression; 5.6% had scores of 15 or more indicating moderately severe depression; and 1.9% had scores of 20 or more indicating severe depression (Table 17).

Based on the U.S. national survey on drug use and health conducted in 2005, 2006, and 2007, 1.5% of men and 3.1% of women aged 65 or older reported a past year major depressive episode (Substance Abuse and Mental Health Services Administration; SAMHSA; 2010). The numbers reported by the participants in this study are comparable to those reported by SAMHSA but not higher, hence the study hypothesis is not supported.

As shown in Table 3, GAD7 scores of the participants had a mean of 2.33 and standard deviation of 3.40. Further, as Table 17 depicts, 6.5% participants reported at least moderate anxiety levels while 0.9% demonstrated severe anxiety. For norms, the *Diagnostic and Statistical Manual of Mental Disorders* (DSM-IV) reported that the one-year prevalence rate is approximately 3% for GAD (American Psychiatric Association, 2000). Löwe et al. (2008) on the other hand reported that approximately 5% participants had a score of 10 or more and 1% had scores of 15 or higher. These numbers are comparable but not higher as hypothesized.

Qualitative Analysis

To understand the activities that seniors usually engage in and the organizations of which they are members, the participants were asked to specify the places they visit, the frequency of visit and the purpose. Socializing (36.5%), praying (21.1%), shopping or accompanying others on shopping trips (14.8%), and walking (11.8%) are the most frequent activities for which AI seniors go out of their homes. Family outings, visiting libraries, medical appointments, jobs, and pursuing hobbies and personal interests are some of the other reasons. Most activities are carried out weekly (32.9%) or one to two times a month

(29.8%), while some are practiced daily (15%). Temples or Gurudwaras, senior centers, family or friends' homes, neighborhood parks, and shopping centers are the usual locations that AI seniors visit.

Open-ended Questions: Themes. Only those participants who self-administered the survey ($N = 109$) were asked to respond to the open-ended questions in the psychosocial questionnaire. Out of the 109 participants, 31 chose to answer the qualitative portion of the survey, and a couple of them also sent their views on the subject in an email. In terms of what would improve their life quality, the following major themes emerged:

1. Spirituality, self-improvement, contentment, meditation and prayer: for example, "Meditation and prayers will keep me happy and will improve my quality of life," and "Spiritual field is life balancing and it bestows the sense of fulfillment in our life."
2. Better physical health, elimination of diseases: examples include, "if God has not given me blindness," and "I am not feeling well due to severe pain in my knees."
3. Improved infrastructure such as transportation, housing, health facilities, and medical insurance: "Cheaper medical insurance," "greater availability of transport," and "there should be senior housing for people from India with reasonable rent" are some examples.
4. Better relations with family members: for example, "I wish my son, daughter in law and grandchildren demonstrate more affection visibly. I feel neglected."
5. Regular activities including volunteering as well as paid opportunities: "To get myself engaged in activities to keep myself busy," and "If I get job and start working, it will help me feeling good" are some of the examples.

In addition to the themes above, the following ideas were also expressed by several participants both as answers to the questionnaire, and in informal talks during the interviews:

1. Opportunity to share life's knowledge and experience: for example, "be able to write a book about my life," and "I need an assistant who can help me with my lifelong work."
2. Opportunity to socialize with individuals of similar age and social strata: for example, "By remaining in group of good friends," and "meet people from the same age group and same social strata."
3. Hope and desire to return to India preferably with children: examples include "I do not want to die in USA," and "Would like to go back to India but with my children which may not be possible."

Thus, despite the small number of qualitative responses, a rich set of themes have emerged. The implications of these results will be discussed in the next chapter.

Summary of Findings
Conducted between July and October, 2011, this study used convenience and snowball sampling to recruit 109 seniors (63 men and 46 women). To allow individuals with language barrier to participate, both self-administered ($n = 38$) and interviewer-assisted ($n = 71$) formats, and Hindi, English, and Bengali as interview languages were used. The study sample was diverse: four religions, 12 native languages, and more than 10 Indian states were represented.

The study hypothesis that AI seniors will experience a loss of autonomy or independence was supported. Specifically, their self-reported mastery was found to be low (47.7% limited mastery, 33.9% moderate mastery, 18.3% heightened mastery); they reported financial dependence on their children or the government (11% independent, 89% dependent); a language barrier that limits their access to services was reported (22.9% strongly agree, 27.5% agree); their access to transportation in the U.S. is statistically significantly lower than what they had in India before migration ($\chi2$ (16) = 63.53, $p < 0.001$), and if they were living in India now ($\chi2$ (16) = 35.207, $p = .004$); and their current financial condition in the U.S. is significantly worse than the condition in India before relocation ($\chi2$ (12) = 22.526, $p = .032$), and if they were living in India now ($\chi2$ (16) = 32.442, p = .009).

Although in direct paired questions, the participants rated their QoL in India ($M = 4.30$, $SD = 0.687$) higher than that in the U.S. ($M = 3.76$, $SD = 0.881$), these differences were statistically not significant ($\chi2$ (12) = 11.322, $p = .502$). However, they admitted being far more isolated, lonely, or left out of things in this country (24.8% strongly agreed, 15.6% agreed) compared to in India (0.9% strongly agreed, 5.5% agreed), and these differences were statistically significant ($\chi2$ (16) = 68.341, $p < 0.001$). Participants also rated their social support in India as far better (51.4% strongly agreed, 17.4% agreed) than what it is in the U.S. (1.8% strongly agreed, 12.8% agreed) while 16.5% were neutral.

The study hypothesis that AI older adults, who are U.S. citizens ($n = 53$) will have higher QoL in comparison to those who are permanent residents ($n = 56$), was also supported: citizens had a statistically significantly higher QoL score for psychological health domain ($F(1, 107) = 2.886$, $p = .092$), and environment domain ($F(1, 107) = 7.905$, $p = .006$) when compared to permanent residents; citizens had better finance ($F(1, 107) = 14.767$, $p < 0.001$) better self-reported English proficiency $F(1, 107) = 2.820$, $p = .096$, and lower isolation ($F(1, 107) = 7.439$, $p = .007$) when compared to permanent residents; citizens also visited India less frequently in comparison to permanent residents: $F(1, 107) = 5.541, p = .020$.

The hypothesis that compared to the general U.S. population, AI seniors will have higher prevalence of depression and anxiety, was not supported: the prevalence was found to be similar but not higher.

The participants were well educated (33.1% graduate, 33% post graduate), and indicated a preference for Indian books, newspapers, and television programs. They also self-identified as Indians (85.3%), and considered India as their home (82.6%). Almost half (46.8%) reported that they visit India every year.

In response to the qualitative question about things that would improve the QoL of the participants, the themes that emerged included spirituality; better physical health; better infrastructure such as transportation, housing, health facilities, and medical insurance; better relations with family members; and regular activities, including both paid jobs and volunteering opportunities. Desire to share life's knowledge and experience, to socialize with individuals of similar age and social strata, and to return to India, preferably with children, was also expressed.

CHAPTER FIVE: DISCUSSION, CONCLUSIONS, AND RECOMMENDATIONS

The present study extends the research on under-researched AI older adults. The literature categorizes the AI senior community into two distinct groups with very different needs: early immigrants who arrived in search of a job or education, and family-sponsored recent immigrants who relocated to unite with their families (NIAASC, n.d.; Prasad, 2009). The empirical research on AI seniors is scarce in the first place, and second, existing studies include both categories of seniors, thereby diluting their focus. This may be the first study that focuses exclusively on family-sponsored recent immigrants. Specifically, the study explores the QoL of AI parents, who have immigrated late in life to be with their adult children.

Further, most of the research conducted so far on Indian seniors has included only English-speaking participants, although the Atlanta study included Gujarati-speaking seniors (Diwan, 2008). By inviting participants who can communicate in Hindi or Bengali, in addition to those fluent in English, this study has been able to reach the population that has so far been neglected by the academic world. Moreover, even those who know English very well can sometimes not participate because their vision has deteriorated with age. Several persons falling in this category participated in this study, thereby increasing the reach of this study.

Based on the study results reported in Chapter 4, this chapter will highlight the major discoveries and findings while linking them with the existing literature. Implications of the study for mental health practitioners and directions for future research will also be discussed.

Discussion

The purpose of the study was to explore the QoL of AI parents living in the SF Bay Area, who have immigrated to live with their adult children. Existing models for measuring QoL of older adults could not be directly applied because of the unique nature of this population: specifically, their Indian heritage and late-life immigration. As a result, a combination of published instruments and a study-specific questionnaire containing psychosocial variables pertinent to this population was used to understand the life quality of these AI seniors.

The original expectation for the number of participants was only 50-75, but the AI seniors welcomed the study. Not only did they participate with enthusiasm, they also recommended it to their friends, allowing the research target to be improved. Although the study was finally closed at 109 participants, it should not be too difficult to recruit larger numbers of participants for future studies.

Participant Diversity: Representation of Indian States

Reflecting the diversity of India, the participants of this study came from more than 10 Indian states and spoke 12 native languages. However, the number of immigrants from each state did not correspond with the population of that state in India. For example, although Punjab and Gujarat have only 2% and 5% of India's population (Government of India: Ministry of Home Affairs, 2011), in the study, 23.9% Punjabis and 20.2%

Gujaratis participated. Part of this could be attributed to convenience or snowball sampling methods adopted, but this also suggests that the AI senior population in the Bay Area is dominated by Punjabis and Gujaratis. That these two communities also seem to have better infrastructure and social support for seniors could be a contributing factor in this.

For example, there are specific senior groups targeted only towards Gujaratis and temples frequented mostly by the Gujarati community. Similarly, *gurudwaras* (Sikh-temples) cater mainly to Punjabi Sikhs, and they also offer special programs and support for seniors. Not all Punjabis, however, follow the Sikh religion. The study sample had 26 Punjabi participants, out of which 14 were Sikhs, 11 were Hindus, and one was Jain.

Further, it seems that older adults from some states of India migrate while parents from other states simply prefer visiting this country. As Bengali was one of the interview languages, special efforts were made to recruit Bengali participants. It was, however, very difficult to identify Bengali older adults who were permanent residents or citizens, despite good connections in the community, including family and friends of the researcher. Eventually, participants were recruited at the *Durga Puja* celebrations, the biggest cultural festival of Bengal. When AI parents start visiting the U.S. prior to immigration, their inability to find other age-cohorts belonging to their community and speaking their native language could be a factor that deters them from immigrating.

Demographic Factors

An interesting finding of this study was that the participants were highly educated: 33% were post-graduates while another 33% had a bachelor's degree, and 8% had some college education (Table 2). Similar results were reported for the Atlanta study of AI seniors, where English-speaking participants were even more educated, with 58% post-graduates, and 35% having some college or a graduate degree (Diwan, 2008). In contrast, only 17% participants of the AAFNY study (Mui et al.,

2006), and 38% of Gujarati speaking participants of Atlanta study (Diwan, 2008) had post-high school education. Diwan had even speculated that family sponsored AI parents will have lower education, but as a group, participants of the present study defy that speculation. It is, however, important to remember that the current study sample was not homogeneous: several participants confided during the interviews that they are illiterate, or that they have very little formal education.

Despite both husbands and wives participating separately in the research, only 65.1% of the participants were married while the rest were widowed (Table 2), which indicates that a sizable number of AI older adults living in the Bay Area are widowed. This supports the finding reported by other studies (Rangaswamy, 2000), and informally confirmed by study participants, that one reason for immigration is the death of the partner. Left alone, older adults feel more secure moving in with their sons or daughters, as expressed by one of the participants of Miltiades (2002) study, who chose to stay in India with her husband: "My sons and daughters are American citizens, so they have some facilities. So, I want my husband to go there [to America] and stay with my daughter when I die. I don't want him to stay alone" (p.49).

The self-reported proficiency in English was lower for women compared to men with 76.2% men and only 34.8% women agreeing or strongly agreeing that they communicate very well in English. Further, 42.9% men and 60.9% women agreed or strongly agreed that the lack of English proficiency prevents access to services. Moreover, based on the mastery scale scores, limited mastery was shown by 39.7% men and 58.7% women, moderate mastery by 34.9% men and 32.6% women, and heightened mastery by 25.4% men and 8.7% women.

Overall, both men and women had low or limited mastery, but women performed worse than men. This gender difference in mastery and English proficiency can be attributed to patriarchal and hierarchical Indian culture (Chandra et al., 2009; Kalavar, 1998; Shreshtha, 2010) where men occupy a superior position, and women are taught to follow the "rule of three obedience" (Mui & Shibusawa, 2008); that is, they must obey their fathers before marriage, husbands after marriage, and sons when widowed (Miltiades, 2002).

Men, on the other hand, are taught to protect their sisters, daughters, wives, and mothers through various traditions while following their fathers, uncles, and elder brothers. Further, sons are encouraged to study while women are often denied education (e.g. Kalavar, 1998), which explains women's lesser proficiency in English.

Multilingual Capability, Hindi as the Most Common Language

The diversity of India in terms of native language was reflected in the study sample as participants spoke 12 different native languages (Table 4). Despite this diversity, Hindi, the national language of India, emerged as the most common and well-understood language with 52 out of 109 people (48%) choosing it as a language they are most comfortable in. Further, more than half the participants (52.3%) chose more than one language, supporting the finding of other researchers that many Indians have multilingual capability (e.g. Rangaswamy, 2000).

Most participants stated that they speak their native language, as well as Hindi or English or both. Sometimes, the native language of a neighboring state, or of the state they grew up in if different from the native state, was chosen. It is important to note that they were responding to "Which language do you feel most comfortable communicating in?" If instead, they were asked to specify all the languages they can interact in, perhaps the response would have included more languages, and perhaps a higher percentage would have chosen Hindi. Nevertheless, for mental health professionals, finding Hindi as the most common language has significant implications, which will be discussed in a later section.

Theoretical Models

In Chapter 2, two studies (Brockmann, 2002; Grewal et al., 2004) relevant to QoL models for older ethnic immigrants were discussed. Findings of this study support the factors identified in both these studies. Specifically, political and legal context, identity or sense of belonging, social support, and material resources, the four factors identified by Brockmann, were important for the participants.

Further, out of the six factors that influence QoL according to Grewal and colleagues, five that were found important in this study are having a role, support networks, financial resources, health, and independence. The sixth factor, "having time" was perhaps not so important because most participants had ample free time, and were more interested in meaningful activities and social connections to fill this time. One reason for this difference is that this study focused on late-life immigrants while Grewal et al. studied those who migrated to England decades ago, and were now approaching retirement.

Proposing QoL Model for AI Senior Immigrants	1. Political and Legal Context
	2. Autonomy or Independence
	• Mastery or Self-Efficacy in New Culture
	• Access to Transportation
	• Financial Dependence
Extension of	• Dependence due to Language Barrier
	3. Social Support Network
Brockmann (2002):	4. Sense of Identity or Belonging
QoL Model of Older Ethnic Immigrants in Europe.	5. Meaningful Role
Grewal et al. (2004): Influences on QoL.	6. Health

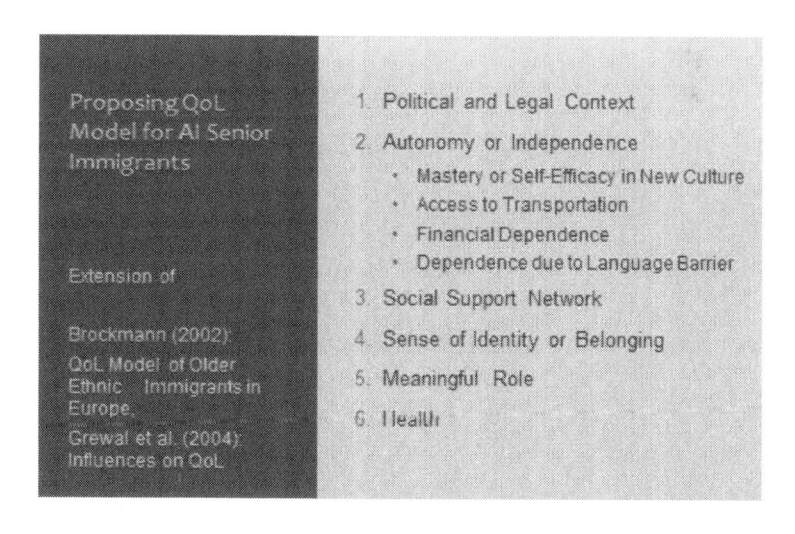

Figure 14. Proposed QoL Model for AI Senior Immigrants

Building on the model of Brockmann, this study proposes the following key issues that impact the QoL of AI seniors: (a) political and legal context, (b) autonomy or independence, (c) social support network, (d) sense of identity or belonging, (e) meaningful role, and (f) health. Autonomy or independence is further subdivided into mastery or self-efficacy in the new culture, access to transportation, financial dependence, and dependence due to language barriers. Thus, "material resources," identified by Brockmann and Grewal et al., is subsumed within autonomy. The proposed model is shown pictorially in Figure 14.

The key difference between the present study and the two European studies (Brockmann, 2002; Grewal et al., 2004) is in the study population. The Eurpoean older immigrant studies focused on the equivalents of "early immigrants" in this study. As a result, issues related to late-life immigration such as isolation, lack of transportation, language barrier, and lack of knowledge of available resources are more pertinent for the present study population. These will be further discussed in the next few sections.

QoL: United States versus India

The study hypothesized that AI older adults will experience a loss of autonomy or independence after immigration, which was supported by the results. Their self-reported mastery is low; they are financially dependent on their children or the government; many have a language barrier that limits their interaction and communication; and they were more easily able to move around in India compared to the U.S. Thus, on several levels, their life quality has deteriorated because of the late-life immigration.

Transportation. On the question of access to transportation in the U.S., participants were more dissatisfied than satisfied, and 63.8% disagreed or strongly disagreed that they have the transportation to go wherever they want to go

(Table 12). Further, riding with their families is the most common mode of transportation for 41.7% of the participants (Table 9). In contrast, they reported far better access to transportation that allowed them to go wherever they wanted to go in India, both before they immigrated (75.9% strongly agreed) and if they were living there now (69.4% strongly agreed). This difference in access to transportation in the U.S. and India was found to be statistically significant through chi-square analysis.

These results confirm the previous study findings that lack of mobility is one of the biggest challenges for the study population (Mui & Cross, 2003a; Prasad, 2010; Rangaswamy, 2000; Trang, 2009). In the AAFNY study, for example, 85.2% Indian seniors had reported that their children helped with the transportation needs (Mui & Cross, 2003a). Further, 49 out of 99 Indian seniors had reported that they required transportation help in visiting doctors or clinics, which is almost double of what general New York city elders reported (28%).

The participants of this study expressed similar views in the qualitative portion of the survey. One participant, for example, wrote, "The greater availability of transportation may help me to move about whenever I need," while another shared, "Having more easy transportation would be welcome as it would enable more frequent visits to friends."

Inability to move independently forces AI seniors to depend on their children or grandchildren, thereby, impacting their sense of self-efficacy. Further, their movement is restricted to weekends, when the working adult children have some free time unless they use public transportation.

In India, many of these participants were used to chauffeur driven cars at their command, so it is likely to be a big leap for them to get accustomed to using public transportation. Further, many of the sponsoring children are doing well in Silicon Valley, and so they live in large houses in the suburbs with poor public transportation. Moreover, the bus stop is likely to be at a distance from their home, and many seniors are afraid that they may fall, or their physical health may not allow them to walk. Para-transportation services like Outreach in Santa Clara County are a good alternative, but many lack any knowledge about it. This has important practice implications, which will be discussed in a later section.

Financial dependence. The study hypothesis that participants would be financially dependent on their children or the government was supported as only 11% were found to be financially independent while the balance 89% were dependent (Table 10). Further, 70.6% participants were receiving Medi-Cal (Medicaid), which reflects the federal poverty levels, and has been used in the literature as a proxy for inadequate finances (Mui & Shibusawa, 2008). These results are consistent with other studies that have reported economic dependence as a major challenge for older immigrants (Burr et al., 2009; Prasad, 2010).

Further, amongst different Asian ethnic groups studied, Indians (72%) were found to be the most likely group to receive financial assistance from children in the AAFNY study (Mui & Cross, 2003a). While comparing their financial condition in India and the U.S., statistically significant differences were found, and the participants were far more financially independent in India, both before immigration and now.

It is important to understand in this context that many AI immigrants had good jobs and were financially secure in India, allowing them to pay for a quality education for their children, which in turn was the stepping stone towards their journey to Silicon Valley. As a result, having to depend on their children for even small needs is difficult for them as expressed by one participant, "They [we] do not like to ask children for money," and supported by other studies (Lamb, 2009a).

Isolation. When asked to rate the QoL in India and in the U.S., although the numbers were higher for India (Table 14), the differences were statistically not significant. However, as Table

15 shows, participants admitted being far more isolated, lonely, or left out of things in this country (24.8% strongly agreed, 15.6% agreed) compared to in India (0.9% strongly agreed, 5.5% agreed), and these differences were statistically significant. Participants also rated their social support in India as far better (51.4% strongly agreed, 17.4% agreed) than that in the U.S. (1.8% strongly agreed, 12.8% agreed) while 16.5% were neutral (Table 15).

The fact that there was significant difference for isolation and social support questions, but not for overall QoL, might mean that when asked general questions, the study sample prefers to say everything is going well. Therefore, to understand aspects of their lives, both practitioners and researchers will need to ask specific, direct questions.

Leaving behind their social capital in India, and experiencing social isolation in the U.S. are some of the biggest challenges in front of the study population, a finding that is corroborated by other studies (e.g. Kalavar, 2003; NIAASC, n.d.; Ryan et al., 2003). This isolation is further enhanced because of the language barrier. An interesting finding in this context is that although 58.7% agreed or strongly agreed that they communicate very well in English, 50.4% also agreed or strongly agreed that English is a barrier in their access to various services (Table 11). Many of the participants attributed this seeming conflict to their inability to understand the American accent. Further, their Indian accent is not well understood by mainstream Americans.

Frequent visits to India. A surprising result of the study was that 46.8% of the participants (57.1% residents, 35.8% citizens) travel every year to India (Table 5). A further 24.8% (19.6% residents, 30.2% citizens) visit every two years. Only 10.1% stated that they travel less than once in four years. When one considers that an extended trip to India stops the SSI for recipients, putting them into further economic hardship, it indicates a strong pull towards their home country that is able to withstand the financial implications.

Other scholars have studied this phenomenon of alternating between the country of origin and the adopted country (*pendeln* in German), and called it a positive strategy used by older immigrants (Brockmann, 2002). Because it mitigates the disadvantages of living in either country, and allows them to draw on the resources of both countries, many immigrant older adults in the U.S. as well as in Europe adopt this strategy.

Further, both in informal discussions and in written responses, a desire to return to or at least die in India emerged. One participant shared, "I do not want to die in USA." This is particularly interesting as these seniors seemed to be aware that this may not be feasible. In the words of another participant, "[I] would like to go back to India but with my children which may not be possible."

Similar sentiments to return back but only if accompanied by the children have been expressed not just in other AI older adult studies (e.g. Nandan, 2005), but also older immigrant studies in Europe. Calling it the "myth of return," Brockmann (2002) points out that this is a goal that older immigrants desire but are unable to achieve for various reasons. Along with the wish to stay with children, health-care system in the host country is another common reason put forward by the immigrants.

In the context of the desire to return to India, it is, important to note that individual variations exist: for some participants, the life in the U.S. is better, while for others, there is no difference. From this last category, one participant of this study shared, "I am enjoying my life and I do not find any difference in living in USA or in India."

QoL of AI Seniors and the Population Norms for WHOQOL-BREF

Hawthorne et al. (2006) had published preliminary population norms for WHOQOL-BREF for different age-groups, gender, and health status. The authors had suggested that these norms can serve as guidelines for researchers while interpreting their results. When taken as a group, the participants of the present study had lower QoL on three out of four domains when compared to the population norms reported by both the Hawthorne study and the Noerholm study (as cited in Hawthorne et al., 2006), However, as reported in Chapter 4, significant differences were found between AI citizens and permanent residents on psychological and environment domains, and in both these domains, citizens outperformed the norms whereas permanent residents had the lowest scores.

Specifically, in the environment domain, citizens had the highest score (M = 78.1, SD = 11.4) followed by the Hawthorne study (M = 75.1, SD = 13.0) and the Noerholm study (M = 74, SD = 16), whereas green-card holders reported the lowest scores (M = 71.6, SD = 12.9). Similar results were reported for psychological health domain, with citizens (M = 71.36, SD = 14.9) having higher score than in the Hawthorne study (M = 70.6, SD = 14.0) and Noerholm study (M = 69, SD = 16), and the permanent residents (M = 65.96, SD = 18.0) trailing behind everyone. These results support the study hypothesis that citizens will have a higher QoL compared to residents. As described in literature review, the rationale behind this is that citizens have been in this country for longer and therefore have better environmental support, including access to social benefits.

For the physical health domain, the scores for the Noerholm study (M = 77, SD = 17) and the Hawthorne study (M = 73.5, SD = 18.1; Hawthorne et al., 2006), were much higher compared to the present study (M = 67.6, SD = 19.6), implying that Indian seniors lag behind in physical health. The results, however, were just the opposite on the social relationships domain as this study was at the top (M = 72.18, SD = 15.5) followed by the Hawthorne study (M = 71.5, SD = 18.2), and the Noerholm study (M = 69, SD = 18).

One explanation of the results could be that AI seniors are more satisfied with their social relations. An alternative possibility is that seniors are unwilling to admit that they are dissatisfied with their social relations because it might mean betraying the family. Considering that filial piety is of paramount importance in the collectivistic Indian culture and that individuals are supposed to sacrifice self-interests in favor of the family interests (Durvasula & Mylvaganam, 1994; Gill, 2008; Khanna et al., 2009; Nandi, 1980), the second alternative seems to be a more plausible explanation.

It is important to note that the norms of the Hawthorne and the Noerholm studies are based on research on Australian and Danish population (Hawthorne et al., 2006), and there are inherent confounds in attempting to make cross-cultural comparisons regarding psychological constructs, such as QoL, which are culturally construed. Further, notable age-group and sampling differences between the study samples bring further uncertainty to such comparisons. Still, one wonders whether the results discussed above reflect an actual difference between various nationalities, or they are simply a result of age-group differences and sampling strategy.

Note that the Hawthorne study data includes the random community sample data collected for devising the WHOQOL-OLD instrument discussed in Chapter 2. Further, Hawthorne and colleagues had reported that domain scores decreased slightly with advancing age in their study, but in the comparison above, the scores for the general category were used because single scores for age 60 and above were not available. Despite the differences in the population characteristics, it is interesting to note that the participants of the present study had domain scores similar to available norms, and that in two domains, the norms were between the scores of citizens and permanent residents.

Another important point that should be considered in this context is whether Indians' belief in karma affected the responses. The karmic theory attributes a current adverse situation to past bad karmas or karmic debt (e.g. Shrestha, 2010). That is, when something bad happens to people, it is considered to be a result of bad actions in the present life or past lives. Further, to finish or nullify bad karmas, one is supposed to accept whatever life hands out. The WHOQOL-BREF has several sections where participants are asked to respond on a 5-point scale from "very dissatisfied" to "very satisfied." Here particularly, many did not want to entertain the idea of choosing dissatisfied or very dissatisfied for any question, and kept saying, "it's fine; I'm satisfied."

Perhaps, this is because indicating dissatisfaction could be perceived as non-acceptance of karma, bringing on further negative experiences. Further, as Jeste and Vahia (2008) pointed out, self-contentment, control over desires, and renouncing materialistic and physical pleasures are considered as attributes of wisdom according to *Bhagavad Gita*, the Hindu holy book, which could be another reason AI seniors express satisfaction with life-situations. The desire to look good in the eyes of the interviewer, a problem common to studies relying on self-reports (e.g. Campbell et al., 1976) could be another reason for such a preference.

Impact of the Political and the Legal Context

The third research question looked at the politico-legal context in which AI immigrants arrive in this country, and examined how societal environment affects QoL of these seniors. In her proposed model for QoL of older ethnic minority immigrants in Germany, Austria, and the UK, Brockmann (2002) had identified the political and legal context as one of the four key life domains that impacts QoL of immigrants. The literature review examined in detail the evolution of various immigration laws in the last half century, and how they impacted and continue to influence AI immigrants in general, and older adults arriving on family sponsorship in particular.

Although it is difficult to operationalize the nuances of social, political, and legal environment, the citizenship status gives an indication of such influence because a number of benefits available to senior citizens have been rescinded particularly for immigrants living on a green card through the 1996 act of PRWORA (Burr et al., 2009; Majmundar, 2003; Torres-Gil & Treas, 2009). After a residency period of five years, seniors qualify for citizenship, which eventually qualifies them for Medicare, Medicaid, and other benefits. In California, however, Medicaid is called Medi-Cal, and is available to permanent residents (Health Consumer Alliance, 2008).

While researching in early 1990s, Rangaswamy (2000) had found that many seniors became permanent residents for travel convenience as well as to qualify for benefits. By the late 1990s, however, the scenario changed and citizenship became a prerequisite, not just for benefits but also for reducing the prohibitive cost of health care. As a result, seniors immigrating after the enactment of welfare reform and immigration acts of 1996 are often left with no option but to take the citizenship. In the present study, out of 11 participants who reported having no health insurance, nine were permanent residents while only two were citizens.

This study hypothesized that AI older adults who have acquired U.S. citizenship will have higher QoL in comparison to those who are permanent residents. On several dimensions including psychological health, environmental domain, finance, and feeling of isolation, this was indeed found to be true. In addition, citizens had better English proficiency and they traveled less frequently to India when compared to permanent residents: perhaps their connection with the home country is somewhat weaker, and they are more adapted to this country.

Moreover, citizens are no longer as dependent on extramural refueling (Akhtar, 1999) discussed in Chapter 2 as are permanent residents. It was, therefore, no surprise that more green-card holders self-identified as Indians (77.4% citizens, 92.9% permanent residents) rather than Americans (5.7% citizens, no permanent residents) or Indo-Americans (11.3% citizens, no permanent residents) (Table 5). The balance of 5.7% citizens and 7.1% residents chose multiple identities.

Also, when asked about their home country, 91.1% green-card holders chose India as the home country compared to 73.6% citizens. These results indicate that the connection with India, although still strong for citizens, is certainly not as strong as that of permanent residents. Living longer in the U.S., citizens have better environmental and social support here, and many have accepted their adopted country as their new homeland. As a result, they do not feel the need to visit India as frequently as permanent residents. An alternate explanation could be that with the passage of time, their connection with family and friends in India may have weakened (Nandan, 2007; Rangaswamy, 2000).

Further, as reported in literature review, longer length of stay in the U.S. was associated with lesser acculturative stress in some studies (Hans, 2002), but poorer health (Diwan & Jonnalagadda, 2001), higher depression, and acculturative stress (Mui & Kang, 2006; Mui & Shibusawa, 2008) in other studies. Better psychological and environmental health of citizens compared to permanent resident found in this study, is thus congruent with the findings of Hans (2002), but inconsistent with the findings of other studies reported above.

Prevalence of Depression and Anxiety

Based on PHQ-9 and GAD-7, the prevalence of depression and anxiety among AI seniors was found to be similar but not higher when compared to general U.S. population, as hypothesized. That is, the findings of this study are in contrast to previous studies that report higher depression among Asian older adults (e.g. Markides et al., 2009, Mui & Kang, 2006). In part, this can be attributed to the stigma of mental health in the AI population (Durvasula & Mylvaganam, 1994; Lai & Surood, 2008; Patel, 2005) whereby mental health issues are kept within the family, hidden from the society. Seeking help from professionals is regarded as bringing shame and disgrace to the family, and is therefore taboo. While verbally administering the instruments, participants seemed averse to admitting negative experiences: When words such as depression were mentioned, often, the immediate answer was, "I don't have that. I am fine."

The PHQ-9 has a question that asks the frequency of the feelings of "Thought that you would be better off dead or of hurting yourself in some way." Considering that thoughts of self-harm are derided in the Hindu culture, it was no surprise that participants seemed unwilling to entertain that they have such thoughts. Because the effect of bad karmas is supposed to persist from one life to the next, destroying the current body simply means that one needs to take another birth to pay the karmic debt. Further, it is possible that AI older adults resort to spirituality to deal with adverse conditions. One participant, for example, shared:

> Stop having any negative view about things happening around you. If apparently a negative thing seems to have happened, recollect and understand and then try to find a method so that it may not repeat. Never put the blame on others.

Another participant expressed similar views, "I now understand that small annoyances kill us like slow poison. I have now a good control for not being annoyed by small annoyances." Further, even though the PHQ-9 and the GAD-7 have been translated in Indian languages (see Chapter 3), in order to assess depression and anxiety on AI individuals, perhaps newer tools need to be devised that are more in tune with Indian culture.

This is especially important because psychological constructs such as depression and anxiety are culturally bound, and in Indian culture, the society looks down upon not only the person with a mental illness, but also the entire family. Hence, the instruments designed to measure depression and anxiety should take into account how they are expressed in Indian culture.

Connection with Children and their Families

The participants' immigration to the U.S. was sponsored by their families and the primary reason for their relocation was to unite with their families. It was, therefore, no surprise that 96 out of 109 participants are living with their children. Consistent with the findings of other researchers (Bowling, 2005; Diwan, 2008; Mui & Cross, 2003b; Smith et al., 2004), this study found that having a good relationship with their families was uppermost in the minds of the participants, who fell into two categories. In the first group were those who already had good connection with their children: with satisfaction and pleasure, they repeatedly emphasized that their children will do anything for them.

The second group consisted of those who wished that their relationship would improve, and had two subgroups. Most participants belonged to the first subgroup: they were still living in the homes of their children but felt isolated, ignored, or taken advantage of. A few outliers formed the second subgroup of those who had to move out, and were living alone. In several such cases, a soured relationship with their daughters-in-law was the cause, and these parents lamented the separation, as expressed by one of the participants:

> Generally I feel bad and depressed due to wrong attitude of my daughter-in-law. She has not visited us for the last 5 years and also not allowed us to visit/see our grandchildren. If she changes her attitude and meets us occasionally along with one grandchild, it will be much beneficial for our health.

These sentiments are similar to those expressed in other studies on Asian older adults (Kalavar & Van Willigen, 2005; Mui & Shibusawa, 2008; Rangaswamy, 2000). Further, seniors miss the warm relationships that grandparents usually have with their grandchildren in India. As reported in the literature, some AI older adults have immigrated to assist in the parenting of their grandchildren (e.g. Kalavar & Van Willigen, 2005). When young, there is usually a good bonding between the generations, but as one participant shared, "Children when grow enough, they do not have any attachment with grandparents." He further commented, "Grandparents in USA are not the part of family." The hurt and mental anguish that seniors feel because of this severed relationship has also been reported by other researchers (e.g. Kalavar & Van Willigen, 2005). Some grandparents even return back to India when the grandchildren no longer need the child-care (Miltiades, 2002).

For many older adults, passing on their culture to the next generation provides meaning to life but for this population, that avenue is often not open. Their grandchildren have adopted American values and American culture, and in many cases they do not even know the native language, and therefore, cannot even communicate with their grandparents. This inability of the grandchildren to speak in the native language and their discarding traditional Indian culture increases the gulf between the generations, as expressed by a participant in another study: "I don't understand their world, and they cannot relate to my past. We are in one house with little in common." (Kalavar & Van Willigen, 2005, p. 223)

Peer Relationships, Meeting Places

An opportunity to interact with peers of same age-group, language, and culture is important to this community. In the words of one participant, "May be having to meet people from the same age group and same social strata" would improve the QoL. As a result, those who are able to go to AI senior centers regularly seem to be happier. Popular AI senior groups in the Valley include ICC in Milpitas, Friends Of Same Wave Length (FOSWL) and ICC in Cupertino, The Hub in Fremont, Fremont Senior Center at Elizabeth Lake where both INSAF and ICC groups meet, and senior groups at Fremont Temple, Jain temple, and Vaishnav Temple (Haveli) in Milpitas. Participants were recruited from all of these locations. Additionally, there are various spiritual groups that meet at different temples or spiritual centers that immigrant Indian parents regularly visit alone or in company of their adult children.

An ingenious solution. As most AI seniors do not have independent transportation, their mobility is quite restricted. Further, as one participant remarked, "there is no place where they [we] can meet without paying fees." A surprising discovery that improved the planned recruitment strategy of this study was the way the AI older adults have overcome the transportation and the financial barrier. Many have started meeting on daily basis in local parks or shopping centers, which serve the dual purpose of providing exercise and giving them an opportunity to interact with same-age peers. Those who are unable to walk because of poor health or those who live in parts of Bay Area where the AI population density is lower, however, cannot benefit from such informal gatherings.

In the context of meeting locations and peer relationships, another interesting point was observed. Early immigrants, the category of AI seniors that has been excluded from this study because they came to the U.S. for job or education rather than family reunification, often act as advocates for the study population of recent immigrants. Although most attendees at various AI senior centers are recent immigrants or non-immigrant visitors from India, some early immigrants also attend regularly. Familiar with the American culture, these early immigrants often take lead in managing the senior centers, and advocating for seniors' issues whether that is in the Bay Area or on the East Coast. Several members of the executive committee of NIAASC, an AI seniors' advocacy association founded in the aftermath of 1996 Welfare reforms (see Chapter 2), for example, are early immigrants.

Stay Here or go Back?

Not just the seniors but the entire AI community struggles with the question of whether to continue living here in the U.S.

or to pack their bags and return to India. For immigrant parents, India offers some independence, especially if they belong to higher socioeconomic class. The public perception is that immigration leads to upward social mobility and improved standard of living, which in turn, improves the QoL of the immigrant. For many study participants, however, late life immigration has resulted in reduced social capital, isolation, and perhaps, downward social mobility.

Gans (2007) defined social mobility as "the movement to a higher or lower class or status position" (p. 154). Based on this definition, one can see that AI immigrant seniors have several losses: their traditionally high position in the family hierarchy is reversed: in India they were the decision makers, and were sought because of their experience and wisdom, but in the new land they must go to their children for advice, transportation, and help in communication due to the language barrier. They have also lost their economic independence and sense of self-efficacy, and are now dependent on their children and/or the government, an especially difficult transition as many have come from middle to upper middle class in India (Rangaswamy, 2007). Loss of extended family and friends, and not having meaningful role or work resulting in a sense of being unwanted, are further challenges. It was, therefore, no surprise when one participant shared:

> In my view seniors having their money, pension income and a place to live in India will have better life there than in USA. In India all sorts of help is available. Single seniors can live in old-age home while here assisted living is very costly.

Similar sentiments were expressed by another senior: "Only those parents who can afford (financial and healthwise) to live independently in the USA should consider emigrating to USA. In all other cases it is Just a Gamble." For most seniors, however, going back is simply wishful thinking, a dream that is not likely to come true, especially because they want their children to relocate with them. But the adult children want to remain close to their children (grandchildren of seniors), who have grown up in this country, and have adapted to the American culture. For most of these grandchildren, the United States is their home, and India only an exotic place to be visited once in a while. Thus, these complex intergenerational ties may keep the immigrant parents tied to the U.S. thereby adding a new color to the tapestry of this country. It is, therefore, time that the society in general, and the Indian community in particular, recognizes and honors the contributions of AI immigrant seniors while understanding and addressing their concerns and needs.

Implications for Practice

The results of this study have several implications for social-work and mental-health practitioners that will be discussed in this section. In order to reduce health disparity and provide quality services for ethnically diverse population, it is important that they are offered services in their native languages (Khanna et al., 2009; Mui & Shibusawa, 2008).

As 6.6% of the population in Santa Clara County is of AI origin (U.S. Census Bureau: American Fact Finder, 2011), one might expect the county to offer linguistically appropriate services to the AI community. The reality, however, is that none of the Indian languages are included in the five languages (English, Spanish, Chinese, Vietnamese, and Tagalog) identified by the county in which services must be provided (Santa Clara County Mental Health Department (SCCMHD], 2010). Further, the AI group is not among the eight racial and ethnic groups (African-American, African Immigrants, Chinese, Filipino, Latino, Native American, and Vietnamese) for which Ethnic and Cultural Community Advisory Committees (ECCACs) have been created to improve outreach in the community (SCCMHD, 2010).

One reason for this is that the AI community is linguistically very diverse. In this study, for example, 12 different native languages were identified with just 109 participants. Nevertheless, as discussed earlier, 48% of the participants identified Hindi as one of the languages that they are most comfortable communicating in. The percentage might be much higher if we consider individuals who are able to understand and communicate in Hindi even though it is not their most comfortable language. Further, native speakers of Punjabi or Gujarati who participated in this study were able to communicate in Hindi with the researcher. As a result, the county could consider including Hindi in the list of languages in which they offer services. The AI community could also advocate with various counties for such inclusion.

Further, as discussed earlier, one of the discoveries of this study is that AI older adults meet in local parks and shopping centers, places of worship, and senior centers. It will be very beneficial to newcomers as well as long-term residents unaware of such meetings in their neighborhood, if these local meeting locations are compiled and publicized. Researchers and practitioners could also benefit because these locations could serve as the sites for reaching this population to recruit participants or provide services.

Moreover, considerable stigma toward mental health conditions exists in the study population. Social-work and government agencies whose charter is to improve public health or help seniors could work toward reducing this stigma by disseminating information and conducting educational campaigns. These agencies include the mainstream organizations such as the National Alliance on Mental Illness (NAMI) and the Council on Aging, as well as seniors' associations in the Indian community such as ICC and INSAF.

Mainstream agencies have so far not been able to make inroads into the Indian community. NAMI in Santa Clara County, for example, has a vibrant, linguistically and culturally appropriate support network for several other Asian groups including Chinese and Vietnamese, but none for the AI group at the time of this writing (early 2012). Similarly, the Council on Aging Silicon Valley had advisory representation from all major Asian groups except the AI group till early 2012 when the author joined them. These agencies could also make information about entitlements, benefits, and services including para-transit transportation, Medicare, and Medi-Cal available in Indian languages, especially Hindi.

Common to all elderly immigrants, lack of knowledge about available benefits and services is one of the major challenges for the study population (Kalavar, 2003; Mui & Shibusawa, 2008; Prasad, 2010; Trang, 2009). Not only do the seniors and their families and caregivers need to know about their availability, they also need help with the application process, if eligible.

Considerable thought and attention needs to be given to understand how to reach this under-served population. The interested agencies may have to devise diverse ways in which to push the needed information to the AI senior community. One possibility is to capitalize on the success of the innovative CAPS program (CAPS services, n.d.) of the city of Fremont in collaboration with the city of Newark and Union City, discussed in Chapter 2. Volunteers from 12 different ethnic, faith-based, or social rights organizations act as advocates for the seniors in their community in the CAPS program. Speaking in the seniors' native languages and mindful of their cultures, these trained volunteers provide information about local resources and services on diverse subjects such as transportation, housing, health insurance, social security, financial aid, legal aid, and immigration to the seniors and their families.

A free resource book, *The How-To Guide for Immigrant Seniors* (City of Fremont Human Services, 2009), has also been published to help them in becoming familiar with the rules and regulations associated with insurance, taxes, transportation, housing, banking, citizenship, employment, medical, and legal services.

Modeled after the success of CAPS program and funded by the Council on Aging, the Senior Peer Advocate program has been introduced in late 2011 in Santa Clara County by the Health Trust and its partners (Health Trust, 2011). Recognizing the value of peer-to-peer assistance, the volunteers in the SPA program are older adults themselves; hence they understand the issues faced by their age-cohorts. Other cities and counties in the area may help in improving the QoL of their senior immigrants by replicating the services offered by CAPS and SPA programs.

Directions for Future Research

One of the exploratory goals of the study was to find the factors that affect QoL, and possibly even predict it. The large number of variables, however, made the sample size ($N = 109$) relatively too small so that there was not enough power in the study to conduct traditional regression analyses. A larger research study could overcome this barrier and find factors impacting QoL.

Although many participants were recruited from various senior centers, temples, cultural event locations, and senior groups in local parks, sustained efforts were made to recruit home-bound seniors by reaching out through various email groups as well as through snowball methodology in which participants were asked to refer other potential candidates. As a result, approximately 10 - 15 seniors who are mostly home-bound participated in this study. Future studies could improve in this area so that the voices of such seniors become more prominent. Further, instead of convenience sampling, more scientific sampling methodology such as area probability sampling used in the AAFNY study (Ryan et al., 2003) could be employed, which would allow better generalization of results.

Another recommendation is that future studies include the city in which the participants live. This will allow analysis of where the study population is concentrated, and efforts could then be made to provide services where they are needed the most while devising strategies to improve the outreach in other cities. Further, though the Bay Area is an ethnic hub for the AI community, the density of the AI population varies significantly in different cities. Future studies could, therefore, compare the QoL of individuals residing in different cities.

Moreover, studies that span different parts of the U.S. could compare the QoL of seniors in different ethnic enclaves and remote locations. This is especially significant because the social benefits available to the immigrants fall under the purview of the states, and hence vary widely across the country (Burr et al., 2009).

This study specifically omitted parents who are visitors and have not immigrated to this country, but such visiting parents were present alongside the potential participants in each recruitment location. For parents who choose to stay behind in India, the emigration of their adult children has profound psychological and social impact, which was the subject of Miltiades (2002) study. Future research could include these visitors, and compare their perspectives and QoL with that of permanent residents and citizens. This is particularly important because the line between immigrants and visitors is blurred— many immigrant parents choose to spend several months a year in India while many visitors visit the U.S. every year or two.

As discussed in an earlier section, many seniors are attached to a senior center or a temple or a neighborhood park, where they are able to meet and interact with their age-cohorts. They may be visiting this place every day or just once a week, but it offers a sense of community and belonging that seems to play a significant role in the lives of AI seniors, as they have something to look forward to. Others who do not have such connections seem to feel more isolated and out of place in this country. In informal conversations, the participants spoke highly of such centers but the effect of such connections was not studied formally. Future research could investigate whether such connections are a factor in improving QoL of AI seniors.

As discussed earlier, good relations with their families is of paramount importance to AI seniors. Future studies that include both the AI parents and their host adult children, therefore, could be very beneficial. Perhaps focus groups that discuss the perspectives of both groups could result in potential solutions for the challenges that AI seniors face.

Conclusions

Based on the study results, several conclusions can be drawn regarding AI parents who immigrate in late life to live with the families of their adult children. This section will summarize some of these conclusions including the major challenges that the study population faces, and the steps that can be taken towards their solution. Further, keeping in mind that one of the goals of this study was to make a small opening in the closed walls that surround the AI older adult community, this section will present typical characteristics of the population under study. A QoL model that extends the existing model on older ethnic immigrants, and identifies the key domains impacting the QoL of AI seniors will also be outlined.

Based on the study experience, if one is asked to speculate about and paint a picture of a typical AI parent living in the SF Bay Area who has immigrated in late-life to unite with the family, then the foremost point to keep in mind is that individual variations are significant, and must be taken into account. Nevertheless, typical members of the study population are likely to have the following characteristics: an equal chance of being male or female; possibly highly educated; living with the families of sponsoring children; and equally likely to be citizens or green-card holders. Further, one in three or four persons is likely to be widowed, and every second or third such parent is likely to be Punjabi or Gujarati.

Financially dependent on children or government, these immigrant AI seniors have limited mobility due to restricted access to transportation, and face a language barrier either because of the differences in American and Indian accents, or due to lack of knowledge of English. Although well placed in India with good social connections, such Indian seniors are isolated and have very limited social circle in this country. They would like to socialize with others who have the same culture and beliefs; that is, those who speak the same native language and observe the same festivals. Further, such immigrant parents have limited knowledge of social services or benefits, and how to avail them.

Self-identifying as Indians, many immigrant seniors still consider India as their home country, and visit it at least once in two years if not every year. They have immediate or extended family in India with whom they feel close and therefore keep in touch regularly. Engrossed in Indian culture, AI seniors dress in traditional Indian clothes, love to watch Indian television, and read Indian newspapers, books or magazines. They regularly walk around the neighborhood, and possibly practice yoga and *pranayams*. Further, spirituality is important to them, and their belief in karma motivates them to accept life the way it is offered without complaining. Some of the characteristics such as high-education, and reasonably high socioeconomic status in India, are in direct contrast to the prevalent beliefs about immigrants.

Chapter 2 discussed that there is no consensus on the definition of QoL in the literature, and that QoL is an amorphous, value-laden term that can only be defined in the context of the individuals' culture. Although it depends on the factual or objective conditions, the individuals' subjective evaluation of these conditions is far more important in determining their QoL. This study, therefore, focused on the perceptions of AI immigrant seniors about their lives. Further, considering that QoL is a general term that could encompass anything and everything (Andrews & Withey, 1976), this study specifically zeroed in on how late-life immigration affected the QoL of the participants.

Based on both the literature and the participants' perspectives, some of the major challenges in front of the AI senior immigrant community are (a) social isolation which is intensified if the spouse is no longer alive; (b) financial dependence; (c) lack of access to transportation; (d) language barrier resulting in dependence for communication; (e) lack of knowledge about available social services such as para-transit transportation, availability of Indian books and movies in local libraries, and free English classes; (f) difficulty in obtaining affordable health insurance especially when they first arrive, or in the first five years after getting a green card while they await eligibility for citizenship; (g) emotional distance with the family, especially grandchildren due to different rates of acculturation among family members; and (h) lack of meaningful role that might cause a feeling of being unneeded and unappreciated. These challenges are not unique for Indians; rather, they are shared by other Asian immigrants (e.g. Mui & Shibusawa, 2008). Figure 15 summarizes these challenges.

Major Challenges / Shared by Other Senior Asian Immigrants	
	1. Isolation
	2. Financial Dependence
	3. Lack of Access to Transport
	4. Language Barrier
	5. Lack of Knowledge about available services (Para-transit Transport, Library, English classes, senior groups' meeting)
	6. Health Insurance (State Dependent)
	7. Emotional distance with Family
	8. Lack of Meaningful Role

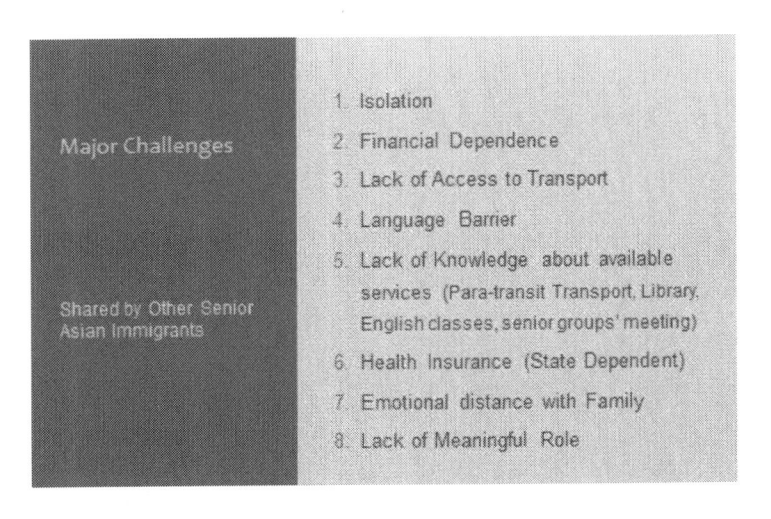

Figure 15. Major Challenges faced by AI Senior Immigrants

Although visitors were excluded from this study, whether it was senior centers or temples or parks or cultural events, there were as many seniors on visitors' visa as there were citizens and residents. In informal discussions, many of these visiting parents were quite clear that visiting the USA is fine but they will definitely not want to live here on permanent basis. The major causes reported were forced social isolation and dependence on children that living in this country entails. Similar sentiments were expressed by participants in the study by Rangaswamy (2000).

In order to combat the challenges described above, the possible next steps towards solutions include:

1. Creation of a directory of places seniors visit (formal and informal): This would be helpful for newcomers moving to the region as well as seniors who are already residing in that locality but are unaware that other seniors regularly meet in that area.
2. Representation in mainstream agencies: Some of the agencies include:
    - Council on Aging and other similar organizations: First steps towards this have been taken and the author is now a member of the Advisory Committee of Council on Aging Silicon Valley
    - NAMI
    - County Ethnic and Cultural Communities Advisory Committees
    - Aging Services Collaborative in Santa Clara County
3. Advocating for services in Hindi
4. Working with Outreach and other transport agencies: As isolation is one of the biggest concerns of AI immigrant seniors, an affordable way of commuting will really help in reducing the isolation
5. Creation of resource Lists: A list of resources that are relevant to the cultural needs of AI seniors can be compiled. This could, for example, include nursing homes or assisted

living homes where Indian food is available; or crisis hotlines where one can talk anonymously.
6. Psycho-education: This could include informing seniors about services already available in various Indian Languages
7. Forming volunteer groups: The need to find meaning in life can be met if seniors engage in volunteer activities for the causes they believe in. In informal discussion, several seniors indicated that they tried to offer their services on volunteer basis but did not receive encouraging response from non-profit organizations as well as from formal institutes such as school districts. One such senior who is a physician stated that he goes to India every year for several months as agencies are more receptive in India and he is able to carry out volunteer activities there.
8. Building awareness in Indian community in Silicon Valley: Of paramount importance is to start the dialog within Indian community, and to raise awareness about the issues that seniors face. To that end, first steps have been taken. Philanthropist and social entrepreneur, Manjula Gupta, recently produced a television show highlighting the needs of the seniors in her award winning "Chai With Manjula" series (Chai With Manjula, n.d.). The show focused on late immigrants, the population of this study, and the results of the present research were summarized there. The program was aired on the public television channels of various Bay-Area cities in 2012, and is available online at http://www.chaiwithmanjula.com/media/SeniorsfromIndia.html

Findings of this study were consistent with the QoL model for older ethnic migrants (Brockmann, 2002) and the key factors that influence QoL of older adults across different ethnic groups (Grewal et al., 2004). Extending the model proposed by Brockmann, this study proposes that six key domains impact the QoL of seniors: (a) political and legal context, (b) autonomy or independence, (c) social support network, (d) sense of identity or belonging, (e) meaningful role, and (f) health. Further, there are four subfactors for autonomy or independence: mastery or self-efficacy in the new culture, access to transportation, financial dependence, and dependence due to language barrier. These domains and subdomains as well as the eight major problems identified above highlight the importance of late-life immigration on the QoL of AI seniors.

Epilogue

Contrary to the popular perception that immigration results in better living and upward social mobility, for the study population, late life immigration has depleted their social capital and in many cases resulted in downward social mobility. Many have lost their independence, sense of self-efficacy and self-confidence, and are now dependent on their children or government. Although they educated, motivated, and enabled their children to immigrate and get established in the United States, often their contributions are neither remembered nor recognized. The AI community in the Bay Area has come a long way in the last 20 years. It is building roots and establishing support structures. Now is the right time to understand and address the concerns and needs of AI immigrant seniors and to recognize and honor their contributions.

REFERENCES

Abramson, T., Trejo, L., & Lai, D. (2002). Culture and mental health: Providing appropriate services for a diverse older population. *Generations, 26*(1), 21. Retrieved from Psychology and Behavioral Sciences Collection database.

Administration on Aging [AOA], Department of Health & Human Services. (2009). *Historical Evolution of Programs for Older Americans.* Retrieved from: http://www.aoa.gov/aoaroot/aoa_programs/oaa/resources/History.aspx

Administration on Aging [AOA], Department of Health & Human Services. (2010). *Older Americans Act.* Retrieved from: www.aoa.gov/aoaroot/aoa_programs/oaa/index.aspx

Agarwal-Narale, T. (2005). *Mental health of South Asian women: Dialogues with recent immigrants on post-migration, help-seeking and coping strategies.* Retrieved from Proquest Dissertations and Theses database. (AAT MR22697)

Aggarwal, A. N., Agarwal, R., Gupta, D., & Jindal, S. K. (2010). Validation of a Hindi translation of mini asthma quality of life questionnaire in North Indian patients with bronchial asthma. *The Indian Journal of Chest Diseases & Allied Sciences, 52*, 83–89. Retrieved from http://medind.nic.in/iae/t10/i2/iaet10i2p83.pdf

Akhtar, S. (1999). *Immigration and Identity: Turmoil, treatment, and Transformation.* Northvale, NJ: Jason Aronson Inc.

America.gov: Engaging the World. (n.d.). *Books: History.* Retrieved from: http://www.america.gov/publications/books.html

American Psychiatric Association. (2000). *Diagnostic and Statistical Manual of Mental Disorders, Fourth Edition, Text Revision.* Washington, DC:American Psychiatric Association.

Andrews, F. M., & Withey, S. B. (1976). *Social indicators of well-being: Americans' perceptions of life quality.* New York, NY: Plenum.

Badruddoja, R. (2007). *The ABCD conundrum: What does it mean to be a South Asian-American woman?* Retrieved from

Proquest Dissertations and Theses database. (AAT 3319415)

Balkrishna, A. (2007). *Yog: In synergy with medical science*. Hardwar, Uttarakhand, India: Divya Prakashan.

Bandura, A. (1977). Self-efficacy: Toward a unifying theory of behavioral change. *Psychological Review, 84*(2), 191–215. Retrieved from http://www.des.emory.edu/mfp/Bandura1977PR.pdf

Bandura, A. (1994). Self-efficacy. In V. S. Ramachaudran (Ed.), *Encyclopedia of human behavior, Vol. 4* (pp. 71–81). New York, NY: Academic Press. Retrieved from http://www.des.emory.edu/mfp/BanEncy.html

Barron, A. M. (2000). *Life meanings and the experience of cancer: Application of Newman's research method and phenomenological analysis*. Retrieved from Dissertations & Theses: Full Text database. (AAT 3008589)

Batalova, J. (2009). Immigration reform in the United States: Raising key questions. *Generations, 32*(4), 73–79. Retrieved from Academic Search Premier database.

Beckerman, N., & Corbett, L. (2008). Immigration and families: Treating acculturative stress from a systemic framework. *Family Therapy, 35*(2), 63–81. Retrieved from PsycINFO database.

Berry, J. W. (1990). Acculturation and adaptation: A general framework. In W. H. Holtzman, & T. H. Bornemann (Eds.), *Mental health of immigrants and refugees: Proceedings of a conference sponsored by Hogg Foundation for mental health and World Federation of mental health* (pp. 90–102). Austin, TX: Hogg Foundation for Mental Health.

Bhattacharya, G. (2008). Acculturating Indian immigrant men in New York City: Applying the social capital construct to understand their experiences and health. *Journal of Immigrant & Minority Health, 10*(2), 91–101. Retrieved from Academic Search Complete database.

Bijlani, R., Vempati, R., Yadav, R., Ray, R., Gupta, V., Sharma, R., et al. (2005). A brief but comprehensive lifestyle education program based on yoga reduces risk factors for cardiovascular disease and diabetes mellitus. *The Journal of Alternative and Complementary Medicine, 11*(2), 267–274, doi:10.1089/acm.2005.11.267.

Bowling, A. (2005). *Ageing well: Quality of life in old age*. New York, NY: Open University Press.

Bowling, A. (2009). Perceptions of active ageing in Britain: Divergences between minority ethnic and whole population samples. *Age & Ageing, 38*(6), 703-710. Retrieved from CINAHL database.

Brazier, A., Mulkins, A., & Verhoef, M. (2006). Evaluating a yogic breathing and meditation intervention for individuals living with HIV/AIDS. *American Journal of Health Promotion, 20*(3), 192-195. Retrieved from PsycINFO database.

Brockmann, M. (2002). Towards a model of quality of life for older ethnic minority migrants in Germany, Austria and the UK. *European Societies, 4*(3), 285–306. doi:10.1080/1461669022000013577.

Brommer, S. J. (2004). *"We walk with them": South Asian women's organizations in Northern California confront domestic abuse*. Retrieved from Proquest Dissertations and Theses database. (AAT 3136874)

Brown, P. L. (2009, August 30). Invisible immigrants, old and left with 'nobody to talk to.' *New York Times*. Retrieved October 2, 2010, from http://www.nytimes.com/2009/08/31/us/31elder.html?_r=2&pagewanted=3

Brown, I., Friefeld, S., & Schiller, C. (1993). *Quality of life for persons with developmental disabilities: An annotated bibliography*. Retrieved July 10, 2010, from The Centre for Health Promotion, University of Toronto website: http://www.utoronto.ca/qol/biblioint.htm

Brown, R., & Gerbarg, P. (2005). Sudarshan kriya yogic breathing in the treatment of stress, anxiety, and depression: Part II- clinical applications and guidelines. *The Journal of Alternative and Complementary Medicine, 11*(4), 711–717. doi:10.1089/acm.2005.11.711.

Brown, S., Bean, F., & Bachmeier, J. (2009). Aging societies and the changing logic of immigration. *Generations, 32*(4), 11-17. Retrieved from Academic Search Premier database.

Burke, A., & Marconett, S. (2008). The role of breath in yogic traditions: Alternate nostril breathing. *Biofeedback, 36*(2), 67–69. Retrieved from Academic Search Complete database.

Burr, J. A., Gerst, K., Kwan, N., & Mutchler, J. E. (2009). Economic well-being and welfare program participation among older immigrants in the United States. *Generations, 32*(4), 53–60. Retrieved from Academic Search Premier database.

Campbell, A., Converse, P., & Rodgers, W. (1976). *The quality of American life: Perceptions, evaluations, and satisfactions.* New York, NY: Russell Sage Foundation.

Carlin, J. (1990). Refugee and Immigrant Populations at Special Risk. In W. H. Holtzman, & T. H. Bornemann (Eds.), *Mental health of immigrants and refugees* (pp. 224-233). Austin, TX: University of Texas Press.

Carr, A. J., & Higginson, I. J. (2001). Are quality of life measures patient centered? *British Medical Journal, 322*(7298), 1357–60. (Document ID: 74107945).

Center for Immigration Studies. (1995). *Three decades of mass immigration: The legacy of the 1965 immigration act.* Retrieved July 21, 2010, from http://www.cis.org/articles/1995/back395.html

Chai With Manjula. (n.d.). *A show about giving.* Retrieved August 15, 2011, from http://chaiwithmanjula.org/

Chandler, J. F. (2009). *The use of social and temporal comparison to explore the process of quality of life evaluation in older adults.* Retrieved from Proquest Dissertations and Theses database. (AAT 3390543)

Chandra, P., Satyanarayana, V., Satishchandra, P., Satish, K., & Kumar, M. (2009). Do men and women with HIV differ in their quality of life? A study from South India. *AIDS and Behavior, 13*(1), 110–7. (Document ID: 1620120851).

Chattopadhyay, S. (2005). Spiritual and religious themes in psychiatric management: A proposed 'biopsychosocial' model. *Internet Journal of World Health & Societal Politics, 2*(1), 13–21. Retrieved from Academic Search Complete database

Chokkanathan, S. (2009). Resources, stressors and psychological distress among older adults in Chennai, India. *Social Science & Medicine, 68* (), 243–250. (Document ID: 10.1016/j.socscimed.2008.10.008).

Choudhry, U. (2001). Uprooting and resettlement experiences of South Asian immigrant women. *Western Journal of Nursing Research, 23*(4), 376. Retrieved from Academic Search Complete database.

City of Fremont Human Services, Aging and Family Services Division. (2009). *The how-to guide for immigrant seniors.* Retrieved from: http://www.capseniors.org/The_How-To_Guide_for_Immigrant_Seniors.pdf

Cloninger, S. (2008). *Theories of personality, understanding persons.* New Jersey: Pearson Education Inc.

Community Ambassador Program for Seniors. (n.d.). *CAPS Demographics and History: Tri-City Demographics.* Retrieved July 19, 2010, from http://capseniors.org/history.html

Community Partnerships for Community Ambassador Program for Seniors [CAPS]. (n.d.). *CAPS Services.* Retrieved July 19, 2010, from http://capseniors.org/services.html

Community Partnerships for Older Adults. (n.d.). *Demographics.* Retrieved September 21, 2010, from http://cpfoa-stage.musk.usm.maine.edu/resources/levelthree.aspx?sectionGUID=d1274277-fa64-4de2-a5cf-6c1c2d45f697 and http://cpfoa-stage.musk.usm.maine.edu/aboutcpfoa/

Council on Aging Silicon Valley. (2009). *Senior services directory, Santa clara county: A compendium of resources for seniors, family members and caregivers.* San Jose, CA: Council on Aging Silicon Valley

County of Santa Clara. (n.d.). *History of the County*. Retrieved August 15, 2009, from http://www.sccgov.org/portal/site/scc/chlevel3?path=%2Fv7%2FSCC%20Public%20Portal%2FCounty%20Connection%2FAbout%20the%20County%2FHistory%20of%20the%20County

Cross, P. (2003). Demographic and economic profile. In *Asian American elders in New York city: A study of health, social needs, quality of life and quality of care* (pp. 12–27). New York, NY: The Asian American Federation of New York.

Da Silva, G., Lorenzi-Filho, G., & Lage, L. (2007). Effects of yoga and the addition of Tui Na in patients with fibromyalgia. *Journal of Alternative & Complementary Medicine, 13*(10), 1107-1114. doi:10.1089/acm.2007.0615.

Danhauer, S., Tooze, J., Farmer, D., Campbell, C., McQuellon, R., Barrett, R., et al. (2008). Restorative yoga for women with ovarian or breast cancer: Findings from a pilot study. *Journal of the Society for Integrative Oncology, 6*(2), 47–58. doi:10.2310/7200.2008.0008.

Daniels, R. (2007). The immigration act of 1965: Intended and unintended consequences. In U.S. Department of State publication, *Historians on America: Decisions that made a difference* (pp. 76–83). Retrieved from http://www.america.gov/publications/books/historiansonamerica.html

Das Gupta, M. (1999). *Identities, interests and alternative spaces: A transnational perspective on South Asian political participation in the United States.* Retrieved from Proquest Dissertations and Theses database. (AAT 9917908)

Deepak, A. C. (2004). *Identity formation and the negotiation of desire: Women of the South Asian diaspora in the United States.* Retrieved from Proquest Dissertations and Theses database. (AAT 3115342)

Department of Homeland Security. (2010). *Yearbook of immigration statistics: 2009: Table 2: Persons obtaining legal permanent resident status by region and selected country of last residence: Fiscal years 1820 to 2009*. Retrieved August 24, 2010, from the Department of

Homeland Security website: http://www.dhs.gov/files/statistics/publications/LPR09.shtm and http://www.dhs.gov/xlibrary/assets/statistics/yearbook/2009/table02.xls

Derry, C. A. (1996). *The relationship of acculturation to attitudes inhibiting Indian-Americans from seeking mental health services*. Retrieved from Proquest Dissertations and Theses database. (AAT 9623537)

Dissart, J., & Deller, S. (2000). Quality of life in the planning literature. *Journal of Planning Literature, 15*(1), 135. Retrieved from Academic Search Premier database.

Diwan, S.. (2008). Limited English proficiency, Social Network Characteristics, and Depressive Symptoms Among Older Immigrants. *The Journals of Gerontology: Series B Psychological sciences and social sciences, 63B*(3), S184–91. Retrieved from ProQuest Psychology Journals. (Document ID: 1507374751).

Diwan, S., & Jonnalagadda, S. (2001). Social Integration and Health Among Asian Indian Immigrants in the United States. *Journal of Gerontological Social Work, 36*(1/2), 45–62. Retrieved from SocINDEX with Full Text database.

Diwan, S., Jonnalagadda, S., & Balaswamy, S. (2004). Resources Predicting Positive and Negative Affect During the Experience of Stress: A Study of Older Asian Indian Immigrants in the United States. *The Gerontologist, 44*(5), 605–14. Retrieved from ProQuest Psychology Journals. (Document ID: 730766121).

Donesky-Cuenco, D., Nguyen, H., Paul, S., & Carrieri-Kohlman, V. (2009). Yoga therapy decreases dyspnea-related distress and improves functional performance in people with chronic obstructive pulmonary disease: A pilot study. *The Journal of Alternative and Complementary Medicine, 15*(3), 225–234. doi:10.1089/acm.2008.0389.

Durvasula, R., & Mylvaganam, G. (1994). Mental health of Asian Indian: Relevant issues and community implications. *Journal of Community Psychology, 22*(2), 97–108. Retrieved from Psychology and Behavioral Sciences Collection database.

Elliott, D. J., Trier, P. M., & Stein, N. (1986). Mastery, stress, and coping in marriage among chronic pain patients. *Journal of Behavioral Medicine, 9*(6), 549–558. Retrieved from http://www.springerlink.com/content/q505830r37l75973/

Exchange-rates.org - World currency exchange rates and currency exchange rate history. (n.d.). *Indian Rupees (INR) to 1 US Dollar (USD)*. Retrieved from: http://www.exchange-rates.org/history/INR/USD/T

Farver, J., Bhadha, B., & Narang, S. (2002). Acculturation and psychological functioning in Asian Indian adolescents. *Social Development, 11*(1), 11–29. doi:10.1111/1467-9507.00184.

Felce, D., & Perry, J. (1995). Quality of Life: Its definition and measurement. *Research in Developmental Disabilities, 16*(1), 51–74. doi:10.1016/0891-4222(94)00028-8

Fernandez, L. (2005, July 12). Elderly immigrants face strain of aging in a strange land. *Knight Ridder Tribune News Service*, p.1. Retrieved from ProQuest Newsstand. (Document ID: 866080641)

Freedman, T. G. (1991). *Women's stories: The symbolic meaning of breast cancer*. Retrieved from Dissertations & Theses: Full Text database. (AAT 9134410)

Frisch, M. (1994). *Quality of life inventory*. Retrieved from Mental Measurements Yearbook database.

Gans, H. J. (2007). Acculturation, assimilation and mobility. *Ethnic and Racial Studies, 30*(1), 152–164. doi:10.1080/01419870601006637.

Gauntlett, K. A. (2009). *Characteristics of late-life happiness: The cognitions, behaviors, emotions, and attitudes of happy individuals during late-life development*. Unpublished doctoral dissertation, Argosy University, San Francisco Bay Area Campus – California.

Gee, G., & Ponce, N. (2010). Associations between racial discrimination, limited English proficiency, and health-related quality of life among 6 Asian ethnic groups in

California. *American Journal of Public Health, 100*(5), 888–895. doi:10.2105/AJPH.2009.178012.

Ghosh, M. (2007). *Effects of acculturation on young adult South Asian-Indians.* Retrieved from Proquest Dissertations and Theses database. (AAT 3286265)

Gill, N. K. (2008) *East Indian immigrants' experiences and psychotherapy in the United States: A comprehensive survey of the literature and proposed model for working with this population.* Unpublished doctoral dissertation, Argosy University, San Francisco Bay Area Campus – California.

Gokal, Shillito, & Maharaj, 2007). Positive impact of yoga and pranayam on obesity, hypertension, blood sugar, and cholesterol: A pilot assessment. *The Journal of Alternative and Complementary Medicine, 13*(10), 1056–1057. doi:10.1089/acm.2007.0679

Gopinath, S. (2005, January). *Foreign exchange regulatory regimes in India: From control to management.* Address by Deputy Governor at the Conference organized by the Forum for Free Enterprise at Mumbai, India on January 25, 2005. Retrieved from Reserve Bank of India website: http://rbidocs.rbi.org.in/rdocs/Speeches/PDFs/60912.pdf

Gorski, T. (1989). *Understanding the twelve steps: An interpretation and guide for recovering people.* New York, NY: Prentice Hall Press.

Government of India: Ministry of Home Affairs, Office of the Registrar General & Census Commissioner. (2011). *Census 2011: Home / Provisional Population Totals India.* Retrieved from: http://www.censusindia.gov.in/2011-prov-results/prov_results_paper1_india.html

Government of India: Ministry of Social Justice And Empowerment. (2007). *The maintenance and welfare of parents and senior citizens bill.* Retrieved from: http://www.prsindia.org/uploads/media/1182337322/scr1193026940_Senior_Citizen.pdf

Greer, P. T. (1998). *Breast cancer: Imaginal realms of meaning.* Retrieved from Dissertations & Theses: Full Text database. (AAT 9913751)

Grewal, I., Nazroo, J., Bajekal, M., Blane, D., & Lewis, J. (2004). Influences on quality of life: a qualitative investigation of ethnic differences among older people in England. *Journal of Ethnic & Migration Studies, 30*(4), 737–761. doi:10.1080/13691830410001699595.

Grewal, M. (2004). *Communicative planning for the marginalized: The case of abused Asian Indian immigrant women.* Retrieved from Proquest Dissertations and Theses database. (AAT 3138161)

Grinberg, L., & Grinberg, R. (1989). *Psychoanalytic perspectives on migration and exile* (N. Festinger, Trans.). New Haven, CT: Yale University Press.

Gupta, R., & Pillai, V. (2002). Elder care giving in South Asian families: Implications for social service. *Journal of Comparative Family Studies, 33*(4), 565. Retrieved from SocINDEX with Full Text database

Gupta-Carlson, H. (2007). *No place to call home: Remapping America's 'Middletown' from a South Asian perspective.* Retrieved from Proquest Dissertations and Theses database. (AAT 3264851)

Haas, B. (1999). Clarification and integration of similar quality of life concepts. *Image: Journal of Nursing Scholarship, 31*(3), 215–220. Retrieved from CINAHL database

Han, J. K. (2007). *Becoming South Asian: An examination of identity, intergroup relations, and responses to 9/11.* Retrieved from Proquest Dissertations and Theses database. (AAT 3264973)

Hans, N. (2002). The role of ethnic identity and acculturation in determining acculturative stress in Asian Indians. *Dissertation Abstracts International: Section B: The Sciences and Engineering, 62*(7-B). 3378.

Haroon, N., Aggarwal, A., Lawrence, A., Agarwal, V., & Misra, R. (2007). Impact of rheumatoid arthritis on quality of life.

Modern Rheumatology, 17(4), 290–295. (Document ID: 1319788081)

Harris-Reid, M. A. (1998). *Coming to America: Immigration, stress, and mental health*. Retrieved from Proquest Dissertations and Theses database. (AAT 9909899)

Harvard Health Publications. (2009). Yoga for anxiety and depression. *Harvard Mental Health Letter, 25*(10), 4–5. Retrieved from Psychology and Behavioral Sciences Collection database.

Hawthorne, G., Herrman, H., & Murphy, B. (2006). Interpreting the WHOQOL-Brèf: Preliminary population norms and effect sizes. *Social Indicators Research, 77*(1), 37–59. (Document ID: 1061583151).

Hayes-Bautista, D., Hsu, P., Perez, A., & Gamboa, C. (2002). The 'browning' of the graying of America: Diversity in the elderly population and policy implications. *Generations, 26*(3), 15–24. Retrieved from CINAHL database.

Health Consumer Alliance. (2008). *Medi-Cal Overview: Chapter Two: Eligibility*. Retrieved from: http://healthconsumer.org/Medi-CalOverview2008Ch2.pdf

Health Trust. (2011). Healthy Aging: Seniors respond to service cutbacks by becoming advocates for their peers. *Health Trust Fall 2011 Newsletter*, 5-5. Retrieved from http://www.healthtrust.org/news/documents/HealthTrust_Fall2011Newsletter_Final.pdf.

Henderson, S., & Whiteford, H. (2003). Social capital and mental health. *Lancet, 362*(9383), 505–506. Retrieved October 16, 2008, from Academic Search Complete database.

Hensel, E. (2001). Is satisfaction a valid concept in the assessment of quality of life of people with intellectual disabilities? A review of the literature. *Journal of Applied Research in Intellectual Disabilities, 14*(4), 311. Retrieved from Academic Search Premier database.

Hepner, K. A. (2003). *The role of experience-expectation discrepancy and depressive symptomatology in quality of life*. Retrieved from Dissertations & Theses: Full Text database. (AAT 3106999).

Hess, G. R. (2006). Liberalization of U.S. policies on East Indian immigration and naturalization. In A. Ruggiero (Ed.), *Coming to America: The East Indians* (pp. 61–65). Formington Hills, MI: Thomson Gale, a part of the Thomson Corporation. (Original work published 1982)

Higgs, P., Hyde, M., Wiggins, R., & Blane, D. B. (2003). Researching quality of life in early old age: The importance of the sociological dimension. *Social Policy & Administration, 37*(3), 239–252. doi:10.1111/1467-9515. 00336.

Hua, V. (2004, April 17). Nation/Asian Indian needs affect elder care. *San Francisco Chronicle*, p. B.3. Retrieved June 25, 2010, from ProQuest Newsstand. (Document ID: 618854421)

Hyde, M., Wiggins, R., Higgs, P., & Blane, D. B. (2003). A measure of quality of life in early old age: the theory, development and properties of a needs satisfaction model (CASP-19). *Aging & Mental Health 2003, 7*(3): 186–194. doi: 10.1080/ 1360786031000101157.

India Community Center. (n.d.). *Seniors Programs*. Retrieved from: http://www.indiacc.org/seniors

Indian Export Import Portal: A complete EXIM guide for businesses. (n.d.). Foreign exchange regulation act, 1973 (Act 46 of 1973), As amended by the Foreign exchange regulation (amendment) act, 1993 (Act 29 of 1993). Retrieved from: http://exim.indiamart.com/act-regulations/fera-1993.html

Jeste, D., & Vahia, I. (2008). Comparison of the conceptualization of wisdom in ancient Indian literature with modern views: Focus on the Bhagavad Gita. *Psychiatry: Interpersonal & Biological Processes, 71*(3), 197–209. Retrieved from Academic Search Complete database.

Joint Venture: Silicon Valley Network (JVSVN), & Silicon Valley Community Foundation (SVCF). (2010). *2010 Index of Silicon Valley*. Retrieved August, 25, 2010, from http://www.silicon

valleycf.org/news-resources/docs/2010%20Index-final.pdf

Jonnalagadda, S., Diwan, S., & Desai, D. (2002). Perceived needs of Asian Indian immigrants in the U.S. *The Gerontologist: 55th Annual Scientific Meeting "Relationships in a Changing, 42*(1), 108-109. (Document ID: 654488241).

Jonnalagadda, S., & Diwan, S. (2005). Health Behaviors, Chronic Disease Prevalence and Self-Rated Health of Older Asian Indian Immigrants in the U.S. *Journal of Immigrant Health, 7*(2), 75–83. doi:10.1007/s10903-005-2640-x

Kalavar, J. M. (1998). *The Asian Indian elderly in America: An examination of values, family, and life satisfaction.* New York, NY: Garland Publishing.

Kalavar, J. M. (2003, Winter). Recent senior immigrants from India. *National Indo-American Association for Senior Citizen's Newsletter, 4.* Retrieved from http://www.niaasc.org

Kalavar, J., & Van Willigen, J. (2005). Older Asian Indians resettled in America: Narratives about households, culture and generation. *Journal of Cross-Cultural Gerontology, 20*(3), 213–230. doi:10.1007/s10823-006-9004-4.

Kallivayalil, D. J. (2006). *Narratives of suffering of South Asian immigrant survivors of domestic violence.* Retrieved from Proquest Dissertations and Theses database. (AAT 3242888)

Khanna, A., McDowell, T., Perumbilly, S., & Titus, G. (2009). Working with Asian Indian American families: A Delphi study. *Journal of Systemic Therapies, 28*(1), 52–71. doi:10.1521/jsyt.2009.28.1.52.

Kobayashi, K. (2003). Do intersections of diversity matter? An exploration of the relationship between identity markers and health for mid- to later-life Canadians. *Canadian Ethnic Studies, 35*(3), 85–98. Retrieved from Academic Search Premier database.

Kochhar, P., Rajadhyaksha, S., & Suvarna, V. (2007). Translation and validation of brief patient health questionnaire against DSM IV as a tool to diagnose major depressive disorder in

Indian patients. *Journal of Postgraduate Medicine, 53*(2), 102–107. Retrieved from Academic Search Complete database.

Kreitler, S., & Kreitler, M. (2006). Multidimensional quality of life: A new measure of quality of life in adults. *Social Indicators Research, 76*(1), 5–33. doi:10.1007/s11205-005-4854-7.

Krishnan, A., & Berry, J. (1992). Acculturative stress and acculturation attitudes among Indian immigrants to the United States. *Psychology and Developing Societies, 4*(2), 187–212. doi: 10.1177/097133369200400206

Lai, D. (2010). Socio-cultural determinants of mental health of elderly immigrants: Lessons learned from Canada. *European Psychiatry, 25*(1), 706. doi:10.1016/S0924-9338(10)70700-8.

Lai, D., & Surood, S. (2008). Predictors of depression in aging South Asian Canadians. *Journal of Cross-Cultural Gerontology, 23*(1),57–75. doi:10.1007/s10823-007-9051-5.

Lal, V. (2006). East Indians establish a political identity. In A. Ruggiero (Ed.), *Coming to America: The East Indians* (pp. 97-103). Formington Hills, MI: Thomson Gale, a part of the Thomson Corporation.

Lamb, S. (2009a). *Aging and the Indian diaspora: Cosmopolitan families in India and abroad.* Bloomington, IN: Indiana University Press.

Lamb, S. (2009b). Elder residences and outsourced sons: Remaking aging in cosmopolitan India. In J. Sokolovsky (Ed.), *The cultural context of aging: Worldwide perspectives* (pp. 418–440). Westport, CT: Praeger Publishers.

Lambert, W. E., & Taylor, D. M. (1990). Language and culture in the lives of immigrants and refugees. In W. H. Holtzman, & T. H. Bornemann (Eds.), *Mental health of immigrants and refugees: Proceedings of a conference sponsored by Hogg Foundation for mental health and World Federation of mental health* (pp. 103–128). Austin, Texas: Hogg Foundation for Mental Health.

Langit, G. F. (2007). *Intergenerational conflict and acculturation with Filipino-American parents and children seeking mental health services.* Unpublished doctoral dissertation, Argosy University, San Francisco Bay Area Campus – California.

Leach, M. A. (2009). America's older immigrants: A profile. *Generations, 32*(4), 34–39. Retrieved from Academic Search Premier database.

Lin, T., & Yao, G. (2009). Evaluating item discrimination power of WHOQOL-bref from an item response model perspectives. *Social Indicators Research, 91*(2), 141–153. (Document ID: 1649421681).

Liu, W. (1980). Foreword. In P. K. Nandi, *the quality of life of asian americans: An exploratory study in a middle-size community* (pp. ix - xiii). Chicago, IL: Pacific/Asian American Mental Health Research Center.

Low, G. (2005). *Quality of life among older adults – A proposed conceptual model.* University of Victoria (Canada). ProQuest Dissertations and Theses. Retrieved from http://search.proquest.com/docview/304983292?accountid=34899

Löwe, B., Decker, O., Muller, S., Brähler, E., Schellberg, D., Herzog, W., & Herzberg, P. (2008). Validation and standardization of the generalized anxiety disorder screener (GAD-7) in the general population. *Medical Care, 46*(3), 266–274. Retrieved from EBSCOhost.

Ludden, J. (2006, May 9). 1965 Immigration Law Changed Face of America. *National Public Radio*, Retrieved from http://www.npr.org/templates/story/story.php?storyId=5391395

Majmundar, H. (2003). *Mapping the maze: A guide to welfare for elderly immigrants.* Palo Alto, CA: H. J. Majmundar.

Markides, K. S., Salinas, J., & Sheffield, K. (2009). The health of older immigrants. *Generations, 32*(4), 46–52. Retrieved from Academic Search Premier database.

Markoff, J. (2009, April 16). Searching for Silicon Valley. *New York Times*, Retrieved from http://travel.nytimes.com/2009/04/17/travel/escapes/17Amer.html?pagewanted=all

Martin, A., Rief, W., Klaiberg, A., & Braehler, E. (2006). Validity of the Brief Patient Health Questionnaire Mood Scale (PHQ-9) in the general population. *General Hospital Psychiatry, 28*(1), 71–77. Retrieved from CINAHL database.

Mazaheri, M. (2010). Overall, and specific life satisfaction domains: Preliminary Iranian students norms. *Iranian Journal of Public Health, 39*(2), 89–94. (Document ID: 2074229411)

Mehta, R. R. (2005). *An exploratory study examining the psychological needs of Asian-Indian clients as perceived by Asian-Indian psychotherapists.* Unpublished doctoral dissertation, Argosy University, San Francisco Bay Area Campus – California.

Mehta, S. (1994). Acculturation and mental health: Asian Indian immigrants in the United States. *Dissertation Abstracts International: Section B: The Sciences and Engineering, 54*(12-B). 6466.

Mehta, S. (1998). Relationship between acculturation and mental health for Asian Indian immigrants in the United States. *Genetic, Social & General Psychology Monographs, 124*(1), 61. Retrieved from Psychology and Behavioral Sciences Collection database.

Mehta, T. G. (2005). *Multiple selves in South Asian adolescents.* Retrieved from Proquest Dissertations and Theses database. (AAT 3177361)

Melwani, L. (2006). East Indians and the impact of the September 11 terrorist attacks. In A. Ruggiero (Ed.), *Coming to America: The East Indians* (pp. 104 - 109). Formington Hills, MI: Thomson Gale, a part of the Thomson Corporation.

Mendonca, L., Nichols, R., & Rajgopal, K. (2000). The bay leads the way. *McKinsey Quarterly,* (1), 10-12. Retrieved from Business Source Complete database.

Miltiades, H. B. (1999). *Filial expression across geographic boundaries: Asian Indian immigrants to the United States and their non-immigrant parents.* Retrieved from

Dissertations & Theses database. (AAT 9951874)

Miltiades, H. B. (2002). The social and psychological effect of an adult child's emigration on non-immigrant Asian Indian elderly parents. *Journal of Cross-Cultural Gerontology, 17*(1), 33–55.

Moffatt, S., & Mackintosh, J. (2009). Older people's experience of proactive welfare rights advice: Qualitative study of a South Asian community. *Ethnicity & Health, 14*(1), 5–25. doi:10.1080/13557850802056455.

Mui, A. (2003). Physical health, mental health, and quality of life. In *Asian American elders in New York City: A study of health, social needs, quality of life and quality of care* (pp. 28–46). New York, NY: The Asian American Federation of New York.

Mui, A., & Cross, P. (2003a). Informal and formal supports. In *Asian American elders in New York city: A study of health, social needs, quality of life and quality of care* (pp. 47–84). New York, NY: The Asian American Federation of New York.

Mui, A., & Cross, P. (2003b). Traditional values, stress, and life satisfaction. In *Asian American elders in New York City: A study of health, social needs, quality of life and quality of care* (pp. 85–115). New York, NY: The Asian American Federation of New York.

Mui, A., & Kang, S. (2006). Acculturation stress and depression among Asian immigrant elders. *Social Work, 51*(3), 243–255. Retrieved from Academic Search Complete database.

Mui, A., Nguyen, D., Kang, D., & Domanski, M. (2006). Demographic profiles of Asian immigrant elderly residing in metropolitan ethnic enclave communities. *Journal of Ethnic & Cultural Diversity in Social Work, 15*(1/2), 193–214. doi:10.1300/J051v15n01-09.

Mui, A., & Shibusawa, T. (2008). *Asian American elders in the twenty-first century: Key indicators of well-being.* New York, NY: Columbia University Press.

Mullins, S. C. (1990). Social services for refugees and immigrants: Issues and problems. In W. H. Holtzman, & T.

H. Bornemann (Eds.), *Mental health of immigrants and refugees: Proceedings of a conference sponsored by Hogg Foundation for mental health and World Federation of mental health* (pp. 167–171). Austin, TX: Hogg Foundation for Mental Health.

Myers, D. (2009). Aging baby boomers and the effect of immigration: Rediscovering the intergenerational social contract. *Generations, 32*(4), 18–23. Retrieved from Academic Search Premier database.

Nandan, M. (2005). Adaptation to American culture: Voices of Asian Indian immigrants. *Journal of Gerontological Social Work, 44*(3/4), 175–203. doi:10. 1300/J083v44n03_11

Nandan, M. (2007). "Waves" of Asian Indian elderly immigrants: What can practitioners learn?. *Journal of Cross-Cultural Gerontology, 22*(4), 389–404. doi:10.1007/s10823-007-9042-6.

Nandi, P. K. (1980). *the quality of life of asian americans: An exploratory study in a middle-size community*. Chicago, IL: Pacific/Asian American Mental Health Research Center.

National Indo-American Association for Senior Citizens (NIAASC). (n.d.). *Issues and aspirations: Indian seniors in the United States of America*. Retrieved June 28, 2010, from http://www.niaasc.org/

National Indo-American Association for Senior Citizens (NIAASC). (2010). *Newsletter Spring/Summer 2010*. Retrieved November 14, 2010, from http://www.niaasc.org/

NRI Realty News. (n.d.). *FEMA rules & policies*. Retrieved from: http://www.nrirealtynews.com/nri-banking/fema-rules.php

Outreach. (n.d.). *Together we ride, mobile management center for Santa Clara County: Frequently asked questions: Senior transportation*. Retrieved from: http://www.outreach1.org/shared_pages/faqs/faq_seniortransportation.htm

Padmanabhan, P. (2010, August). Autumn Blues. *India Currents, 24*(5), 12–15.

Patel, U. N. (2005) *Understanding the under-utilization patterns of mental health services by Asian Indian Americans: A booklet for Asian Indian American physicians*. Unpublished doctoral dissertation, Alliant International University, Los Angeles – California

Pearlin, L., Lieberman, M., Menaghan, E., & Mullan, J. (1981). The stress process. *Journal of Health & Social Behavior, 22*(4), 337–356. Retrieved from Academic Search Premier database.

Pearlin, L., Nguyen, K., Schieman, S., & Milkie, M. (2007). The life-course origins of mastery among older people. *Journal of Health & Social Behavior, 48*(2), 164–179. Retrieved from Academic Search Premier database.

Pearlin, L., & Radabaugh, C. W. (1976). Economic strains and the coping function of alcohol. *American Journal of Sociology, 82*(3), 652–663. Retrieved from http://www.jstor.org/stable/2777343.

Pearlin, L., & Schooler, C. (1978). The structure of coping. *Journal of Health & Social Behavior, 19*(1), 2–21. Retrieved from Academic Search Premier database.

Periyakoil, V. S. (2004). Older Asian Indian Americans. In R. Adler & H. Kamel (Eds.), *Doorway thoughts: Cross-cultural health care for older adults. Volume 1* (pp. 68–79). Sudbury, MA: Jones & Bartlett/American Geriatrics Society.

Pfizer Inc. (n.d.). *PHQ and GAD-7 instructions*. Retrieved January 17, 2011, from Patient Health Questionnaire Screeners website: http://www.phqscreeners.com/instructions/instructions.pdf

Pfizer – PHQ Screeners. (n.d.). *Screener overview*. Retrieved April 6, 2011, from Patient Health Questionnaire Screeners website: http://www.phqscreeners.com/overview.aspx?Screener=03_GAD-7

Phelan, E., Williams, B., Meeker, K., Bonn, K., Frederick, J., LoGerfo, J., & Snowden, M. (2010). A study of the diagnostic accuracy of the PHQ-9 in primary care elderly. *BMC Family Practice*, 1163–71. doi:10.1186/1471-2296-11-63

Pillay, A. A. (2004). *Psychotherapy, psychoeducation, and*

resocialization treatment of male South Asian domestic violence perpetrators. Retrieved from Proquest Dissertations and Theses database. (AAT 3126435)

Poongothai, S., Pradeepa, R., Ganesan, A., & Mohan, V. (2009). Reliability and validity of a modified PHQ-9 item inventory (PHQ-12) as a screening instrument for assessing depression in Asian Indians (CURES-65). *The Journal Of The Association Of Physicians Of India, 57,* 147–152. Retrieved from MEDLINE database.

Portes, A., & Rumbaut, R. G. (2006). *Immigrant America: A portrait (3rd ed.)*. Berkeley, CA: University of California Press.

Power, M., Quinn, K., Schmidt, S., & the WHOQOL-OLD Group. (2005). Development of the WHOQOL-Old module. *Quality of Life Research, 14,* 2197–2214. doi: 10.1007/s11136-005-7380-9

Prasad, R. (1995). *The Bhagavad Gita: The song of God*. New Delhi, India: Motilal Banarsidas Publishers Private Ltd.

Prasad, R. (2009, July). *Residential and other related issues of Indian elders*. Paper presented at the Birhan Convention, Philadelphia, PA. Retrieved June 28, 2010, from http://www.niaasc.org/

Prasad, R. (2010, September). *Mobilization of services for senior citizens of Indian origin: How are we doing and what we have yet to do?*. Paper presented at the 30th Anniversary Convention of the National Federation of Indian-American Associations, New York, NY.

Prutkin, J., & Feinstein, A. (2002). Quality-of-life measurements: Origin and pathogenesis. *The Yale Journal of Biology and Medicine, 75*(2), 79–93. Retrieved from MEDLINE database.

Quality of Life Research Unit. (n.d.). *QOL Concepts: The quality of life model*. Retrieved August 10, 2010, from http://www.utoronto.ca/qol/concepts.htm

Rait, G., & Burns, A. (1997). Appreciating background and culture: The South Asian elderly and mental health. *International Journal of Geriatric Psychiatry, 12*(10), 973–977. Retrieved from Academic Search Premier database.

Raj, A. (2004). Indian diaspora in North America: The role of ethnic networks and organizations. Conference Papers – American Sociological Association, (pp.1–20). doi:asa_proceeding_34827.PDF

Rajiva, M. (2005). *Racing through adolescence: Becoming and belonging in the narratives of second generation South Asian girls.* Retrieved from Proquest Dissertations and Theses database. (AAT NR06742)

Ramdev, S. (2008). *Maharsi Patanjali's Yogadarsana: The yoga philosophy.* Hardwar, Uttarakhand, India: Divya Prakashan.

Ramdev, S. (n.d.). *Yog: Its philosophy & practice.* Hardwar, Uttarakhand, India: Divya Prakashan.

Rangaswamy, P. (2000). *Namaste America: Indian immigrants in an American Metropolis.* University Park, PA: The Pennsylvania State University Press.

Rangaswamy, P. (2007). *Indian Americans: The new immigrants.* R.D. Johnston (Series Ed.). New York, NY: Chelsea House, An imprint of Infobase publishing.

Reimers, D. M. (2006). East Indian immigration increases due to the 1965 U.S. immigration act. In A. Ruggiero (Ed.), *Coming to America: The East Indians* (pp. 74 - 82). Formington Hills, MI: Thomson Gale, a part of the Thomson Corporation.

Reserve Bank of India. (n.d.). *Foreign exchange management (possession and retention of foreign currency) regulations, 2000.* Retrieved from: http://rbi.org.in/Scripts/BS_FemaNotifications.aspx?Id=165

Roshanravan, S. (2007). *South Asian American identity formation and the politics of women of color.* Retrieved from Proquest Dissertations and Theses database. (AAT 3289099)

Rudrappa, S. (2001). *"White in public, Indian at home?": The practices of ethnicity among Indian immigrants in late 20th century United States.* Retrieved from Proquest Dissertations and Theses database. (AAT 3020821)

Ruggiero, A. (Ed.). (2006). *Coming to America: The East Indians.* Farmington Hills, MI: Thomson Gale, a part of the Thomson Corporation.

Ruggles, S. J., Alexander, T., Genadek, K., Goeken, R., Schroeder, M. B., & Sobek, M. (2010). *Integrated public use microdata series: Version 5.0 [Machine-readable database]*. Minneapolis, MN: University of Minnesota.

Ryan, A. S. (2003). Overview. In *Asian American elders in New York City: A study of health, social needs, quality of life and quality of care* (pp. 1–11). New York, NY: The Asian American Federation of New York.

Ryan, A. S., Mui, A., & Cross, P. (2003). *Asian American elders in New York City: A study of health, social needs, quality of life and quality of care*. New York, NY: The Asian American Federation of New York.

Sabl, A. (2009). Aging and immigration: An ethicist's perspective. *Generations, 32*(4), 87–92. Retrieved from Academic Search Premier database.

Samuel, L. (2008). *Disruption, displacement, ambivalence: The making of migrant identities among women in the Keralite diaspora*. Retrieved from Proquest Dissertations and Theses database. (AAT NR39050)

Sandhu, S. (2009). *Engineering the American Dream: An Ethnography of the Culture of Success for Asian Indian Elites in Los Angeles and the Silicon Valley*. Retrieved from Proquest Dissertations and Theses database. (UMI 3347824)

Santa Clara County Mental Health Department. (2010). *Cultural Competence Plan*. Retrieved November 29, 2011 from: http://www.sccgov.org/SCC/docs%2FMental%20Health%20Services%20(DEP)%2Fattachments%2FO_o%2FSanta%20Clara%20County%20CCP%20Full%2011-23-10.pdf

Santamaría, M. J., & Palma, M. (2008). *Immigrant integration in Silicon Valley: Legalization, language acquisition and bridging the cultural gap*. Retrieved August 15, 2010, from http://www.siliconvalleycf.org/grantmaking-strategies/pdf/research-paper-bridging-cultural-gap.pdf

Saxena, S., Chandiramani, K., & Bhargava, R. (1998). WHOQOL-Hindi: A questionnaire for assessing quality of life in health care settings in India. *The National Medical Journal Of India, 11*(4), 160–165.

Saxena, S., Quinn, K., Sharan, P., Naresh, B., Yuantao-Hao, & Power, M. (2005). Cross-linguistic equivalence of WHOQOL-100: A study from North India. *Quality of Life Research, 14*(3), 891–897. doi:10.1007/s11136-004-1084-4.

Saxenian, A. (2002). Silicon Valley's new immigrant high-growth entrepreneurs. *Economic Development Quarterly, 16*(1), 20–31. doi: 10.1177/0891242402016001003

Seeman, M. (2008). Psychosocial notebook: Summary of personal control. Retrieved from http://www.macses.ucsf.edu/research/psychosocial/control.php

Sen, A. H. (2002). *Mapping transnational boundaries: Urban cultural landscapes of South Asian immigrants in San Francisco and Berkeley, 1900--2000*. Retrieved from Proquest Dissertations and Theses database. (AAT 3082398)

Shankar, S. (2003). *Windows of opportunity: South Asian-American teenagers and the promise of technology in Silicon Valley*. Retrieved from Proquest Dissertations and Theses database. (AAT 3089334)

Shannahoff-Khalsa, D., Sramek, B., Kennel, M., & Jamieson, S. (2004). Hemodynamic observations on a yogic breathing technique claimed to help eliminate and prevent heart attacks: A pilot study. *Journal of Alternative & Complementary Medicine, 10*(5), 757–766. Retrieved from Academic Search Complete database.

Shariff, A. (2006). *Gender, acculturation, ethnic identity, and parenting stress among South Asian families*. Retrieved from Proquest Dissertations and Theses database. (AAT MR22200)

Sharma, R. (1998). *Multicultural perspectives on treatment approaches to men of color who batter women: The case of Indo-Canadian men*. Retrieved from Proquest Dissertations and Theses database. (AAT 3112169)

Sharma, A. (2006). *Provision of domestic violence services for immigrant women: A case for re-examining the concept of cultural competence*. Retrieved from Proquest Dissertations and Theses database. (AAT 3243425)

Shrestha, S. (2010). *Quality of life among elderly Nepali women*. The Pennsylvania State University. Retrieved from Proquest Dissertations and Theses database. (UMI 3436101)

Singh, M., Arteaga, S., & Zea, M. (2002). *Factors related to depression and anxiety among East and South Asian American women*. Washington, DC: American Psychological Association, Public Interest Directorate; Women's Programs. Retrieved from PsycEXTRA database.

Smith, A.E., Sim, J., Scharf, T., & Phillipson, C. (2004). Determinants of quality of life amongst older people in deprived neighborhoods. *Ageing & Society, 24,* 793–814. doi:10.1017/S0144686X04002569.

Social Security Online. (n.d.). *Supplemental security income*. Retrieved from http://www.socialsecurity.gov/ssi/index.htm

South Asian Heart Center, El Camino Hospital. (n.d.). *CAD Statistics*. Retrieved from http://www.southasianheartcenter.org/why-southasians/cadstatistics.html

South Asian Heart Center [SAHC], El Camino Hospital. (n.d.). *Mission*. Retrieved from http://www.southasianheartcenter.org/about/mission.html

Spitzer, R., Kroenke, K., Williams, J., & Löwe, B. (2006). A brief measure for assessing generalized anxiety disorder: the GAD-7. *Archives Of Internal Medicine, 166*(10), 1092–1097. Retrieved from EBSCOhost.

Spitzer, R. L., Kroenke, K., & Williams, J. B. (1999). Validation and utility of a self-report version of PRIME-MD: The PHQ primary care study. *JAMA, 282*(18), 1737–44.

Substance Abuse and Mental Health Services Administration [SAMHSA]. (2010). *Mental health, United States, 2008*. HHS Publication No. (SMA) 10-4590, Rockville, MD: Center for Mental Health Services, SAMHSA.

Sue, D. & Sue, D. (2008). *Counseling the culturally diverse: Theory and practice.* New Jersey: John Wiley & Sons, Inc.

Sutherland, G. (2006). East Indians are declared ineligible for U.S. citizenship. In A. Ruggiero (Ed.), *Coming to America: The East Indians* (pp. 53 - 59). Formington Hills, MI: Thomson Gale, a part of the Thomson Corporation. (Original work published 1923)

Taneja, I., Deepak, K., Poojary, G., Acharya, I., Pandey, R., & Sharma, M. (2004). Yogic versus conventional treatment in diarrhea-predominant irritable bowel syndrome: A randomized control study. *Applied Psychophysiology and Biofeedback, 29*(1), 19–33. doi:10.1023/B:APBI.0000017861.60439.95.

Tekur, P., Singphow, C., Nagendra, H., & Raghuram, N. (2008). Effect of short-term intensive yoga program on pain, functional disability and spinal flexibility in chronic low back pain: A randomized control study. *Journal of Alternative & Complementary Medicine, 14*(6), 637–644. doi:10.1089/acm.2007.0815.

Trang, A. (2009). What older people want: Lessons from Chinese, Korean, and Vietnamese immigrant communities. *Generations, 32*(4), 61–63. Retrieved from Academic Search Premier database.

Treas, J. (2009). Four myths about older adults in America's immigrant families. *Generations, 32*(4), 40-45. Retrieved from Academic Search Premier database.

Tri-City Elder Coalition. (n.d.). *Pathways to Positive Aging.* Retrieved from http://www.tceconline.org

Torres-Gil, F., & Treas, J. (2009). Immigration and aging: The nexus of complexity and promise. *Generations, 32*(4), 6-10. Retrieved from Academic Search Premier database.

University of California San Francisco [UCSF], MacArthur Research Network on Socioeconomic Status and Health. (2008). Psychosocial notebook: Personal control. Retrieved from http://www.macses.ucsf.edu/research/psychosocial/control.php

U.S. Census Bureau: American Fact Finder. (1990). *Decennial: Census 1990: 1990 summary tape file 1 (STF 1) - 100-percent data: P007. Detailed race - universe: Persons.* Retrieved September 29, 2010, from: http://factfinder.census.gov

U.S. Census Bureau: American Fact Finder. (2000). *Decennial: Census 2000 Summary File 1 (SF 1) 100-Percent Data: QT-P7: Race Alone or in Combination for American Indian, Alaska Native, and for selected categories of Asian and of Native Hawaiian and other Pacific Islander: 2000.* Retrieved October 19, 2010, from: http://factfinder.census.gov

U.S. Census Bureau Newsroom. (2008a). *Asian/Pacific American heritage month: May 2008.* Retrieved June 18, 2010, from: http://www.census.gov/newsroom/releases/archives/facts_for_features_special_editions/cb08-ff05.html

U.S. Census Bureau Newsroom. (2007). *Household income rises, poverty rate declines, number of uninsured up.* Retrieved June 18, 2010, from the U.S. Census Bureau website: http://www.census.gov/newsroom/releases/archives/income_wealth/cb07-120.html

U.S. Census Bureau: American Fact Finder. (2009). *Data Set: 2006-2008 American Community Survey 3-year estimates, geographic area: United States, population group: Asian Indian alone or in any combination.* Retrieved August 24, 2010, from the U.S. Census Bureau website: http://factfinder.census.gov

U.S. Census Bureau: American Fact Finder. (2011). *Race Reporting for the Asian Population by Selected Categories: 2010 Census Summary File 1.* Retrieved October 28, 2011, from the U.S. Census Bureau website: http://factfinder2.census.gov/faces/nav/jsf/pages/index.xhtml

U.S. Department of Health & Human Services. (2011). *Centers for Medicare & Medicaid Services: Medicaid Program - General Information: Overview.* Retrieved from: https://www.cms.gov/MedicaidGenInfo

U.S. Department of Justice. (n.d.). *Americans with disabilities act of 1990, as amended*. Retrieved from: http://www.ada.gov/pubs/adastatute08mark.htm#12143

Varghese, F. (2005). Extrinsic and intrinsic religiousness and their relationship to acculturation and help-seeking among Asian Indian Pentecostals. Retrieved from PsycEXTRA database.

Verma, R. (2004). *Migration and memory: Reflections on schooling and community by Sikh immigrant youth*. Retrieved from Proquest Dissertations and Theses database. (AAT 3143197)

Watts, A. (1975). *Psychotherapy east and west*. New York: Vintage Books: A Division of Random House.

Weisman, R. (2005, August 8). High-tech talent flows back to India: Those who helped fuel US boom may spur brain drain. *The Boston Globe*, Retrieved from http://www.boston.com/business/technology/articles/2005/08/08/high_tech_talent_flows_back_to_india

Weisman, R. (2006). Many East Indians immigrants are returning to India. In A. Ruggiero (Ed.), *Coming to America: The East Indians* (pp.122–126). Formington Hills, MI: Thomson Gale, a part of the Thomson Corporation. (Original work published 2005)

Whitley, R., & McKenzie, K. (2005). Social capital and psychiatry: Review of the literature. *Harvard Review of Psychiatry*, *13*(2), 71–84. Retrieved from Academic Search Complete database.

Wig, N. (1999). Mental health and spiritual values. A view from the East. *International Review of Psychiatry, 11*(2/3), 92-96. doi:10.1080/09540269974230.

Wiggins, R. D., Higgs, P., Hyde, M., & Blane, D. B. (2004). Quality of life in the third age: Key predictors of the CASP-19 measure. *Ageing and Society, 24*, 693-708. doi: 708708361.

Wiggins, R. D., Netuveli, G., Hyde, M., Higgs, P., Blane, D. B. (2008). The evaluation of a self-enumerated scale of quality of life (CASP-19) in the context of research on ageing: A combination of exploratory and confirmatory approaches.

Social Indicators Research, 89, 61–77. DOI: 10.1007/s11205-007-9220-5

World Health Organization. (n.d.). *Health statistics and health information systems: Definition of an older or elderly person.* Retrieved from: http://www.who.int/healthinfo/survey/ageingdefnolder/en/index.html

World Health Organization (WHO). (1948). *Constitution of the World Health Organization.* Retrieved from: http://www.who.int/governance/eb/who_constitution_en.pdf

World Health Organization. (1996). *WHOQOL-BREF: Introduction, administration, scoring and generic version of the assessment: Field trial version.* Retrieved from: http://www.who.int/mental_health/media/en/76.pdf

World Health Organization, Division of Mental Health and Prevention of Substance Abuse. (1997). *WHOQOL: Measuring quality of life.* Retrieved from: http://www.who.int/mental_health/media/68.pdf

World Health Organization, Division of Mental Health and Prevention of Substance Abuse. (1998). *WHOQOL User manual.* Retrieved from: http://www.who.int/mental_health/evidence/who_qol_user_manual_98.pdf

World Health Organization, WHO Centre for Health Development. (2004). *Ageing and health technical report, Volume 5: A glossary of terms for community health care and services for older persons.* Retrieved from: http://whqlibdoc.who.int/wkc/2004/WHO_WKC_Tech.Ser._04.2.pdf

Yakhnich, L. (2008). Immigration as a multiple-stressor situation: Stress and coping among immigrants from the former Soviet Union in Israel. *International Journal of Stress Management, 15*(3), 252–268. doi:10.1037/a0013002.

Zaeem, L. (2007). *Immigrant adolescents' perceptions and experiences as new Canadians.* Retrieved from Proquest Dissertations and Theses database. (AAT MR33176)

Zittel, K., Lawrence, S., & Wodarski, J. (2002). Biopsychosocial model of health and healing: Implications for health social work practice. *Journal of Human Behavior in the Social*

Environment, 5(1), 19. Retrieved from SocINDEX with Full Text database.

ABOUT THE AUTHOR

Born and raised in a traditional Indian joint family, Dr. Anita Jhunjhunwala Mukherjee strived from an early age to find her identity beyond the predefined gender roles. The three years at the Indian Institute of Science, Bangalore, were a defining period in her life. Not only did she fulfill her dream to be a computer engineer but she also met Animesh Mukherjee, who played and continues to play many roles in her life including that of a mentor, life partner, business partner, and friend.

After finishing Master's in Computer Science from Iowa, Anita went back to India and worked in the software industry in different countries for many years, as a business analyst, design architect, project manager, and an entrepreneur. She immigrated to the United States at the height of dot com boom and stayed to see the bust.

Looking for meaning in life, Anita volunteered with a variety of non-profit organizations including those concentrating on mental health, women's issues, political and democratic reforms, literacy, spirituality, and culture. She counseled people in crisis, facilitated groups and trainings, participated in awareness building and outreach activities, and helped in raising funds by organizing events, managing media relations, and coordinating volunteers. While working extensively with at-risk population, a desire to acquire the necessary professional tools propelled her to complete a doctorate in Counseling Psychology. Her new profession enables her to work for the causes that she believes in such as social justice, and the need to focus on mental health and quality of life rather than physical health and material possessions.

Her research was featured on the award winning television show "Chai With Manjula" (www.Chaiwithmanjula.com/media/SeniorsfromIndia.html) aired on public channels in SF Bay Area in 2012. Her research interests include adjustment and mood disorders, and the role that systemic issues such as migration play in their development. She can be contacted at anitaj@gmail.com.

Made in the USA
Lexington, KY
30 April 2013